Studio Thinking from the Start

THE K–8 ART EDUCATOR'S HANDBOOK

JILLIAN HOGAN / LOIS HETLAND / DIANE B. JAQUITH / ELLEN WINNER

Foreword by David P. Nelson

Illustrations by Nicole Gsell

TEACHERS COLLEGE PRESS

TEACHERS COLLEGE | COLUMBIA UNIVERSITY

NEW YORK AND LONDON

NATIONAL
ART EDUCATION
ASSOCIATION

901 Prince St., Alexandria, VA 22314
800-299-8231 ■ www.arteducators.org

To the teachers and students who make Studio Thinking come alive

---

Additional resources (including teacher-created materials, tables, and links to videos) are available at www.studiothinking.org and/or tcpress.com/studiothinking

Published simultaneously by Teachers College Press, 1234 Amsterdam Avenue, New York, NY 10027 and the National Art Education Association, 901 Prince St., Alexandria, VA 22314

Cover Design: Nicole Gsell
Text Design: Lynne Frost

Library of Congress Cataloging-in-Publication Data

Names: Hogan, Jillian, author. | Hetland, Lois, 1953–, author. | Jaquith, Diane B., author. |
    Winner, Ellen, author. | Gsell, Nicole, illustrator.
Title: Studio thinking from the start : the K–8 art educator's handbook / Jillian Hogan, Lois Hetland,
    Diane B. Jaquith, Ellen Winner ; foreword by David P. Nelson ; illustrations by Nicole Gsell.
Description: New York, NY : Teachers College Press, [2018] | Includes bibliographical references and
    index.
Identifiers: LCCN 2018016980 (print) | LCCN 2018032635 (ebook) | ISBN 9780807776995 (ebook) |
    ISBN 9780807759158 (pbk. : acid-free paper)
Subjects: LCSH: Art—Study and teaching (Elementary—United States).
Classification: LCC N353 (ebook) | LCC N353 .H64 2018 (print) | DDC 372.5/044—dc23
LC record available at https://lccn.loc.gov/2018016980

ISBN 978-0-8077-5915-8 (paper)
ISBN 978-0-8077-7699-5 (ebook)

Printed on acid-free paper
Manufactured in the United States of America

Contents

**Full-color mini-posters that illustrate each of the
eight Studio Habits of Mind appear after page 152**

Foreword

SOME YEARS AGO, a slim volume called *Studio Thinking* was recommended to me. I was a professor teaching courses in both music and humanities, and the book elucidated certain practices that I, as an artist as well as a scholar, was instinctively attempting to incorporate in my classrooms, and it inspired other ideas that improved my pedagogy.

Later, as a university provost, I often recommended *Studio Thinking* and its updated edition, *Studio Thinking 2,* to faculty from various disciplines with an introduction along the lines of, "It is one of the most helpful volumes about teaching practices I've ever seen." Little did I know at the time that I would one day have the privilege of working alongside one of the authors, Lois Hetland.

When the request came from Teachers College Press to pen the Foreword to this new iteration of the text, *Studio Thinking from the Start,* I immediately agreed. I did so because I believe strongly in the value of the *Studio Thinking* lens, and because I want to commend the book—heartily—not only to elementary teachers but also to principals and other administrators who will learn much, as I have, about what makes for a successful classroom.

Studio Thinking isn't just about the art studio. It is about *thinking.* The imaginative and creative work of the studio doesn't really exist without thinking, and the best thinking doesn't really exist without imagination and creativity. The broad value of this work stems from the fact that learning is an art.

Teaching too is an art, and good teachers are always honing their craft. In an age when standardized tests too often force teachers to focus inordinately on the (supposed) product, *Studio Thinking* is a welcome reminder of the significance of process. I appreciate how this book encourages a process rooted in the prospect that learning—artistic and otherwise—begins with the human capacity to "see": to observe, to behold, to imagine. With the current demands placed on teachers (and administrators), a focus on the primary practice of seeing is not only welcome, but necessary.

If we want our students to think, if we want them to learn, we must engage them in habits of mind that cultivate their innate abilities. The habits of artists in their studios can help all of us who teach to hone our techniques in every classroom engaged in the art of learning and can aid administrators to see possibilities to enrich our schools for the sake of learners and teachers alike.

This book has its genesis in the practice of real teachers. Teachers who read it will find much that is familiar. The author-researchers, who are themselves teachers, have learned from teachers and then have given their findings back to the field. Teachers have used the results of that research in their classrooms and then have given more feedback to the researchers, who then have shared the discoveries of that circle of scholarship and practice in this volume, designed especially for elementary educators.

As Jillian Hogan, Lois Hetland, Diane Jaquith, and Ellen Winner illuminate what many good teachers already do, they help us reflect on common practices that are truly beneficial, they make explicit some practices that for many are tacit, and they share what for many may be new practices. These author-researchers help us enter the classroom with a new lens.

To my colleagues in administration, especially superintendents, principals, and university deans of education, I commend *Studio Thinking from the Start.* I recommend you take the time to try on the *Studio Thinking* lens and then consider how it might be useful to the classroom teachers with whom you work. Perhaps read it with a group and try out some of the ideas. See how the habits of mind, studio structures, and studio practices might help you allocate resources and support faculty as they create compelling classrooms that engage every child in the joy of learning.

No work is more important than that done by teachers who prepare our youngest citizens. They cultivate in students the habits of mind that set the course for a lifetime of learning, and yet they receive too little compensation, too little recognition, and not nearly enough thanks.

If you are a teacher, I hope you will see this book as a gift from its authors and the many teachers who have helped shape its content. The knowledge and practices recommended here will help you in your work. As you continue to hone your craft, I hope you enjoy the fruit of your labor with young people who have the potential to create the kind of world we all want to live in.

—David P. Nelson, Ph.D.
President, Massachusetts College of Art and Design
Boston, Massachusetts

Acknowledgments

WE THANK John Landrum Bryant for his belief in our work and the support he has provided over the years through the Bauman Foundation. We are also grateful to Shirley Veenema and Kimberly M. Sheridan for their central contributions to the original development of the Studio Thinking framework.

We have been fortunate to have had the opportunity to visit, speak with, and receive emails and resources from teachers all over the United States. We're grateful for the opportunity to learn from all of you. We especially thank those who gave their time in the compilation of this book:

Dana Adams
David Ardito
Fernando Aguilar
Agusta Agustsson
Caren Andrews
Justin August
Eileen Barnett
Amy Billstrom
Amy Birkan
Tracey Broback
Robin Brooks
Sharron Cajolet
Camille Calica
Hillary Campbell
Carolyn Carr
Alane Paul Castro
Raquel Cardoso
Deborah Clearwaters
Kitty Conde
Rosette Costello
Susan Deming
Brian Dodson
Terri Eichel
Mahsa Ershadi
Alexandra Etscovitz
Caitlin Evans
Demetrius Fuller
Itoco Garcia and faculty
    of Harder Elementary
    School

Cynthia Gaub
Judith Goodwin
Lauren Gould
Chrissy Gray-Rodriguez
Gina Griffiths
Alexis Hamilton Green
Stacie Greenland
Laura Grundler
Nicole Gsell
Jeremy Guidry
Caren Gutierrez
Wynita Harmon
Cammie Harris
Melissa Hayes
Steve Heil
Grace Hulse
Ryan Hynes
Ianthe Jackson
Tana Johnson
Catherine Karp
Samantha Kasle
Leslie Keir
Susan Killebrew
Jessica Kitzman
Holly Bess Kincaid
Richard King
Thomas Knab
Celia Knight
Deborah Kramer

Anne Kress
Heidi Kupferman
Mariah Landers
Ann Ledo Lane
Mandy Lockwood
Pam Lucker
Natalie Maine
Nate Manean
Emily Manning-Mingle
Julia Marshall
Linda McConaughy
Sam Miller
Vanessa Miller
Alicia Mitchell
Constance Moore
Louise Music
Brooke Nagel
Bethany Haizlett Narajka
Kate Nesmith
Ashley Norman
Trena Noval
Mary Olson
Marisol Pastor-Cabrera
Sonal Patel
David Patusco
Christine Phillips
Jocelyn Phillips
Meghan Pierri
Gaia Pine

Rosemary Polizotto
Kathryn Potter
Barth Quenzer
Christine Reed
Emily Roberts
Roni Rohr
Stella Santos
Steve Schaffner
Larraine Seiden
Lindsey Shepard
Mizuho Shiomi
Emily Stewart
Jennifer Stuart
Amy Summa
Katherine Thompson
Gabriel Tsuei
Julie Toole
Bernardo Varela
Beth Warner
Ann Wettrich
Diana Woodruff
Cheryl Wozniack
Ceara Yahn
Elizabeth Young
Dale Zalmstra
and research assistants
    in the Arts & Mind
    Lab at Boston College

Hidden in Plain Sight

IN THE LATE 1980s, the English illustrator Martin Handford created a character known in the United States as Waldo. Dressed in red and white, with large spectacles and a hat, Waldo remains relevant in pop culture today and appears in cartoons, comic strips, and last-minute Halloween costumes. Over the last thirty years, children and adults have spent rainy afternoons poring over Handford's books looking for Waldo hidden in crowded scenes. Where's Waldo?

One of the authors of this book, Jill Hogan, realized in the early 1990s that there is a flaw that keeps the *Where's Waldo?* books from being perpetually entertaining. As a young child, after spending a Christmas afternoon intently inspecting her new gift of a *Where's Waldo?* book, she had found all of the Waldos. She then flipped back to the first page to repeat the fun. But it turned out that going through a *Where's Waldo?* scene for a second time is much less absorbing. Yes, Waldo was still hidden, surrounded by visual clutter. But to the repeat observer, he was hidden *in plain sight.* Once he had been found, he really couldn't be unfound. Jill found her eyes immediately drawn to where she previously had seen Waldo. It was no longer possible to see the pages through fresh eyes—her mind had created a new lens for seeing based on the information she had acquired after solving the puzzle.

STUDIO THINKING: A LENS

We all have ways of thinking that shape how we interpret situations. Whether we call them mindsets, lenses, dispositions, or attitudes, these perspectives frame the outlook with which we approach the world. Those wearing rose-colored lenses bypass faults and immediately find the good in every person. Those with a growth mindset don't dwell upon the difficulties of failures but instead see opportunities to improve. And those who have already solved a *Where's Waldo?* puzzle have information that removes the fun from the game.

The *Studio Thinking* framework is also a lens through which teachers and other observers of classrooms—like administrators, researchers, parents, and policymakers—can view both art and general education environments (Hetland, Winner, Veenema, & Sheridan, 2007, 2013). Like Waldo, the Studio Habits of Mind (SHoM) can't be unseen—once you realize how to recognize these thinking dispositions in artmaking and have words to organize them in your cognition, it's hard to go back to old ways of viewing. Instead of viewing art classes just as a time for "doing things," one begins to realize that art classes are a time for thinking. Studio Thinking pulls artistic thinking to the center—so important for 21st century visual arts education.

In fact, since *Studio Thinking* was first published, more than 17,000 copies of the original and second editions (Hetland et al., 2007, 2013) have been sold, and the Studio Thinking framework has been adopted in schools around the globe. This lens for looking at art classrooms challenges teachers, students, and administrators to move from a focus on artistic *products* and compliant student behaviors (which are easy to see) to a focus on the *processes* of student thinking (which are not always so easy to see). We hope this book helps make this initially hidden process of thinking more apparent to teachers, students, and school communities—so that the Studio Habits of Mind go from hidden to *hidden in plain sight.*

TEACHERS WEIGH IN

The responses of teachers who are using Studio Thinking in their teaching have taught us what makes this framework valuable.

❖ "It's What I Already Do"

Everything I read [in Studio Thinking] rang so true to what I was already doing.

—*Ceara Yahn, K–8 art teacher, Heath School, Brookline (Massachusetts) Public Schools*

I think [Studio Habits of Mind] are and should be an intrinsic part of an art curriculum.

—*Eileen Rotty, K–5 art teacher, Jenkins Elementary School, Scituate (Massachusetts) Public Schools*

Teachers tell us that the Studio Thinking framework is already familiar in their teaching practices. The immediate applicability of these ideas to busy and overloaded teachers is important. Teachers juggle seemingly endless piles of mandates: lists, frameworks, and initiatives. From national, state, and local standards, to district curriculum guidelines, to plans for integrating with classroom teachers, to IEPs and other considerations for exceptional learners, to school initiatives for English and second-language acquisition or developing grit . . . there is a lot that art teachers are asked to consider as they plan and teach. Rather than just another entry on the list of considerations, the Studio Thinking framework zeroes in on processes that are already happening in art classrooms. The purpose of this book is to help teachers and elementary students develop their ability to use this lens as they reflect metacognitively on their practice.

We know the Studio Thinking framework already exists in art classrooms, because the original authors developed it from the bottom up—by systematically observing, videotaping, coding, and analyzing both classes in high schools and interviews with teachers. Many other lists, initiatives, and standards are codified top down, created from theory and beliefs about what should be done rather than from an empirical analysis of what actually occurs. While both top-down and bottom-up approaches are important, our empirical approach reveals that broad and potentially generalizable thinking dispositions are already taught in arts classrooms.

❖ "It Gives Us Language and Legitimacy"

I love being able to explain to others in the field why it is important that we do what we do.

—*Samantha Kasle, K–5 art teacher in the Arlington (Massachusetts) Public Schools*

[Studio Thinking] helps administrators realize that there is thinking involved in art.

—*Agusta Agustsson, art teacher in the Waltham (Massachusetts) Public Schools*

It can be challenging to be an elementary art teacher. While most art teachers believe deeply in what they do and know that their training was rigorous, they too often report feeling dismissed by their colleagues, who think they are teaching a "frill." The Studio Thinking framework gives language to describe the important thinking that goes on in the elementary art studio. Teachers use it to explain the merits of art education to students, parents, colleagues, and administrators. While skeptical colleagues can argue that they have survived into adulthood while being a "terrible painter" or "miserable at drawing," few will accept incompetence at observing, envisioning, or reflecting. This is because the habits of mind in the Studio Thinking framework are ones that we value as a society. While technical art skills, such as shading and color mixing, may be ones that an adult can abandon and still be successful, the thinking habits taught in art classes are useful everywhere. In fact, teachers of all subjects have begun to help students extend use of the Studio Habits of Mind beyond the art studio, as can be seen in Chapter 6.

ABOUT THIS BOOK

The original Studio Thinking project systematically documented eight habits of mind observed in arts-centered secondary schools. Many elementary and middle school teachers found the concepts applicable to their classrooms and adeptly created age-appropriate ways to illuminate Studio Habits of Mind for their students so that they emerged into *plain sight*. This new book is for anyone interested in practical applications of the Studio Thinking framework with elementary and middle school students. We have collected here a set of ideas and resources appropriate for these students, mostly created by innovative teachers who shared their work with us. Many of the ideas can be scaled up by high school teachers.

What this book does not provide is a prepackaged curriculum of ready-to-go lessons. To help explain why not, we return to Waldo. *Where's Waldo?* books do not include answer keys. There is no easy way out—readers must find their own paths to solving the problem. The pleasure of finding Waldo emerges from a process of problem solving and troubleshooting.

Teachers are professionals who constantly identify and solve idiosyncratic problems (which are far more challenging and serious than those posed by finding Waldo) and, to do so, they need respect and autonomy so that they can design what and how they teach. When researchers provide teachers with cookie-cutter curricula, those binders often end up abandoned on a shelf. So we took a different approach. We sought out teachers who had chosen to think through the Studio Thinking lens, and we asked them to share what worked best for them. Their ideas are featured in this book to serve as springboards as readers design their own Studio Thinking–rich approaches appropriate for their particular students and classrooms.

We encourage teachers to take advantage of the "Things to Think About" sections at the end of each chapter. The questions in these sections are meant to support reflection and journaling for practicing teachers and to frame discussion in higher education courses and professional study groups. This book is a starting point for teachers to examine their own classrooms through the Studio Thinking lens and share observations and ideas with colleagues. In this way, thinking is no longer hidden, but illuminated by a spotlight.

DEVELOPING YOUR LENS

You can read this book cover to cover for a comprehensive experience or skip around for inspiration or reference to specific topics or as questions arise in the classroom.

In Part I, Chapters 1 and 2, we introduce the Studio Thinking framework to new readers and to all who wish to expand their understanding of the original work. The framework was originally developed through empirical research in five classrooms in two outstanding Massachusetts arts high schools: Boston Arts Academy and Walnut Hill School for the Arts. These visual arts classrooms were led by five master teachers—Beth Balliro, Jason Green, Kathleen Marsh, Guy Michel Telemaque, and Jim Woodside. We encourage those who want more information about the research that led to the development of the framework to look at *Studio Thinking* (Hetland et al., 2007).

We chose these schools for the first two books as examples of strong arts education—these were classrooms where teachers are exhibiting artists, students have a serious interest in the arts, and arts instruction occurs over many hours per week. We did not choose these specialized contexts because rigorous art programs are the only places these patterns of thinking can be taught. Rather, we chose them to ensure that students experienced enough time in arts classes so that we could identify the many elements of quality arts programs. Of course, the kind of environment found in these high schools is unusual, as compared with the realities of typical elementary art programs. We have since learned from teachers that our framework maps readily onto art programs in non-arts focused schools and at all age lev-

els. We wrote this book to share the elegant ways that many elementary and middle school visual arts teachers have adapted the principles of Studio Thinking to their own settings.

Our framework is a two-part lens for viewing art education, which we describe here in our first two chapters. Studio Habits of Mind are the focus of Chapter 1, in which we describe eight distinct thinking dispositions that emerge in the process of planning, making, interacting with, and assessing art and artists (see Table I.1). In Chapter 2, we describe the four Studio Structures, which are ways that time, space, and interactions are organized in studio instruction (see Table I.2).

In Part II, Chapters 3 and 4 offer written portraits of elementary art teachers who use the Studio Thinking framework regularly. Chapter 3, Portraits of Practice, looks into a typical day in three art rooms to see, hear, smell, and feel what goes on there. In Chapter 4, Portraits of Planning, we peek into the minds of teachers as they negotiate various considerations in their curriculum planning.

Chapter 5, in Part III, takes up the tricky issue of assessment, increasingly required in art classrooms, and shows how teachers might apply formative approaches to assess learning of the Studio Habits. Chapter 6 provides examples of how some teachers use the Studio Thinking framework as a tool for arts advocacy, parent education, and integration with other disciplines.

In Appendices A–E, we share resources that teachers from across the United States submitted to inspire other teachers as they begin or continue to use the Studio Thinking framework explicitly in their teaching. We hope that the activities, forms, and rubrics provided there will help as you introduce the Studio Habits, document your students' learning, and guide them to reflect on their own learning. In Appendix F we provide a reference chart of how the National Core Arts Standards (National Coalition of Core Arts Standards, 2014) and the Studio Habits overlap.

We've taken care to find teachers from many types of schools—public, private, high poverty, middle class, urban, suburban, and rural. We hope that teachers recognize themselves and their settings in these examples and use them as inspiration for classroom and curricular planning and for reflection. To teachers from groups underrepresented here, we're sorry we missed you! Please get in touch with us!

Art teaching, learning, and making are thoughtful and challenging processes. Unlike *Where's Waldo?*, answers, solutions, and contexts in art education are constantly evolving. We hope you take a rainy afternoon (or two, or

TABLE I.1. The Studio Habits and Their Definitions

Develop Craft	**Technique:** Learning to use tools, materials, and artistic conventions
	Studio Practice: Taking care of tools, materials, works, and space
Engage & Persist	Finding personally meaningful projects and sticking to them
Envision	Imagining new artworks and steps to bring them to life
Express	Making works that convey personal meaning and interpreting meaning in the works of others
Observe	Looking closely and noticing
Reflect	**Question & Explain:** Talking about students' work and working processes
	Evaluate: Talking about what works well, what does not, and why, in works by self and others
Stretch & Explore	Playing, trying new things, making mistakes, and learning from them
Understand Art Worlds	**Domain:** Learning about what artists make
	Communities: Learning to collaborate and understanding that artists often work in groups

TABLE I.2. The Studio Structures and Their Definitions

Teacher Presents	Teachers present information to the whole class, often about an assignment or artist
Students at Work	Students work individually or in groups on projects while the teacher circulates the room and has informal conversations with students that serve as a means of formative assessment
Talking About Art	Students look at each other's works or works of artists from outside the classroom and offer descriptive and evaluative comments
Showing Art	Artworks (both drafts and finals) are publicly displayed, often outside of class, and students are involved in planning, installation, and hosting

These tables are available for free download and printing from tcpress.com/studiothinking ten!) with this book and come to your own understandings of the uses and value of the Studio Thinking framework for elementary and middle school teaching.

A NOTE ABOUT "PEDAGOGICAL APPROPRIATION"

The teaching resources you'll find in this book were offered by individual teachers. In an age of Pinterest, Teachers Pay Teachers, social media groups, and classroom blogs, information flows freely. Such resources can serve as a tremendous help to teachers, and we generally view this as a positive benefit of technological progress. However, we recognize and regret that some of the resources that we provide throughout the book may have been the original brainchild of someone else—perhaps even you! Wherever possible, we reference the origins of particular ideas, but we know that we may inadvertently have neglected or misattributed some. If you find one of your ideas here, unreferenced or wrongly cited, we hope you will view this positively—maybe it shows that your work has gone viral and is beyond citation. Please let us know if this has happened so we can correct future editions!

WHERE TO FIND MORE

We were fortunate that so many teachers gave their time to talk to us, sent us resources they've developed, and opened the doors to their classrooms for us to visit. In this book we have included a representative sample of what we collected. Please visit our website, where we have posted the materials that we could not include in the book due to space constraints. We have also created additional web resources, including a file for downloading and printing the Studio Habits and Studio Structures and their definitions, a list of hyperlinks to videos about artists that are discussed in the text, and Appendix F (a reference chart connecting the National Core Arts Standards and the Studio Habits). You can find these at www.studiothinking.org and/or tcpress.com/studiothinking

PART I

Understanding Studio Thinking

CHAPTER 1

The Studio Habits of Mind

IN THIS CHAPTER, we describe the eight Studio Habits of Mind reported in *Studio Thinking* (Hetland et al., 2007, 2013). The term *habits of mind* is currently in common use, and this chapter explains what it means to us, how we define the Studio Habits of Mind (refer to Table I.1), and how these may look in the art classroom.

WHAT ARE HABITS OF MIND?

Habits are behaviors that are hard to change. We all have default settings (brushing teeth before bed, eating a 2:15 p.m. snack, or being a "glass half full" type of person) that we use throughout the day without forethought. Habits, broadly conceived, are natural and automatic and can be good or bad. Children come to school with a variety of thinking habits, some of which are helpful while others close thinking down. It is important to help them develop approaches that support learning. The Studio Thinking framework equips teachers to do that.

The Studio Habits of Mind were developed through empirical research (using close observation and qualitative interviews) in classrooms dedicated to visual arts learning. They capture the way that artists think. When looking at artworks, viewers consider the artist's place in the contemporary discourse about art [Understand Art Worlds: Domain], what the artist means to convey [Express], and what it took to create the work [Engage & Persist; Develop Craft]. Similarly, when making art, artists needn't be reminded to envision a plan—it's an organic part of their process. While few students become professional artists, all can benefit from learning to think like an artist.

Teachers have used the Studio Habits of Mind widely across all grade levels, in arts disciplines and other subjects, and in educational settings in and out of schools, such as museums and community arts centers. When used regularly in elementary schools, students may come to internalize these thinking habits and take them with them wherever they go. When teachers make thinking the center of artmaking, children in elementary schools can become reflective, well-rounded artmakers and develop positive thinking habits from the start.

❖ The Three Parts of a Habit

Habits of mind are *thinking dispositions*. Thinking dispositions have three parts: *skill, inclination,* and *alertness* (Perkins, Jay, & Tishman, 1993). The three parts are equally important for developing quality thinking. A dispositional view of thinking looks at the behaviors and attitudes that are present when students show deep understanding. This gives a more complete picture of what is going on for the student while learning and demonstrating understanding. The Studio Thinking approach asks not just "can students do this?" (skill) but also "will the student invest the time and effort needed to do this well?" (inclination) and "are students aware of the right times to do this and why to do it?" (alertness).

When we talk about skill, we mean competency. Does the child know how to observe? Can she envision? Can she reflect? But this is not the whole story—a student may be competent when given specific directions but may not be motivated to use a particular habit on her own (inclination). Or she may or may not notice when or why that habit would be useful (alertness). For Studio Habits to be fully internalized and to transfer to situations where students are not directed to use them, the student needs to develop not only skill but also the attitudes to put those skills into action—inclination (I want to do it) and alertness (I know when and why to do it). As shown in Figure 1.1, skill, inclination, and alertness interact. When students internalize a habit of mind, they use its interacting parts regularly and automatically.

❖ Broad and Useful Outside the Art Room

Studio Habits are big and broad and are used not only in the art room but also throughout the course of the day—

FIGURE 1.1. Each Studio Habit thinking disposition has three parts: skill, inclination, and alertness.

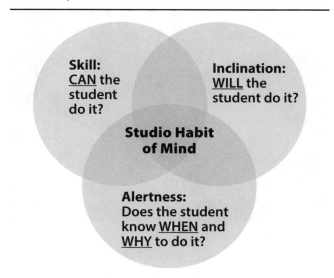

in school and out. Many technical skills, such as preparing a printing plate or mixing colors, are specific techniques used just in the art room. However, the *disposition to Develop Craft*—to acquire the rules of a domain—is a more general habit of mind that can be seen in science, writing, reading, or any other discipline.

A habit learned in art class may or may not generalize outside of the arts. While we might hope for this to happen automatically, it has been difficult to show experimentally (Ritchhart & Perkins, 2005; Winner, Goldstein, & Vincent-Lancrin, 2013). That kind of generalization might occur only when the teacher makes a specific connection across subject areas ("teaching for transfer"). For example, if students learn habits of mind in art classes, other teachers who are in communication with the art teacher can call students' attention to those habits in their own subjects. If students have learned to observe in art class, their science or classroom teachers can remind them to use that habit on nature walks or when studying how animals move. When learning to read, children can be reminded to be alert to times they might want to use Engage & Persist with a new book, even if the opening chapter is challenging. Connections through Studio Thinking can be made in every discipline throughout the school day (see Chapter 6 for examples).

❖ Already There, Hidden in Plain Sight

As discussed in the Introduction, we conceive of the Studio Habits of Mind as a positive "hidden curriculum" in the art class. The thinking dispositions we describe are not ones that teachers need to force into their current curricula; they are already there but may be hidden. Elementary students already use Studio Thinking implicitly, as they plan, organize, make, question, revise, and note their progress in art class. Becoming *aware* of *how* they are thinking with Studio Habits only happens when someone makes these patterns of thinking visible in practice. Students do not need to memorize the list of Studio Habits—that often is not developmentally appropriate in elementary schools. But teachers can use Studio Habit terms interchangeably with more common language and point to displayed signage to help students become familiar with the concepts. For older students, making these concepts more concrete with systematic language may help integrate Studio Habits into everyday artmaking discussions. With a conscious understanding of Studio Habits, students can begin to take charge of their own learning.

Historically, art education has sometimes highlighted the habit Develop Craft, focusing on learning techniques with various media. At other times, Stretch & Explore has been the norm, where students are left to make anything without encouragement to refine. Similarly, Understand Art Worlds often has been a focus of art appreciation. Studio Thinking identifies eight thinking dispositions that teachers address during art classes. Once a teacher begins seeing, articulating, and planning for the thoughtful identification of Studio Habits of Mind in the art curriculum, the habits emerge from their hidden corners and become visible throughout the art room and in children's lives outside of the art room as well.

In the following vignette, we show how Micah uses the Studio Habits as he works on a lesson about identity in art teacher Agusta Agustsson's classroom.

USING THE STUDIO HABITS: MICAH'S SELF-PORTRAIT

As Micah plans and then paints a self-portrait, we can see that he demonstrates a rich array of artistic modes of thinking—he uses all of the Studio Habits.

❖ Class 1

As Micah and his peers enter the classroom, they anticipate a common learning activity, a targeted task called a "Do Now." They find directions in a predictable place on a whiteboard and work on the task independently until the formal start of class. Today, Agusta asks the class to write "me" words about themselves as they enter the classroom, scaffolded by asking students to write three sentences to describe themselves [Envision].

Goals of the Unit [written on the whiteboard]:

The Identity portrait is meant to describe a person.
- Who you are
- What people know you by
- What makes you "YOU"

Agusta offers a brief introduction to the class: "There are lots of ways that artists deal with identity. You are used to portraits [Understand Art Worlds: Domain]. You don't have to talk about yourself in pictures that people could recognize—you could use 'Tokens of Identity' with symbols to represent you [Envision; Express]. Style—the way you dress and wear your hair [Observe]—could be a story [Express]." Agusta shows images of artists who address themes of identity [Understand Art Worlds: Domain]: Frida Kahlo, Faith Ringgold, Kehinde Wiley, Robert Shimora, Barb Hunt, Ramiro Gomez, and Takashi Murakami.

Micah is ready immediately. He gets materials [Develop Craft: Studio Practice] and starts drawing his idea with pencil directly onto the paper without making a sketch first [Envision]. He has represented "artist" by using the schema of a beret, an easel, a palette, and a brush, and he shows "age" through depicting his face with a beard [Express] (see Figure 1.2).

When Micah believes that his pencil drawing is complete [Reflect: Evaluate], he walks over to the paint supplies [Develop Craft: Studio Practice]. Agusta has poured tempera paints into half egg cartons—the primary colors plus white and black. Micah pours brown paint from its bottle, adding it to the primary palette [Envision; Develop Craft: Studio Practice]. He is going to need orange for the kerchief he has drawn around his neck and asks for advice about mixing that [Envision; Develop Craft: Technique]. His teacher picks up a color wheel and prompts him to think about which colors combine to make orange [Observe; Develop Craft: Technique]. He paints in the basic colors for his figure: a blue shirt, blue pants, and a blue beret. Micah mixes an orange color and paints the kerchief [Develop Craft: Technique]. Then he places his painting in the drying rack, cleans his brushes, and returns the paints [Develop Craft: Studio Practice].

❖ Classes 2 and 3

In the following two classes, Micah locates his painting as he enters the classroom [Develop Craft: Studio Practice] and looks at it intently [Observe; Reflect: Evaluate]. He states that he is painting *Me as an Artist in the Future with a Beard* [Express; Reflect: Question & Explain].

In Class 2, he pours extra black and a lot of brown [Envision; Develop Craft: Studio Practice]. Agusta asks him, "What size brushes do you think you will need

FIGURE 1.2. Micah envisions his self-portrait with a pencil drawing.

today?" [Envision; Develop Craft: Technique]. She anticipates that Micah will outline all the objects in his painting with black, because that is a style he prefers [Express]. He selects several brushes and takes newspaper to place under his painting [Develop Craft: Studio Practice]. The paraprofessional in the room asks him if he would like to do the facial details in Sharpie [Envision; Develop Craft: Technique]. "No," he replies, and confidently outlines the figure and the easel with a small brush, returning to the paint area for more black paint [Develop Craft: Technique and Studio Practice; Envision].

Micah later explains that he wanted control in the small area in his painting that features the palette [Envision]. He thinks his coarse brushstrokes might not look right there [Reflect: Evaluate], though he probably could have managed it with a small brush, given that he had already successfully used brushstrokes on the face [Develop Craft: Technique]. He gets markers [Develop Craft: Studio Practice], draws, and then colors in the palette [Develop Craft: Technique]. Then he paints in the floor and the space around the easel. The only spaces remaining to be painted are on the easel and a small rectangle on the wall. Again, he cleans up his materials without prompting as class ends [Develop Craft: Studio Practice].

In Class 3, Micah looks at the paper on the easel in his painting and says he can't decide what to put on it [Envision; Express; Reflect: Question & Explain]. He is then intent and focuses on calm, even strokes [Develop Craft: Technique; Express] that depict a second, smaller self-portrait in a frame on the wall behind the image of the easel within the larger self-portrait [Express]. This time, he starts with a black line painting [although we do not know Micah's range of approaches well enough to be sure, he appears to be using Stretch & Explore]. Next he uses primary colors to mix green in preparation for creating the image on the easel [Envision; Develop Craft: Technique]. He has decided that this painting-within-the-painting will depict his future house for "when I grow up" [Envision]. Micah gets brown and black paint and adds extra yellow to the egg carton paint supply [Envision; Develop Craft: Studio Practice]. He adds details to the background of his future home and lays more yellow over the dried yellow areas to strengthen the color [Reflect: Evaluate; Engage & Persist].

Ten minutes before the end of class, Micah announces that his painting is finished [Reflect: Evaluate] and that he is happy (see Figure 1.3). He cleans up and places his painting in the drying rack [Develop Craft: Studio Practice].

❖ Class 4

Micah reflects, using the form that is routine for his class at the end of every project [Reflect: Question & Explain]:

> *What aspect of your identity did you choose to portray?* [Express]
> "I am very artistic."
>
> *What medium/media did you use and why?* [Express; Develop Craft: Technique]
> "I use paint and markers to get into a little space." [Stretch & Explore] "I wanted the paint colors to be colorful." [Envision; Express]
>
> *What is the first thing you want people to notice about your work?* [Express; Observe]
> "I want [people] to notice that I did a great job." [Reflect: Evaluate]
>
> *How did you solve a problem you encountered?* [Reflect: Question & Explain]
> "My problem was wondering how I would be able to paint the small details." [Envision] "I solved this by using markers." [Stretch & Explore; Develop Craft: Technique; Engage & Persist]
>
> *Describe how you used a Studio Habit.* [Reflect: Question & Explain]
> "I used Envision because I painted myself as an adult." [Reflect: Question & Explain]

The students in the class then participate in a gallery walk in which they give feedback to each other. Micah and his classmates lay the forms they have filled out on tables next to their artworks [Develop Craft: Studio Practice; Reflect: Question & Explain; Understand Art Worlds: Communities]. Classmates walk around looking at each other's work and respond in writing to prompts on another

FIGURE 1.3. All eight studio habits were evident during the creation process of Micah's self-portrait.

worksheet, as shown in the following examples of responses to Micah's painting:

> *Describe the first detail or technique you notice:* [Observe]
> "I noticed you used paint for the whole thing."
>
> *Ask a question. What else do you want to know about this work?* [Reflect: Question & Explain]
> "Is this you in your future house painting?"
>
> *Suggest a title for this work:* [Express]
> "The Painter within the Painting"

After observing Micah carefully over many classes such as these, Micah's teacher knows that she can trust him to work effectively on his own. She anticipates his sustained engagement, expects him to develop artistic ideas without prompting, and knows that he will ask for help when he needs it.

EVEN IF you have never thought about the Studio Habits before, you probably already help your students to develop these thinking dispositions. They have likely been hidden in plain sight in your classroom, as they are in our example from Micah.

Let's now take a look at each of the Studio Habits in detail. In each of the following sections, we provide a definition and a table offering guidance in helping students learn the Studio Habit. We also offer examples from two artists (both historical and contemporary) showing how they use(d) this particular habit. Each habit section also includes a consideration for how the habit is used in other disciplines beyond the art room, and a portrait of an elementary or middle school art teacher helping students to develop that habit.

Develop Craft: Technique and Studio Practice

> Every artist is, first of all, a craftsperson, thoroughly knowledgeable about the materials, tools, and techniques of his or her particular medium and skilled in using many of them.
>
> —*Freeman Patterson (2008)*

Develop Craft has two parts: Technique and Studio Practice. Students are usually attracted by art materials and tools and want to use them. Through modeling, direct instruction, and practice, students learn techniques using tools, materials, and artistic conventions. As they do, they become aware of how technical skills make it possible for them to express themselves. Similarly, when they learn to take care of the art studio and its contents, they recognize the benefits of having what they need when they need it.

DEVELOP CRAFT: TECHNIQUE

Technique is familiar territory to art educators, students, administrators, and parents. Technical skills are often central components of elementary art programs and frequently come to mind first when writing lesson plans. Someone entering an arts classroom for the first time might easily recognize technical skills being taught as the elements and principles of design but may be unaware of other kinds of thinking that are also going on.

Look closely at the workings of a classroom and you will see that the Studio Habit of Develop Craft: Technique cannot be taught alone. Students *observe* how Technique develops. They learn what new media can offer by *stretching and exploring*. They learn to use techniques as the vocabulary and syntax for conveying the meaning that they want to *express*. Videos of artists at work show students how to incorporate techniques successfully into their work and, in doing so, how to appreciate and *understand art worlds*. Teachers integrate the formal elements of art into instruction, including color, line, shape, texture, value, form, and space. They call attention to the ways that mindful use of craft heightens meaning in the artwork through design principles such as balance, emphasis, movement, pattern, repetition, proportion, rhythm, variety, and unity. Teachers help students connect Technique with the goal of *expressing* their ideas and feelings. (See Table 1.1 for guidance in helping students learn Develop Craft: Technique.)

❖ IN THE CLASSROOM: David Patusco Balances Technique and Experimentation

Students from many cultures walk through the sunny outdoor hallways that lead to David Patusco's art room at Garfield Elementary in San Leandro, California. David (see Figure 1.4) is in his first year teaching art, but

---

Artist Connections — Develop Craft: Technique

Albrecht Dürer. German Renaissance artist Albrecht Dürer (1471–1528) was a master of drawing technique. Close-ups of his drawings (such as *Young Hare,* drawn in 1502, or *Rhinoceros,* from 1515) show many distinct kinds of lines all precisely drawn. You can almost feel the fur of a rabbit from the ways he drew the lines. Studying Dürer's meticulous lines can help students begin to use lines in deliberate fashion and to vary their quality to capture different kinds of textures.

El Anatsui. When students are working with 3-dimensional materials and using found objects, they might enjoy studying works by a contemporary artist from Ghana, El Anatsui. Looking closely at his works reveals that they are actually made from myriads of tiny scraps of colored metal held together with wire. As you step back, you cannot see what they are made of, and the works look very different. The skill involved is stunning. Students might assemble a large sculpture out of tiny pieces of found objects so that when you look closely you can see the way they are connected and what the pieces are, but when seen from a distance, the piece looks like one unit.

TABLE 1.1. Develop Craft: Technique

Ways to Talk about the Habit	I Can Statements
• Practice using materials so you can do what you want • Use tools carefully • Practice with techniques and materials	• I CAN use art tools and materials to practice techniques. • I CAN use my artmaking skills to improve my artwork. • I CAN choose specific techniques to express my ideas.

Sample Questions

- What media and techniques can you use to make your work match the image you have in your head? (with Envision)
- How is your [sculpture] like your [drawing]? How is it different? (with Observe)
- Try pressing harder or softer to make different kinds of lines, or try using different kinds of pencils or brushes. (with Stretch & Explore)
- What other [colors, lines, shapes] could you use in your drawing? (with Envision)
- What color do you want there (with Express and Envision), and how can you mix it?
- How will you know you have the color right? (with Observe)
- What could you do to make your drawing feel like it's moving? (with Envision and Express)
- What other [forms, textures, patterns, surfaces] could you use in your sculpture? (with Envision and Stretch & Explore)
- Where is the light coming from? (with Observe)
- How can you arrange or layer [colors, lines, shapes] to make your weaving more interesting to your friends? (with Stretch & Explore and Envision)
- Can you use balance to make your design more interesting to you? (with Stretch & Explore and Envision)
- What other materials or methods could you try? Collage? Recyclables? Paints? Stencils? Cut-outs? Printing? (with Stretch & Explore and Envision)
- How do these artists use [color, shape, line] that might inspire how you do? (with Understand Art Worlds, Observe, and Envision)

How Can Teachers Cultivate Develop Craft: Technique?

- Demonstrate ways to manipulate art tools and materials.
- Plan for ample time so students can explore and practice with materials prior to beginning a final project.
- Invite students to share new techniques they discover with the class.
- Show how artists have used techniques like cross-hatching, shading, outlining, or colors—help students see parallels in their own work.
- Bring students additional materials (e.g., pencils of different hardness) to use as they are working.

he has been a classroom teacher for many years and has participated in his district's Integrated Arts Specialist Program (see Chapter 6).

It is the first half of the year, and 5th- grade students are working on developing craft in drawing. David has described to us how he toggles back and forth between helping students develop Technique and using Stretch & Explore activities to make sure the students don't get too bogged down in just one type of learning. After starting the year with explorations about different types of lines, students are now learning about systematic uses of shapes by drawing manga characters. David anticipates that the explorations with creating different types of lines will carry through to now.

David begins today's class by explaining that today they'll be working on characters that are more realistic and human-like, because that's what some of the students requested. By honoring their wishes, David has motivated the students. Students will learn to draw hair, eyes, and facial features for manga characters. In the next class, they'll combine the different skills to design their own characters. He gives them some explicit guidelines:

FIGURE 1.4. David Patusco addresses his class.

We're going to break this down into lots of pieces . . . the first guideline we're going to draw is for the eyes, and it's a vertical line right down the middle of the head. This next guideline is halfway through the bottom of the circle and the eyeline—that's for the nose. Our last guideline is halfway between that line and the bottom, and that's for our mouth.

The students then create facial features. They also observe the technique used to make glimmer on the eyes in one of the manga models, and then try their hand at creating similar eyes. As the Teacher Presents structure wraps up and Students at Work begins, David returns to the push and pull between developing craft and expressing individuality, and he encourages students to add a hat or earrings or other accessories to their characters.

David acknowledges to the class that besides developing craft in their drawing, they need to use other Studio Habits. He emphasizes how learning new types of art can be hard and tells them to work through challenges because trying something new for the first time can result in an "ugly" product [Engage & Persist]. David uses images of drafts from Disney and Pixar drawings to show students how their works are similar to those created by professional cartoonists [Understand Art Worlds].

DEVELOP CRAFT: STUDIO PRACTICE

The art classroom is a busy studio space that requires meticulous organization, because many students use it every week. When students enter the classroom, it is already set up for them to learn. Everyone can get right to work because the tables are clear of other students' work and materials are prepared and accessible. Part of students' responsibilities as members of the art community is to return the room to the condition in which they found it when they entered, or better. Teachers hold students accountable for consistently established cleanup routines.

When students learn to maintain all areas of the art studio—the tools, materials, artworks, and classroom spaces—they are developing the disposition Develop Craft: Studio Practice. Like adult artists, students learn to access and return tools and materials to designated spaces, maintain artworks-in-process, and contribute to the general care of the art studio spaces (see Table 1.2).

❖ Connections to Other Disciplines

Everything has a craft that must be learned—school subjects like reading, writing, and arithmetic, as well as activities outside of school like chess, baking, video gaming, and soccer. And everything has tools and materials that need to be cared for—writers must care for their pencils and notebooks, cooks must care for their pots and spices, baseball players must care for their bats and mitts. Visual arts are just like these other disciplines. Developing craft can be thought of as a general kind of habit that students can put to work not only in the art studio but in every area of their lives, even though specific practices vary by discipline.

Students can easily relate to those who develop craft in their personal fields of interest. For instance, Olympians and other professional athletes are often well known to students, and they are excellent examples of people who have developed craft in their disciplines. Simone Biles, 2016 Olympic gold medalist in the gymnastics all-around competition, needed to learn precise skills that met standards determined by the gymnastics community. She also needed to ensure that her equipment was ready when she needed it. She continues to develop her technique and practice to the point of excellence.

❖ IN THE CLASSROOM: Christine Phillips Helps Students Maintain the Studio

In late August in Newton, Massachusetts, art teacher Christine Phillips greets her 1st-graders in a temporary building while her school undergoes construction. The periphery of the meeting area rug is surrounded by 24 large laminated red dots on the floor. She invites them to sit "criss-cross on a red dot quiet spot." Christine begins

TABLE 1.2. Develop Craft: Studio Practice

Ways to Talk about the Habit	I Can Statements
• Take care of your environment. • Be a generous art classroom citizen. • Organize and care for tools, materials, and the studio environment. • Respect yourself, others, and your studio. • Do more than your share.	• I CAN take good care of art tools, materials, and artworks. • I CAN organize my workspace. • I CAN put everything away in the right places. • I CAN put works away carefully so they don't get damaged.

Sample Questions

- How did the studio look when you arrived?
- I wonder if there's a better way to arrange your materials?
- What if you place your brushes and water cup right next to your painting hand so you don't drip onto your painting?
- What happens in your regular classroom when things do not get put away in the right places?
- What might happen if the last art class hadn't put materials back for you?
- How can we make sure your artworks are kept safe?

How Can Teachers Cultivate Develop Craft: Studio Practice?

- Establish clear setup and cleanup routines for each kind of medium, teach these to students explicitly, and ask them to help you hold each other to these routines. Follow through relentlessly!
- Model how to take care of tools; for example, demonstrate how to wash paint brushes by pressing them into the palm of your hand under running water until the water runs clear; wash clay tools in a bucket next to the sink so the sink doesn't clog.
- Ask students to sit after they finish cleaning and reflect together for 1 minute on what the tools and materials look like after use compared to when they entered the room.
- Remind students that they need to take care of themselves and their peers by paying attention when handling and storing hot and sharp tools (scissors, glue guns, and exacto knives).

the lesson, which focuses on Studio Practice. Last year in kindergarten, all materials were available on each table; but now, as 1st-graders, these children must take full responsibility for gathering and setting up materials. Using the Responsive Classroom format (Center for Responsive Schools, 2016), Christine begins with a message that she reads aloud from the whiteboard:

Hello Artists,

Artists take care of their materials. Today you will practice choosing drawing materials from the shelf. You will also put them back on shelves at cleanup time.

☺ Ms. Phillips

Christine's expectation is that students take ownership of their studio, as adult artists do when they develop craft through studio practice. These children will be Christine's

students for 6 years, and they need to internalize good habits for studio management.

"Everyone point to where you can find paper." The children point to shelves holding various sizes and weights of paper. "All of our drawing materials will be here," Christine says as she points to several sets of low shelves. "Today we will have a couple of people practice getting out materials and returning them." Following her direction, a volunteer places a piece of drawing paper on a table. Christine repeats the exercise, holding up picture labels as a request for them to find and retrieve regular markers (in boxes) and then thin ones (in round cups) as students practice modeling the expected behaviors.

"At the end of class, who is going to put all of these things away? Not me!" Christine announces. The entire process is repeated in reverse, as students return the items to the shelves while their classmates watch. After modeling setup and return of materials, she invites students, one

---

Artist Connections — Develop Craft: Studio Practice

Joe Fig. Contemporary artist Joe Fig has created wonderful miniature models of modern and contemporary artist studios and painters' tables. (Use a search engine to find his works, *Studios: Historical Artists, Studios: Contemporary Artists,* and *Studios: Painters' Tables,* 2013–2016.) These works provide a window into the ways many different artists have organized their workspaces. Students can see well-organized spaces, with tools and paints in accessible places. They will also see images of artists stepping back and observing (and likely reflecting) on their works. Additional depictions of artist studio spaces can be found through Internet searches.

Betye Saar. In a 2017 video tour of her studio with the *Los Angeles Times,* Betye Saar shows her room of sorted and labeled treasures (not unlike the typical elementary school art room!). Because Saar is a "maker of objects" (she works in assemblage and collage), she is also a collector of items for her works. She describes how walking around the studio and touching or adjusting her displayed objects allows her the freedom to feel like she is playing—and this is sometimes how her artworks begin. The collections in Saar's studio focus on her go-to symbols for her artwork (clocks for time, ships for slave ships, blackbirds for segregation and discrimination, and Aunt Jemima, whom she has liberated into a figure of power in previous work). Saar's studio serves as an inspiration to her, and it helps her make her art.

---

at a time, to select their paper and drawing materials. A student forgets to use two hands to carry the markers and Christine gently reminds him. Soon every table is filled with children who are drawing and sharing materials.

The 1st-graders take their new responsibilities seriously. When a box spills, several children immediately help their classmate pick up all the markers. Later, someone knocks over the electric pencil sharpener. A student asks Christine for a dustpan and brush and sweeps up the shavings. As the Students at Work segment nears an end, Christine rings a chime and asks, "What do you need to do before you go to the rug and look at a book?" A child responds, "Put your crayons and markers on the shelf in the right spot." Students then clean up and place their drawings on the rug to go home or on a shelf to be continued in the next class. Christine steps back to assess how well students have returned materials to their places, indicated by photos on the shelves that match photo labels on each container. "Artists, I am looking at the drawing shelves, and I notice that everything is put back in the right spots. That means we can all find everything next time" (see Figure 1.5).

Christine invests significant time at the beginning of each year to teach—and periodically re-teach—studio practices throughout the elementary grades. She cannot assume that students remember how caring for the studio works. She shows students labels (words and photos) and other storage systems; each time a new material or tool is introduced, she models how to care for it and points out where it belongs. Most of her older students have internalized these studio practices and require few reminders about the expectations for cleanup. By reducing time in transitions, this model of organization and efficiency allows more time for Students at Work and Talking About Art sessions.

FIGURE 1.5. Christine Phillips assists a 1st-grade student as he returns materials to the right places.

Engage & Persist: Finding Passion and Sticking with It

I long so much to make beautiful things. But beautiful things require effort—and disappointment and perseverance.

—Vincent van Gogh (1882)

Engage & Persist refers to how artists find ideas and materials that matter deeply to them and how they commit to sticking with their projects over long periods of time. Engagement requires identifying something to work with that is of personal importance. These ideas or materials may come from students' experiences and memories or from interest in others' works in art or other disciplines. Persistence means facing challenges, keeping going, and learning from each challenge rather than giving up. These two parts combine into one Studio Habit because we see them as intertwined: engagement drives persistence, and persistence deepens engagement.

Artists must be passionate about their ideas; unless they engage, they cannot persist! Trying to finish by will alone usually doesn't work—when the going gets tough, the will gets tired. Without engagement, students run out of the commitment needed to finish challenging projects; teachers need to structure lessons with multiple entry points so students can connect with ideas that matter to them.

To keep students from giving up, sometimes it helps to suggest a break: work on another project, or turn to a sketchbook to envision and stretch and explore until the student feels ready to return to the original project. Encourage students to work through discouragement, self-doubt, and frustration (see Table 1.3).

◆ Connections to Other Disciplines

Engage & Persist is important in all school subjects and in all areas of life. As the adage goes, "Quitters never win, and winners never quit." *Harry Potter* series author J.K. Rowling is not a quitter and clearly practices Engage & Persist. Her preparation began, some might say, when she wrote her first story at the age of 6, and her first novel at

---

Artist Connections — Engage & Persist

Pablo Picasso. Pablo Picasso's painting *Guernica* (1937) went through many, many stages, all documented in Rudolf Arnheim's book *The Genesis of a Painting: Picasso's Guernica* (2006). Just type "Guernica stages" into a search engine to view various stages of the painting. It's fun to identify changes along the way (notice how the arm of the warrior started out upright and ended up lying down; notice how the sun changed into an electric light; notice the change in the horse's position), and then to think about why Picasso made these changes (Arnheim presents his own answers in the book). Students might wonder why Picasso was not satisfied with his first drafts and why he kept persisting. Clearly the theme of this painting—the horrors and injustices of war—was something that engaged Picasso deeply. Was this why he persisted through so many drafts?

Sarah Sze. Sarah Sze is a contemporary American sculptor who creates large structures out of ordinary objects like string, wire, broken glass, computer screens, and torn pieces of paper. The structures are complex and meticulously created. An article by Robin Pogrebin (2015) in the *New York Times* describes how Sze spends a full month installing the work when she prepares her pieces for an exhibition, taking care with the placement of each piece. Everything must be precise yet also give the appearance of randomness. This is a clear example of patient and dedicated persistence.

age 11 (Lavache, 2017). From there, she continued to make plans that would allow her to find success; while struggling to make ends meet, she spent hours writing in her local café when her young daughter was asleep, and she did not let multiple rejections deter her from continu-ing to send her manuscript to publishers. Rowling's ability to keep her goal in sight resulted in a treasured book series that has helped millions of children learn to read and love literature.

TABLE 1.3. Engage & Persist

Ways to Talk about the Habit	I Can Statements
• Be inspired by ideas you care about (Engage). • Try your hardest (Persist). • Troubleshoot problems (Persist). • Stick with it (Persist). • Pursue meaningful work (Engage) and resolve problems as they arise (Persist). • Recognize when you need to re-engage or continue persisting, and use strategies to get back in the groove.	• I CAN bring what I care about most into my artwork. • I CAN connect with and commit to my work. • I CAN use my skills to go deeper into my art. • I CAN stick with my art by problem-solving when challenges come up. • I CAN manage my time to finish an artwork.

Sample Questions

- What inspired your artwork? (with Express)
- What fascinates you lately? What have you found yourself noticing and paying attention to? Objects? Images? People? Games? Shows? (with Observe)
- This reminds me of the time you worked for six classes on one drawing and did not give up. What did you learn from that? (with Reflect: Question & Explain)
- You stick with things you know you're good at [maybe it's math or singing or soccer]. How do you keep yourself going when it gets hard? (with Envision)
- You just did something really hard by attaching all these parts together. How can you do that in this next step? (with Envision)
- What else could you work on for a while to clear your head? (with Envision)

How Can Teachers Cultivate Engage & Persist?

- Understand that our fast-paced world sets children up to expect instantaneous rewards and makes them both eager AND impatient. Give students permission, encouragement, and reminders to slow down, take a break, or change focus to a different part of the work to defuse their frustration.
- Differentiate assignments with accommodations so that each child can perform at optimal levels and use multiple entry points into each assignment.
- Avoid rote exercises that are disconnected from expressive work, such as color wheels or value charts. These may teach specific technical skills if students pay attention, but they seldom elicit strong student interest by themselves. Students are engaged and motivated to gain skills when they need them in preparation for a desirable endeavor (e.g., exploring the expressive qualities of different color combinations).
- When students identify what is holding them back, problem-solve with them to find alternative routes toward completion.
- Map all of the steps and show students how much they have already accomplished.
- Introduce strategies for developing persistence like working on several pieces at once, taking breaks when stuck, using challenging constraints from games (e.g., lists of random actions selected by rolling dice, whirling a spinner, or drawing cards from a deck), and self-imposed challenge limits (e.g., work with your non-dominant hand; paint, sculpt, or draw with eyes closed or drawing covered).

❖ IN THE CLASSROOM: Demetrius Fuller's "Magical World of Art"

Demetrius Fuller, veteran art teacher at the Sokolowski Elementary School in urban Chelsea, Massachusetts, doesn't just have a classroom—he strives to create a "magical world of art," as the sign outside his door reads. Fourth-graders appear at the door—quiet, attentive, and ready to hang on Demetrius's every word. And, indeed, Demetrius's words, often set to music or nestled into his stories, don't disappoint.

Demetrius sees habits of mind as lenses through which to look at artistic behaviors. In his first year of teaching, he created two characters for his students—The Brave Artist [originally Stretch & Explore and Develop Craft], who persists through challenges and isn't afraid to try something new; and The Focused Finisher [Engage & Persist], who persists to get things done. As he says, "Characters are the best way to do it, because kids remember characters and songs. It gets in their heads."

Eventually, and partly inspired by Studio Habits of Mind, Demetrius's characters expanded into a band of "HOMies." Demetrius uses these characters in unique ways to help show his students all that artists do. Each HOMie has an accompanying catchy theme song, which Demetrius plays on his ukulele (see Figure 1.6). The HOMies and their descriptions are shown in Figure 1.7.

Today, the 4th-graders are thinking about how Georgia O'Keeffe displays attributes of the HOMies. Demetrius reads to the class the imaginary letter he created as though it were written by O'Keeffe and asks them to think about which HOMie she most sounds like.

Dear Magical World of Art,

I, Georgia O'Keeffe, think I should be a HOMie because I started painting in a new way. I looked very closely at things from nature: I ZOOMED IN. I think it makes you notice things you wouldn't normally notice. Here I am, at age 73, after a lifetime of practicing. I am holding one of my many paintings of animal bones. I loved to show the sky through the holes in the bones. My friend Jean Toomer, who was a writer, said I painted the universe "through the portal of a bone." I think that was nice. Do you agree?

Sincerely,
Georgia O'Keeffe

FIGURE 1.6. Demetrius Fuller strums his ukulele while singing the theme songs he wrote for each HOMie character.

After Demetrius reads the letter, student hands pop up to volunteer what HOMies *they* recognize in O'Keeffe's letter. "She's the Triple Practicer [Develop Craft], because she practices every day." "Inventor Innovator [Stretch & Explore], because she's the first one who zoomed in." "Brave Artist [Engage & Persist], because she tried hard at new things." The students then put their heads down and vote for their "best choice" for O'Keeffe. The students carry the lens of the HOMies to looking at their own work [Observe; Reflect: Evaluate], inspecting a finished piece and then writing evidence about why they might call themselves a particular HOMie.

By creating characters, Demetrius created an engaging frame through which children can talk about their artwork and artistic behaviors. Providing kid-friendly language like this allows Demetrius to meet the students at their level and help them engage deeply in their artistic endeavors.

FIGURE 1.7. Demetrius Fuller's HOMie characters

Main Idea	Key Details	HOM-Sweet HOMie	Habit of Mind*
You tried your hardest!	• If you messed up, you KEPT ON GOING. • You turned a mistake into SOMETHING NEW. • You LEARNED from your MISTAKE.	**BRAVE ARTIST** 	**Engage & Persist** Learning to embrace problems within the art world or of personal importance, to develop focus conducive to working and persevering at tasks.
You told a story with your art!	• You used pictures to TELL A STORY. • You can EXPLAIN your artwork. • You pretended your story was real.	**STELLAR STORYTELLER** 	**Express** Learning to create works that convey an idea, a feeling, or a personal meaning.
You invented something new!	• You invented a NEW SOLUTION to a problem. • You invented a NEW WAY of doing something. • Your art is UNIQUE.	**INVENTOR INNOVATOR** 	**Stretch & Explore** Learning to reach beyond one's capacities, to explore playfully without a preconceived plan, and to embrace the opportunity to learn from mistakes.
You used your imagination!	• You VISUALIZED your art in your mind-cloud. • You thought, "WHAT IF this were real?"	**CAPTAIN OF THE CLOUDS** 	**Envision** Learning to picture mentally what cannot be directly observed and imagine possible next steps in making a piece.

FIGURE 1.7. Demetrius Fuller's HOMie characters *(continued)*

Main Idea	Key Details	HOM-Sweet HOMie	Habit of Mind*
You practiced, practiced, practiced!	• You CONCENTRATED, ignoring distractions. • You tried to GET BETTER at using the media. • You didn't let yourself be lazy.	**TRIPLE PRACTICER** 	**Develop Craft** Learning to use tools, materials, and artistic conventions; and learning to care for tools, materials, and space.
You inspected your artwork, reflecting on how to make it better!	• You took the TIME to quietly look at your artwork. • You asked yourself, "How can I make this EVEN BETTER? What parts should I REVISE?"	**INSPECTOR REFLECTOR** 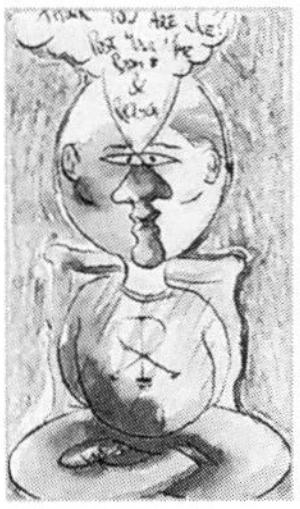	**Reflect** Learning to think and talk with others about an aspect of one's work or working process, and learning to judge one's own work and process and the work of others.
You found clues hidden in someone else's artwork!	• You looked carefully at something in the world, finding its hidden details. • You searched for CLUES about an artwork's MEANING.	**EAGLE-EYE DETECTIVE** 	**Observe** Learning to attend to visual contexts more closely than ordinary "looking" requires, and thereby to see things that otherwise might not be seen.
You learned from art history!	• You paid close attention when learning about a FAMOUS ARTIST. • You thought about what you could LEARN from a famous artist. • You got INSPIRATION for your own art.	**ART HISTORIAN EXTRAORDINARIAN** 	**Understand the Art Community** Learning to interact as an artist with other artists (i.e., in classrooms, in local arts organizations, and across the art field) and within the broader society.

*Adapted by Demetrius Fuller from *Studio Thinking: The Real Benefits of Visual Art Education* (Hetland, Winner, Veenema, & Sheridan, Teachers College Press, 2007).

Envision: Imagining and Planning

I close my eyes in order to see.

—*Paul Gauguin (Boone, 1992, p. 278)*

Even as teachers begin describing a project, students often start to envision how their own artwork might look, murmuring ideas to one another. "I'm going to make a dinosaur!" "Mine's going to be red for the Red Sox." "I want mine to be a ninja. How do you draw a ninja?" Eager to start, students may be inclined to settle for the first idea that comes to them. A series of strategically planned exercises—pair-shares or thumbnail drawings—can move their imaginations from obvious to more unusual possibilities. This stage in creative design thinking is called ideation through divergent thinking (as opposed to convergent thinking, where everyone's ideas are the same). As young artists envision, they consider multiple dimensions based on the assignment's parameters and visualize what they might do.

Envisioning does not end once the initial idea for an artwork is set. Artists continue to envision throughout the artistic process. As the artwork progresses, students observe and reflect on what is happening. They plan midprocess in order to envision their next moves. This Studio Habit can be taught directly to students by modeling "What if?" questions that guide them in envisioning next steps, as shown in Table 1.4. Students can ask each other these types of questions, too, to help peers develop ideas.

Divergent thinking practices open the mind to multiple possibilities, but students may be reluctant to revisit envisioning once they get started. Initial ideas, whether pictured mentally or sketched, are not binding contracts and usually evolve as the work progresses. Reminders to pause as students work—to observe, reflect, and re-envision what comes next—support the inclination to envision and build students' alertness to sources for new ideas. Stepping away from the artwork or having someone hold it for viewing from a distance helps student artists plan where to focus their attention (tied to Observe). This critical step in the process gives artists the opportunity to engage and persist further, refreshed with new ideas about their work.

Artist Connections — Envision

Georges Seurat. Post-impressionist French painter Georges Seurat developed a kind of painting called pointillism. If students look closely at one of his paintings, they will see that each area is composed of dots of pure color. As they step back, the colors blend together. How could Seurat have known which colors to use to create the mixed color effect? He had to be envisioning in his mind how the two colors would look when blended!

Chris Jordan. Contemporary artist Chris Jordan makes art with a social message. His art is not only fascinating to look at but is also intended to wake us up and get us to act! In *Blue* (2005), part of *Running the Numbers II,* in which he makes a point about waste and pollution, he depicts what appears to be a painted human figure, but when you look closely, you see that this figure is created entirely by plastic bottles— 2 million of them. How could Jordan have known where to put each bottle unless he could envision how the final product would look from a distance? To make a point about the problem of students dropping out of school, he created a composition of children's blocks that spells out "Education is the most powerful weapon we can use to change the world. Nelson Mandela." Zooming in on this work, *Building Blocks,* shows that each block is made up of thousands of smaller blocks. There are 1.2 million blocks here, and that's how many students drop out of high school every year in the United States! Chris Jordan could not have known where to place each of those blocks without the ability to envision the whole.

TABLE 1.4. Envision

Ways to Talk about the Habit	I Can Statements
• Make a plan. • Picture it in your mind. • Imagine your final artwork. • Visualize multiple ideas for an artwork in your sketchbook and, later, next steps as your piece evolves. • Let your plan change as you work. • Think about what to do next. (Where is the work asking for attention?)	• I CAN picture ideas in my mind for my artwork. • I CAN get ideas for my artwork by sketching and planning. • I CAN decide on next steps by asking, "What if . . . ?" • I CAN let my ideas change as I work.

Sample Questions

- What if you play with the clay first to try out some ideas, to see what you like? (with Stretch & Explore and Develop Craft: Technique)
- Turn and talk to the person sitting next to you about your idea. Then listen to his or her ideas. (with Understand Art Worlds: Communities)
- Take a walk around the room and see what other students are working on. That might help you envision what to do next. (with Engage and Understand Art Worlds: Communities)
- Tell me about your plan—what's next?
- What if you add more shading so the light areas stand out—can you make it contrast? (with Develop Craft: Technique)
- You like the patterns on this part. What if you let this other area dry so you can paint patterns on top of that, too? (with Develop Craft: Technique)
- What if you balance this edge against that piece so the structure can stand upright? (with Develop Craft: Technique)
- What if you turn the paper upside down and look at it that way? (with Observe)

How Can Teachers Cultivate Envision?

- When introducing a new assignment, invite students to share their initial ideas with the class.
- Use envisioning practices regularly in journals, sketchbooks, thumbnail sketches, and group or pair-share brainstorming.
- Before they start their pieces, ask students to think about and make thumbnail sketches or mock-ups of multiple ideas for how they want their work to look.
- Ask students to look closely at their work and ask themselves, "What could I do to make this different?"
- Show students work from other artists that changed during the process from their initial ideas into the final piece.

❖ **Connections to Other Disciplines**

Those who envision at the Walt Disney Company—designers, artists, architects, and engineers for parks, rides, and resorts—have a special name; they are called *Imagineers*. Disney Imagineers operate under the principle of "blue sky speculation," which means that ideas are encouraged without restrictions for practicality or feasibility (Kerzner, 2013). Being encouraged to imagine so many possibilities has resulted in attractions one might never have thought possible. Disney Imagineers make it possible for millions of families around the world to step into imaginary lands and experience what appears to be magic—but it is really just the result of lots of envisioning (Hench & Van Pelt, 2009).

❖ **IN THE CLASSROOM: Imagining Possibilities with Roni Rohr**

"What could this be?" teacher Roni Rohr asks as she holds up an object for 6th-graders at Eldorado Community School in New Mexico. Today's prompt comes from an unfinished "taper-mâché" (tape over newspaper) arma-ture for a sculpture that was abandoned by someone in another class. It resembles a strange flower, with petal-like forms jutting out from a central point. Students first reply with the obvious: a flower, sun, tree, peacock. Roni instructs them to open their sketchbooks to a new page and draw some of their ideas for the "taper-mâché" form (see Figure 1.8). Students envision as they draw their responses, soon returning to the circle to share. Their interpretations have expanded to include an "odd bug," a "French flower with a mustache," and a "chicken with high heels and fishnet stockings." Roni smiles at the last idea and models how to take it further, saying, "Maybe you made a cartoon of a chicken with high heels . . . but [then] you say, 'No, that's not serious enough for me.' So you flip the page, you envision, and then you change the chicken's body and give the high heels some shoelaces." She pulls out her own sketchbook and opens to a page of drawings that she calls "serious doodles" that help her to process ideas as she envisions new artworks. Some students like the serious doodle approach and work on these throughout class; others continue with works in progress.

Later that day, Roni approaches kindergartners during the opening meeting with a similar spirit of imagination and whimsy. In a quiet voice, she announces, "We are all going to paint now. Everyone, close your eyes and imag-ine your favorite color." Eyes shut around the circle, and children call out their favorite colors. "Mmmm, your col-ors are delicious," Roni exclaims to the giggling 5- and 6-year-olds. She tells them to open their eyes and contin-ues as children stand in the circle, listening.

"You are all holding paint brushes, really big paint brushes, so huge that you have to hold your paintbrush with both hands. Now, dip your paintbrush in the paint—really swoosh it around in there—and swing it up to the sky." As Roni speaks, she exaggerates the movements, and the children follow her actions, loosely swinging their shoulders as they swish their brushes in the imaginary paint jars.

"We are painting a huge landscape. I see a light blue sky. I see fluffy white clouds, lavender mountains, and red

FIGURE 1.8. Roni Rohr talks about imagination and envisioning with her students.

hills. Keep swooshing your brush—move it under and over the other colors you see. Do you see that blue next to the yellow—blend them together—see that luscious green? Try moving your brush up and down to mix more colors—what do you see now?" Children call out the names of colors in their imaginary landscapes. Roni con-cludes by saying, "We are picturing ideas by imagining a landscape. I can't wait to see what ideas you have for your own artworks today."

Roni leads the children to three centers to show them their choices for the day: drawing, "dotting" with large and small paint markers, and construction with Legos. At the end of class, children share their artworks and Roni responds enthusiastically, "Look at all this work! How did you do this?" Children share their ideas, including a sun and moon, fantasy animals, "a pony with me and my friend riding up in the air to Bubble Gum Candy World," and a carefully planned design for an orange juice maker. Roni brings the kindergarten sharing to a close by asking, "An orange juice maker! How many people would like a nice, cold glass of orange juice right now?"

Express: Finding Meaning

A painting with just technique is dead.

—Jim Woodside (as the Studio Thinking team recorded him saying to his painting class, Fall 2004)

Jim Woodside, artist and instructor at the Walnut Hill School for the Arts (one of the two schools featured in our first *Studio Thinking* book [Hetland et al., 2007]), makes it clear to his students that without expression, artworks do not come alive. Children need to know that when they make art, it needs personal meaning. Guiding them to look to their experiences for what they may want to convey in their work and listening to the ideas of others develops their alertness to different kinds of expression. When they see that their work can illuminate ideas, stories, feelings, and perspectives to others, they are motivated to continue seeking meanings that they want to express. Students can easily be shown how the simplest to the most complex arrangements of elements express themes such as joy, sorrow, conflict, anger, movement, loudness, silence, emptiness, and so on. Children, and many adults, carry the misconception that "expression" refers only to feelings—but emotion is just one of many possible meanings in art. Another misconception is that meaning has to be there from the beginning—but meaning often evolves with the work.

Consider the following expressions of meaning:

- A kindergartner re-enacts the wedding of a favorite aunt through drawing.
- A 3rd-grader incorporates the colors of the Mexican flag into a weaving to connect with his family's culture.
- A 5th-grader expresses "courage" through gesture in a clay sculpture of a horse.

During Students at Work, a teacher might comment on a student's contrasting lines and say, "These people over here that you drew with thick markers really stand out. What is going on between them and the other people back here that you drew in pencil?" In response, the student elaborates on a good guy–versus–bad guy theme and explains that he wanted the pencil lines to indicate that the

---

Artist Connections — Express

Shahzia Sikander. Pakistani contemporary artist Shahzia Sikander paints and then covers the painting with tissue paper, putting more drawings on top of that, and creates space through layers of veils. In an interview republished at Art21 in 2011, entitled "*Chaman*," she explains why: "The idea of veiling and revealing here becomes important because a lot of my work is deeply personal." This is a good example of how artists express meanings in their work that are powerfully important to them.

Roxanne Swentzell. The clay figures sculpted by Native American sculptor Roxanne Swentzell speak to universal human emotions. Swentzell learned about clay at an early age:

> I come from a long lineage of Santa Clara Pueblo potters—my mother was a potter, her mother was a potter, and so on. But for me, art was my first language. As a child, I had a speech impediment, and this language problem led me to create clay figurines, to express myself. That is how I started my art career—trying to communicate. Today, these figures still tell my story—even though I have learned to speak since then!

One figure that appears often in her work is the *koshare*, a clown in Pueblo culture. The job of the koshare is to relay difficult messages to members of the community through humor and mime. For Swentzell, her figures reflect this tradition, serving a similar purpose—using clay from the earth to communicate and bring balance to the world (Godrèche, 2013).

TABLE 1.5. Express

Ways to Talk about the Habit	I Can Statements
• Show what you think and feel—your artwork tells others what is important to you. • Communicate thoughts, opinions, and/or emotions. • Tell a story with your art. • Use experiences, perspectives, and beliefs to add meaning to an artwork. • Let the meaning grow and change as your work develops.	• I CAN put meaning into my artwork by including what is important to me. • I CAN communicate my ideas through my artwork. • I CAN interpret meaning in other artists' artworks. • I CAN discover the meaning as I make my work.

Sample Questions

- How is this artwork important to you [the artist]? (with Engage & Persist)
- Does this work remind you of anything? Tell me about that. (If no, "Well, let me tell you things it reminds me of—that may spark ideas for you.") (with Envision and Understand Art Worlds: Communities)
- The direction of your brushstrokes can show us how you feel about something. (with Develop Craft: Technique)
- What colors can you choose to show that this is a scary [or friendly] monster? (with Envision and Develop Craft: Technique)
- What do you hope other people will think when they look at your work? Why will they think that? (with Reflect: Question & Explain and Envision)

How Can Teachers Cultivate Express?

- Frame Talking About Art questions to help students focus on meaning in their artworks, balancing the sessions to highlight ideas and how craft helps them convey that meaning.
- Plan open-ended assignments and then encourage students to make connections to personal interests.
- Ask students to look at their work and think about whether it could be more exciting if they put more feeling into it—soft, hard, dreamy, joyful, curious? How could they do this?
- Listen attentively as students talk about their ideas. Ask others to paraphrase what a student just said and ask the student if the paraphrase captures what they meant.
- Invite students to title each other's work with sticky notes.

bad guys' power was fading as the good guys took over the world. For any students who are reluctant to explore meaning in works, ask them to start by describing colors and shapes, which usually leads to interpretations of meaning. Repeated exposure and discussions about artwork—particularly contemporary work, which is so conceptual—reinforces the value of meaning-making in art class (see Table 1.5).

❖ Connections to Other Disciplines

Much to say we all have.

Yoda, the beloved character from George Lucas's *Star Wars*, has plenty to say, but he doesn't speak much. When he does, we may hesitate a second, but then it all makes sense once our brains process his unique way of using language.

Like invented languages, the visual arts are forms of communicating that aren't as direct as spoken language. It requires alternative ways of forming and understanding expressions that make us think a little harder. Humans have participated in these "convoluted" and "inefficient" means of communicating forever—through music, through fictional languages like those of *Star Wars, Star Trek,* and the *Lord of the Rings* trilogy, and even through making funny faces to make a friend laugh.

❖ IN THE CLASSROOM: Ceara Yahn's Students Express Their Identities

The large wall of windows in Ceara Yahn's art room at the Heath School in Brookline, Massachusetts, looks out on the picturesque and tree-covered suburbs of Boston. Ceara is in her third year teaching full time in Brookline.

FIGURE 1.9. Daphne constructed a collage showing a coat of arms.

It is the start of the school year, and Ceara's older students are all working on a unit that allows them to express themselves. Ceara was inspired by the Olympics from the previous summer. She describes the rich visual impact of the games—uniforms, flags, and color patterns that represent the world's countries. The Olympics were an accessible and concrete starting point for a connection to a personal coat of arms project.

The project started by having students closely observe coats of arms that were created in recent history and learn about connections to the imagery of the country. Bolivia's coat of arms, for example, contains llamas and mountains, both of which are common there. After that, Ceara assigned a brief worksheet to help students brainstorm what they wanted to express visually about themselves. She says,

> [Students] brainstormed images from their homes, from their neighborhoods, from their families, to try to pull together a lot of small pictures that would make a big picture of who they are. So that was the ultimate goal . . . self-expression and self-representation . . . and how can you show who you are through the images you choose and the way that you depict them and combine them?

Fifth-grader Daphne describes her love of the ocean as the centerpiece of her coat of arms (see Figure 1.9). She thoughtfully determined how she wanted to shape the inside of the ocean. "I didn't want [the blue and white papers, collaged to signify waves of the ocean] to be jagged . . . I wanted to give it a different feeling . . . it should be smooth and flowing, so I have a lot of curves. Like the ocean." She made similarly expressive artistic decisions in her separation of the shoreline from the sun rays. "I didn't want it to go straight across. That would be boring. So I wanted it to be a little bit different, and you could envision this in lots of ways—like it's a wave coming down, or just the shape of the ocean. It also gave me more space so I could put more things in the ocean." Daphne felt this shape was unique and important, and she reports making the artistic decision to express that by using oil pastels, so it would stand out to the viewer. The "things" that Daphne put in the ocean were concrete representations of her interests: animals, music, clothing, sports. How should the viewer know that these are important to Daphne? "I made the [sun]light shining on the things that I like, so it would show that they are good things."

In this project, students were able to access personal expression both through concrete subject matter (in the way Daphne depicts symbols of her interests) and with more abstract artistic decisions to express feeling, mood, and relative importance (as Daphne did when she thoughtfully shaped her waves or placed the sun to show the "goodness" of the things she depicted).

Observe: Looking Closely

Paying attention all the time is a very interesting way to go through the day.

—*Stephen Shore (MoMA, 2017)*

Observe is a Studio Habit with tremendous potential for growth in the elementary years. Children have the capacity to be strong observers: they can make fine discriminations among colors, textures, lines, patterns, and forms. These kinds of observations can become content for future works when teachers help students connect their observations with the process of making art. Art teachers expand students' capacities for mindful observation through frequent modeling of ways to observe in the classroom. For example, a teacher calls attention to shadows that bend across a snowbank to describe subtle changes in form seen from the classroom window. This type of demonstration shows students that we can look without seeing; but if we look closely, we can see things we had not noticed before (see Table 1.6).

Drawing or painting from direct observation is excellent practice for hand–eye coordination [Develop Craft: Technique] and to identify colors, form, textures, and line in the model. Some teachers ask students to use viewfinders or jewelers' loupes to simplify and abstract objects under observation. The Studio Habit of Observe goes beyond traditional observational drawing to include other ways to notice details and phenomena worthy of artistic exploration. In addition to a model or object under observation, students may observe such things as the following:

- How their artworks have changed over the year
- New processes and techniques as demonstrated by the teacher or created during Stretch & Explore activities
- Peers' ways of working
- Classmates' finished artworks
- Selected artwork of contemporary and past artists

❖ Connections to Other Disciplines

Humans are a visual species and constantly on the lookout to take in new sensory information, especially through vision. Comedians like Jerry Seinfeld and Ellen DeGeneres have built careers on noting their keen observations. Often asking, "Have you ever noticed . . . ?" these jokesters make us laugh simply by calling attention to things we may have once seen but not truly observed or thought about.

More seriously, many medical schools have begun incorporating slow looking at paintings as a way to train doctors to look closely at their patients to notice symptoms (Naghshineh et al., 2008). Rather than turning immediately to their screens to check lab results, medical schools are encouraging doctors to look directly at their patients, noticing texture of hair and skin, facial expression, tone of voice, body posture, and other qualitative markers that may provide clues to illness.

Artist Connections — Observe

Leonardo da Vinci. Renaissance artist Leonardo da Vinci was fascinated by the structure of the human body. He studied every aspect of it, such as bones and muscles, and he made countless sketches of human anatomy. The sketches were made from corpses that he dissected in order to understand just how the body was put together. Paradoxically, his meticulous observations of lifeless bodies undoubtedly enabled him to paint the human figure with a vivid sense of life. Type "da Vinci anatomical drawings" into a search engine to reveal many examples.

Anish Kapoor. *Cloud Gate* (2006) is a huge outdoor sculpture in Chicago created by Anish Kapoor, a British artist born in India. It is made out of steel and has a shiny surface like a mirror. Nicknamed "The Bean" from its shape, the curves of the sculpture distort the reflections of the surrounding buildings and of the visitors who are viewing it. All straight lines curve, geometry is transformed, and we see the world in a new way.

TABLE 1.6. Observe

Ways to Talk about the Habit	I Can Statements
• Use your detective eyes. • Look closely. • Watch mindfully. • Take your time when you look. • Take it all in—let it soak in. • Walk your eyes back and forth over the surface like you were a tiny ant so you see everything.	• I CAN notice details in the world around me. • I CAN view my own work closely to find areas to keep and to improve. • I CAN examine other artists' artworks to get ideas.

Sample Questions

• How does this look from across the room?
• What captured and holds your attention in this work?
• What happens if we look at this artwork upside-down?
• What do you notice first when you look at this? Why?
• If you could touch this [museum] artwork, what do you think it might feel like?

How Can Teachers Cultivate Observe?

• Maintain a curiosity table with changing collections of unusual objects for children to examine and draw.
• Model the difference between drawing things schematically (e.g., a circle for a head) and drawing things carefully observed (e.g., heads are not really circles! Look for the bumps and turns).
• Demonstrate tools and conventions that lead to closer looking, such as viewfinders of various shapes and sizes, magnifying glasses, jewelers' loupes, microscopes, looking from a distance or through binoculars, and intentionally blurring vision by squinting.
• Discuss student work to uncover areas where the student might look more closely.
• Show works by artists and discuss how carefully the artist observed the subject matter. Encourage students to point out details in the artwork.
• Play games that encourage observation (e.g., "I'll time you for one whole minute as you look at this work. Then take turns telling your neighbor the new things that you saw after looking that you did not see at first.").

❖ **IN THE CLASSROOM: Chrissy Gray-Rodriguez Continues to Learn with Her Students**

Chrissy Gray-Rodriguez, art teacher at the K–8 Garvy Elementary School in Chicago, Illinois, is constantly involved in formal professional development. As the only art teacher in her school, she seeks out programs run by local museums or cultural organizations so that she can network and talk shop with other art educators. Some of these professional development opportunities have led her to think more deeply about Studio Habits of Mind, and recently she has developed exit tickets for her older students that incorporate them.

A glance around the room reveals lots of evidence of Studio Habits. At the front whiteboard, signs and definitions appear for each Studio Habit, with asterisks Chrissy marks at the start of class—foreshadowing which Studio Habits will be important that day. At the side of the room, students have created posters with drawn understandings of each Studio Habit (see Figure 1.10).}

Today happens to be a day with lots of observation lessons. Third-grade students are working on individualized soup cans inspired by the work of Andy Warhol, while middle schoolers are working on drawing realistic self-portraits inspired by the photographs of David Gomez-Maestre. As students work from models (prints of Warhol's works or of their own faces in individual mirrors), eyes dart back and forth between the model and their own drawings (see Figure 1.11). A boy makes a discovery—"at the top of the can, it looks like the Willis Tower and the Hancock Building!" After some explanation, the students turn their heads to look at the shading on the top lip of the can, which resembles a city skyline on its side. Chrissy constantly reminds students to look closely and

FIGURE 1.10. Chrissy Gray-Rodriguez stands in front of her wall display of Studio Habits, which includes student-created definitions, prompts, and visual depictions of each habit.

gives strategies for careful noticing. "I wonder how your soup can looks from across the room? Maybe try putting it on the whiteboard and taking a few steps back to observe?" "We're drawing what we observe—not what you think you know!"

Observing is an activity some may take for granted—art is visual and looking may seem obvious. But in Chrissy's classroom, each of the Studio Habits, including Observe, is discussed systematically in the language she introduces. By being explicit and using consistent words for discussing Studio Habits, it is more likely that these ways of thinking become a bigger part of students' metacognition.

FIGURE 1.11. Student Jovana observes herself carefully in the mirror while creating a self-portrait.

Reflect: Question & Explain and Evaluate

No art is less spontaneous than mine. What I do is the result of reflection and the study of the great masters.

—*Edgar Degas (Moore, 1891, p. 313)*

Reflections, those conversations we all carry on with ourselves and with others, guide artists as they work and evaluate. Artists reflect upon many aspects of their work as it evolves. Elementary art teachers model how to reflect on in-process works by talking through a series of internal questions and decisions that arise as students create art. There are two ways student artists reflect in the art room. First, Reflect: Question & Explain occurs as students observe and think about what is happening in their artwork so that they can envision next steps. This Studio Habit is also in play as they talk about and interpret their

own and others' work in Talking About Art sessions. Second, students are using the habit of Reflect: Evaluate when they make judgments about the quality of their work or the works of others.

REFLECT: QUESTION & EXPLAIN

Throughout Students at Work sessions, teachers move systematically from child to child to provoke students to question and explain. Left to their own, children may spontaneously rush through artmaking without focused thinking. Question & Explain slows down the work process as student artists pause and contemplate their work-in-process. Modeling the habit of Reflect brings mindfulness into the process. Students at this level benefit by open-ended prompts to develop reflective thinking about their artwork, such as "tell me how it's going" or "what's going on in your watercolor?" The teacher can stop class briefly during Students at Work sessions and use a prompt to ask students to pair-share about their work (see Table 1.7).

With practice, most students learn to integrate self-questioning practices into their working habits, eventually without prompting. Talking aloud to a peer is one way to invite a second set of eyes to consider what has been done so far. Some teachers have found it best to ask these kinds of reflective questions in the midst of studio work (not only after cleanup), to give students time to make changes during the same art class.

When the artwork is finished, students continue to question and explain as they present their work in Talking About Art sessions. Students reflect as they write artist statements that describe narratives behind their works, personal meaning, the creative process, or goals for further work. Repeated opportunities to talk about their work solidifies students' reflective skills as they envision next steps. Noting missteps as well as successes helps to guide future actions.

◆ IN THE CLASSROOM: Question & Explain Through the Years with Anne Kress

Anne Kress teaches art classes for Kindergarten–Grade 6 at the Merriam School in the Acton-Boxborough District in Massachusetts. Like many elementary art teachers, she modifies her expectations and assignments across grade levels. Here we see a snapshot of how Reflect: Question & Explain looks at different age levels in her classroom.

On a humid morning in June, kindergartners enter the art room for a class shortened by an upcoming assembly. Anne takes advantage of this time to give students a chance to speak with each other about their artwork. To prepare them for conversations that will happen in table groups of four students, Anne models how to talk about artwork with her puppet, Sproing (see Figure 1.12). Anne and Sproing model how to choose one of the two artworks on their table, deciding what to share about how it was made and listening quietly while a peer is talking. "What was Sproing doing while I was reflecting?" she asks. Students quickly volunteer: "He wasn't talking" and

TABLE 1.7. Reflect: Question & Explain

Ways to Talk about the Habit	I Can Statements
• Retrace your steps—think backward. • Consider the choices you made. • Describe and explore choices for in-progress and finished artwork. • Tell me how you got here and what you did.	• I CAN ask questions about my artwork in progress. • I CAN reflect on how I've created my work and envision the next steps I want to take. • I CAN explain my decisions to others and describe what I did.

Sample Questions
- What part of your work seems incomplete? (with Express, Observe, and/or Envision)
- Tell me what you've done so far, and what you might do next. (with Envision)
- What are your next steps going to be? (with Envision)
- How are you using that [tool, material, process]? (with Develop Craft: Technique)
- What's this work [student's own or other artist's] about? Describe what you see that makes you think that. (with Observe, Express, and Understand Art Worlds)
- Let's look at this artist's work together—I think it has ideas for you. Can you tell me what connects in this piece to your work? (with Understand Art Worlds: Domain, Observe, and Envision)

How Can Teachers Cultivate Question & Explain?
- Generate a list of questions students can ask themselves as they work. Post the list where students can read it—on a bulletin board or whiteboard so it's easy to see or on small cards at each workstation.
- Encourage students to pair-share briefly during studio time, with or without prompts.
- Show students that when they think about the decisions they are making as they work, they may realize how a decision led them astray. Once they notice that, they can revise, ultimately resulting in a better work.
- Implement routines for older students to write about their process in exit tickets or journals.

FIGURE 1.12. Anne Kress models Talking About Art with her puppet, Sproing.

"He didn't say anything except 'thank you' at the end." This guidance allows all children a chance to share their process in quick ways that give everyone the opportunity to talk. Andrew tells his classmates of his Joan Miró–inspired artwork, "I like this one because it's hard and I like hard things. You should know it's not done. It needs more colors." More complex conversations about artwork happen as a whole class when Anne facilitates a back-and-forth about what children see in a famous artwork she projects on the screen.

When the class leaves, Anne shows us how formats for Question & Explain can change by bringing out examples from older students. Fourth-graders are much better able to write and reflect systematically about their process than the younger students. She encourages them to think about the steps required to complete an artwork. In her mini-book, student Hannah reflects on the various parts of creating a coil pot (see Figure 1.13).

Anne expects her oldest students to think more deeply about their creations, and she uses the Studio Habits of Mind to structure their artist statements. Sixth-grader Jonah created a wire sculpture of a guitarist and com-

---

Artist Connections — Reflect: Question & Explain

Vincent van Gogh. Vincent van Gogh wrote over 600 letters to his brother, and in many of these he was reflecting on his artworks (van Gogh, 1884). Here is an excerpt showing reflections on how he mixes color:

> A dark colour may seem *light,* or rather give that *effect*; this is in fact more a question of *tone.* But then, as regards the real *colour,* a reddish-grey, hardly red at all, will appear more or less red according to the colours next to it. And it is the same with blue and yellow. One has to put but a very little yellow into a colour to make it seem very yellow if one puts that colour in or next to a violet or a lilac tone. I remember how somebody tried to paint a red roof, on which the light was falling, by means of vermilion and chrome, etc.! That didn't work.

Faith Ringgold. Contemporary artist Faith Ringgold makes quilts, combining them with painting and using them to tell stories. In the PBS series *Craft in America,* Ringgold reflects about creating her artwork *Tar Beach.* "As an artist, I have a story to tell. And I think I also need to tell it in words, as well as images." She explains her process:

> Each time I made a quilt, I would first decide the background color. So I know for this case, it's blue so this whole piece of canvas would be attached to the wall of my studio . . . so then, I would go to my favorite upholstery store and I would get . . . cotton duck, finely, finely woven, very good quality. Cotton duck canvas. Not linen! Because linen is not appropriate for painting on with this acrylic without gesso. And there is no gesso here . . . and I would pick several patterns of very well made and colored upholstery fabric so I didn't have to worry about fading and stuff like that. (Gunther, 2012)

FIGURE 1.13. Fourth-grader Hannah writes and draws the steps of making a clay pot in her mini-book.

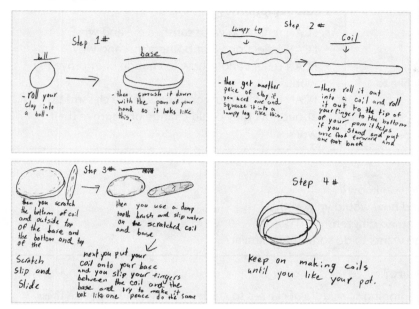

Step #1
<u>Ball</u>
roll your clay into a ball
<u>Base</u>
then smush it down with the [palm] of your hand so it looks like this

Step #2
<u>Lumpy Log</u>
then get another [piece] of clay if you need one and squeeze it into a lumpy log like this
<u>Coil</u>
then roll it out into a coil and roll it out to the tip of your finger to the bottom of your [palm] it helps if you stand and put one foot forward and one foot back

Step #3
<u>Scratch Slip and Slide</u>
then you scratch the bottom of coil and outside top of the base and the bottom and top of the . . .
then you use a damp tooth brush and slip water on the scratched coil and base
next you put your coil onto your base and you slip your fingers between the coil and the base and try to make it look like one [piece] do the same . . .

Step #4
keep on making coils until you like your pot

mented, "A lot of the time, I paused to envision what my hands look like when I'm playing guitar. Sometimes I stopped because I wasn't sure what to do, but I engaged and persisted, and a lot of times when I finished a step in the sculpture, I reflected on what I had done and what I needed to do next."

As examples from Anne's class show, using the Studio Habit of Reflect differs strikingly for younger versus older children. Anne's expectations for how deeply students reflect keep increasing as students grow.

REFLECT: EVALUATE

The Studio Habit Reflect: Evaluate requires students to develop two ways of working with judgments of quality. One way is learning to hear discussions of their own work as potentially useful suggestions from others. Initially, students may be very sensitive and perceive all non-praise as negative, even if the responses are constructive and helpful. Teachers may choose to surround critical suggestions with positive feedback until the evaluation process is better ingrained in classroom culture. The second way students evaluate in the art classroom is by learning to judge others' work based on criteria and then articulating their views honestly but kindly. Both ways mean that "evaluating" is a sophisticated disposition for young children, who develop it gradually over time. (See Table 1.8.)

Teachers first need to help children move beyond assessment of works as something they "like" or "don't like"

or, phrased another way, as a dichotomy between "good" and "bad." To do so, teachers can help students expand the number and types of characteristics and qualities that they can name and describe. Much can be described about artworks, even though there will always remain some level of "gut feeling" that defies verbal explanation. Thinking routines such as "See, think, wonder," or "Looking 10 × 2" are very useful in this regard. More information about thinking routines can be found on the website for the Visible Thinking Project at Project Zero (n.d. b) at the Harvard Graduate School of Education.

At the simplest level, a work is successful to the extent that it conveys meaning to viewers [Express]. That is, works need to evoke responses from those who experience them. Students need to realize and internalize appreciation for how their own works make others feel or think and, also, for how works by others make them feel and think.

Teachers can help students develop a further level of sophistication by pointing out ways in which technique creates expression and thus meaning—craft is the vocabulary and syntax by which artists convey what they intend. By bringing craft and expression into interaction, students recognize why acquiring technique is important.

General evaluative comments such as "Good job!" and "That's great!" are empty praise without enough specificity to be useful. It is more helpful for teachers to focus on one or more visible features of a student's artwork or work process—things that students can change. Here are some examples:

TABLE 1.8. Reflect: Evaluate

Ways to Talk about the Habit	I Can Statements
• Identify what is good about a work. • Identify what is not working, and why. • Identify areas that seem incomplete. • Identify areas that bother you and that you'd like to change.	• I CAN reflect on what satisfies me and why. • I CAN reflect on what bothers me, and why. • I CAN reflect about how to change or improve my work. • I CAN offer helpful comments to my classmates about how they could change or improve their work.

Sample Questions

- What part of your work is going well? How do you know?
- Where do you want to improve or change, and how would you do that?
- If you could do this over again, what might you do differently?
- What advice would you give to someone who wants to do something similar?

How Can Teachers Cultivate Reflect: Evaluate?

- Schedule Talking About Art sessions at the beginning or middle of classes so students have time to revise their work in response to suggestions from peers and teacher.
- Avoid empty praise and ask students instead to think about specifics you and their classmates point out and about what is succeeding, what is distracting, and what is not.
- Model ways to ground self-evaluations in specific reasons, such as "These shapes really stand out, because the background is a different color."
- Show students artists' works that were rejected at first but that, over time, came to be appreciated. Duchamp's *Fountain* is one, van Gogh's works are another, the Impressionists a third. Evaluations can change over time!

- "This part over here seems less developed. Was this intentional, or do you think you need to work on this part some more?"
- "I see that you have layered textures on the outside of the bowl. Do you think that the colors you chose for your glaze help us see these patterns, or do you think they make it harder to see them?"
- "You are thinking about adding a base to your sculpture. How do you think that will change it?
- "Some of your prints are lighter than others. Which do you think are most successful?"

❖ **Connections to Other Disciplines**

People make evaluative decisions constantly and try to defend them. Consider a conversation between two friends deciding on dinner.

> "I was hoping we could go to Alfredo's tonight."
> "Alfredo's? That's not really what I had in mind."
> "What's wrong with Italian?"

> "Nothing's wrong with Italian, but the last time we went to that restaurant, the food was cold when it got the table. Also, there's usually a line for dinner and I'm really hungry. Also the pasta there is really heavy and makes me feel too full. I'd rather get Chinese food."

Discussions like these happen regularly between friends, parents and children, and teachers and students. Students have experience in defending their evaluations of other matters, often with creativity and sophistication—why a favorite (but old and ratty) pair of pants should be in the rotation of school clothes ("I like them"; "they're comfortable"; "they look cool"), why special allowances should be made to delay bedtime for a sporting event (making a connection to a similar exception made for a sibling), or why a second dessert is sometimes warranted ("There was a lot of walking, and I really worked up an appetite."). The process of making an evaluation of a situation and defending that decision is ever-present in our lives, similar to the classroom evaluations made of artworks and work habits.

Artist Connections — Reflect: Evaluate

Julie Mehretu. Contemporary painter Julie Mehretu carefully examines her near-finished large painting *Mural* in the Art21 (2010) video by the same name. She describes how she felt her work was complete until she looked at it in a new way. The work is positioned indoors, but in front of glass windows so there are two ways to experience the work—from inside and outside—and she wants to make sure "they don't battle each other." When Mehretu thought her work was complete, she viewed it from the outside; she was dissatisfied by the size and proportions of some of her shapes from that view. Changing her work, even when she thought she was almost finished, is a natural part of her process:

> The way the whole painting was structured from the beginning, there was no part of it that was completely determined ever. It was always the beginning lines, and the next shapes, so it was always this additive process with certain shapes I knew I wanted to include but wasn't sure where, when, how.

Mehretu's process shows that she is constantly evaluating her work to make decisions about its current state.

Susan Rothenberg. In the Art21 video *Memory* (2005), contemporary painter Susan Rothenberg provides us with a wonderful example of self-evaluation in which she looks at a painting and realizes that something is not right, and then goes about revising it. But sometimes, and infrequently, a painting is quick and needs no revising.

> I keep looking at this painting and thinking why I can't just nail it, just make it be whatever it's supposed to be and move on. So it's constant reviewing, and I can't say what makes me say that's wrong, that stays, that goes, this should be longer. It's sitting there and looking and going, uh oh, I have to do something, and it had to be done with color. This one's been bugging me for, it's been around the studio for four or five months on and off reworked, . . . it's closer I think now to where I can leave it. It's very few paintings that come fast and sharp.

❖ IN THE CLASSROOM: Agusta Agustsson Scaffolds Opportunities for Reflection

In Agusta Agustsson's choice-based classroom in urban Waltham, Massachusetts, two 6th-grade girls hover around their collaborative sculpture, a cardboard horse festooned with orange flowers. "How will you know when you are finished?" a visitor asks. "When it looks good—colorful and unique—so unique we don't know what it is. We are going to add more decorations and cover up all the glue and close everything up." Her friend adds, "We get better ideas working together. We change and compromise. She wants ears but I don't want ears, so we make something like this to replace them. Originally, we had this ribbon around its neck. She said it didn't look good, so we cut it off." This conversation, a combination of explaining and evaluating, is ongoing as these girls work and assess how well they are expressing their intended concept.

The girls are rising to their teacher's expectations for creating personal and original work that is also carefully crafted. They have uploaded written reflections and photographs of their work to Google Classroom (see Figure 1.14), and soon they will participate in a gallery walk, in which student artworks are arranged on tables and a sign on the whiteboard reminds students about the What–How–Why goals (Rutherford, 2012) of peer feedback:

- **What:** Artists give and get specific feedback from peers
- **How:** Artists write and read specific feedback from peers
- **Why:** Artists grow when they consider the opinions of others

Each student's work is accompanied by worksheets with spaces to "tell," "ask," "give," and "suggest," a variation of the

FIGURE 1.14. A student determines that his work is finished and uploads a photo to Google Classroom.

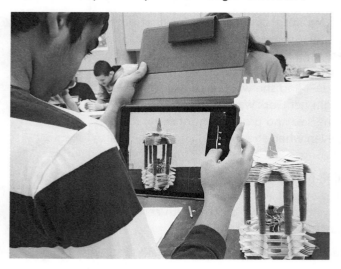

Tell–Ask–Give (TAG) model for feedback (Rog & Kropp, 2004). As students rotate, they pause to examine and reflect on each of four different artworks. They choose an empty box on the worksheet sitting beside the work, write a comment, and sign their names. Each box designates a different type of response. One of the artworks, a watercolor painting of a bird with the background sketched lightly in pencil (see Figure 1.15) receives these peer comments:

> **Tell**—describe the first detail or technique that you notice. *The first detail I noticed is how she blended the watercolors together and created texture with it.*
>
> **Ask** a question. What else do you want to know about the work? *Are you going to add a background?*
>
> **Give** advice. What area needs improvement—what could the artist do? *I think you should add more colors to the bird's feathers to make it prettier.*
>
> **Suggest** a title for this work. Remember to be creative! *Masked Hummingbird*

After students return to their seats, Agusta directs them to star the response that is most helpful and to keep the form in their folder. They add the peer feedback to their artist statement forms. Later, the student artist reflects on her completed painting of the bird, using Agusta's reflection framework:

> **Inspire:** I was inspired by the beautiful wildlife of Jamaica, especially the *Trochilus polytmus,* or doctor bird as is it usually called. The beautiful bird is the

focal point of the painting. I was also inspired by the watercolor paintings of New England winters. I felt a need to try and recreate the purple and blue scenery shown in them.

> **Imagine:** I used graphite pencil and watercolor. I used the graphite pencil to envision the drawing as well as sketch it out. I decided to use watercolor to create texture when it came to the bird's feathers and the trees surrounding it.

> **Create:** I overcame the challenge of trying to blend the colors of not only the bird, but also the scenery around it. When I would place the color into the paper and try to blend with [a] clean brush, the colors would run into another. After this happened many times, I decided to stop trying to fix it. I would only place a color down on the paper near another color that would look good together, so if they ran the colors would look together.

> **Reflect:** I learned a bit about myself when making this piece. The message really hit home with me and who I am. The fact that I am an immigrant and in a place that I sometimes feel like I don't fit in [has] never been more clear. I have drawn my feelings on paper, and it has never made [me] realize how much I feel like this.

Agusta scaffolds multiple opportunities for conversations and thoughtful writing to engage students in reflective practices (see Appendix B). The two sides of Reflect—Question & Explain and Evaluate—are intertwined as students observe to consider their expression and craft. With practice, this process becomes more fluid as students consistently examine their art to identify strengths and areas for improvement, both in their work and in themselves as artists.

FIGURE 1.15. A painting and feedback sheet are displayed in the Gallery Walk.

Stretch & Explore: Play, Use Mistakes, and Discover

I never know really what I'm doing. I have a little inkling of where to start and I'll know when something's finished, but along the way there's lots of diversions and dips and weaves.

—*Cornelia Parker (Howitt, 2013)*

Stretch & Explore comes easily to children and pre-adolescents, who naturally play to learn. The art classroom is a safe place to take risks, initiate ideas, learn to use mistakes as sources of new ideas, and discover new techniques—all part of Stretch & Explore. This Studio Habit is at the heart of problem solving and problem finding, because in play, students push familiar boundaries to see what lies beyond. Stretch & Explore is "mucking about." In doing so, student artists often make mistakes—and they learn that when doing serious exploratory work/play, error is inevitable. Instead of seeing mistakes as something to avoid and worrying that people will think they're "dumb," they learn to see them as opportunities—for new ideas and for figuring out how to improve what didn't work. They often hit upon an idea or process during times they use Stretch & Explore, and these discoveries hold potential to engage their curiosity and commitment.

Staying open to possibility and developing comfort with ambiguity increase with practice, and play is practice.

The opportunity to play before settling into a longer term commitment with a project also allows students to familiarize themselves with the properties of an art material—what it can and cannot do—in service to the art that they want to create. The youngest children see exploratory mark-making as an end in itself; older students may envision how they might use exploration to achieve a goal. Some teachers scaffold "material explorations" with graphic organizers or page guides in sketchbooks that students turn to when starting work with a new medium. Divergent thinking guides students to reach beyond the obvious for solutions that are anything but ordinary. "What if?" questions, similar to those used while envisioning, provide variations for new ways of working.

When students step outside their areas of comfort, they stretch to think beyond the obvious instead of settling for easy, surface answers. For some, stretching may be difficult—a student who feels successful in one medium may fear failure with a new one. It is a challenge to unlock minds that are resistant to Stretch & Explore with art materials and ideas. Teachers encourage low-stakes play,

---

Artist Connections — Stretch & Explore

Claude Monet. Claude Monet was the founder of the Impressionist movement in painting. He rejected the style of the day—very realistic painting. He wanted to show the effects of light on the color of objects. He also wanted to show how things looked in the mist and the rain and through smoke and steam, and how things looked different outdoors as the light changed. Monet painted a series of haystacks and a series of paintings of the Rouen Cathedral in France, each at different times of the day. His paintings, with their thick brushstrokes, give you the *impression* of how things look but do not show objects in realistic detail. Because these paintings were in such a radically new style, critics attacked them as sloppy and unskilled. Now, of course, Impressionism is revered.

Diana Al-Hadid. Syrian-born artist Diana Al-Hadid often works with a team of artists to construct large-scale sculptures and installations. Unusual materials such as fiberglass, foam, wax, plaster, and steel can be used to challenge the laws of gravity (Pollack, 2012). As Al-Hadid's ideas emerge, she reevaluates her work at each stage, revising her plan as she sees how form evolves. By stretching and exploring new ways of working with known materials, the artist expands her understandings of both materials and ideas that guide her as she delves into unforeseen directions (Art21, 2015).

TABLE 1.9. Stretch & Explore

Ways to Talk about the Habit	I Can Statements
• Inquire freely! • Make new mistakes and use them to diagnose and as resources for new ideas. • Play. • Experiment and discover. • Remain open-minded to possibilities. • Troubleshoot problems. • Be open to new ways of working and curious about what might happen.	• I CAN take risks and try things I have never done before. • I CAN play with materials and techniques to discover new ways of working. • I CAN explore concepts to find new ways to express my ideas. • I CAN use my mistakes to find new ideas and to figure out where I could change how I work.

Sample Questions

- What if you tear the edges of paper for collage?
- What if you draw with your eyes closed, or with your nondominant hand, or upside-down?
- What if you weave with braided yarn?
- What if you attach pieces of paper together without glue or tape?

How Can Teachers Cultivate Stretch & Explore?

- Provide ample time for students to play with novel media before making a commitment to an artwork or project.
- Design routines for exploration—cards that students can choose randomly from a deck to try different things, or dice to roll to select choices from a list, or pages with directed guidelines for exploring materials in different ways.
- Demonstrate how a failed attempt can result in multiple new directions.
- Design mini-challenges to introduce new media, such as five different ways to make a piece of cardboard stand up.
- Model "What if?" questions and teach children to use these questions as they Stretch & Explore.

flexible thinking, and willingness to believe that there are many promising outcomes (see Table 1.9). The Studio Habit of Stretch & Explore brings authenticity, new learning, and, potentially, increases confidence in artistic processes.

❖ Connections to Other Disciplines

Some of the best inventions are the result of experimenting—and sometimes arise from mistakes. Very often, scientists, inventors, or engineers come up with something brand new when they remain open to possibilities that were not their original intention. In fact, the discovery of penicillin, and the invention of plastic, sticky notes, and the microwave oven all originated through happy accidents (Cyran & Gaylord, 2012). None of the scientists and inventors involved had set out to create these outcomes—but because they remained open to possible other uses of errors, they discovered or created new, powerful, and useful products.

❖ IN THE CLASSROOM: Around the Room with Cynthia Gaub

Several years ago, toward the end of the school year, Cynthia Gaub realized that she had never gotten to printmaking in her curriculum. Her urban district, Everett, Washington, does not have an elementary art program, so many of her students first experience artistic media and techniques for using them in Cynthia's middle school. To facilitate printmaking experiences before the year ended, Cynthia decided to introduce multiple types of printing in an "around-the-room" (or, round-robin) activity, with a focus on basic skills. Each table, covered in butcher paper, had boxes of supplies, written directions, and paper cut to 4 × 5". A rope around the room's perimeter held drying prints with clothes pins. After experimenting with stamping, monoprinting, collographs, foam, stencils, screen printing, and carving techniques, all students bound their collection of prints into a book (Gaub, 2016).

Her success with this approach inspired more around-the-room experiences at the start of the following school year; she used this approach to introduce students to various art media and techniques. It enabled her students, whose prior art experiences range from none to many, to enter into the activities at their own levels.

Cynthia introduces each material and tool, vocabulary, and directions through signage at each of the tables. Students work for most of the first class, with one rotation at one table. Because she sees students daily, on the next day Cynthia reminds students of her expectations for their rotation, and they pick up where they left off, going from table to table (see Figure 1.16). At the end of class, she facilitates a discussion on challenges and exciting discoveries.

Students stretch and explore with drawing, painting, and collage for two classes before Cynthia assigns a broad theme for which students select their media from among these three choices. Later in the semester, she introduces sculpture and clay through an around-the-room activity for a week prior to an assignment on a theme. She also offers technology, printmaking, and fiber, as time permits.

Over time, Cynthia recognized that her students were growing steadily in developing craft, but their artistic thinking was not advancing at the same rate. Because she wanted students to be able to identify the many types of thinking that direct their decisionmaking through the common language of Studio Habits, she designed a Studio Habits around-the-room activity for six of the eight Studio Habits. Students use worksheets and sketchbooks to note vocabulary, discoveries, and ideas as they visit

FIGURE 1.16. Cynthia Gaub talks with students who are exploring watercolors.

each of these centers (see Appendix A for Cynthia's lesson plan).

After Cynthia's students became familiar with the around-the-room expectations, it was not difficult to implement a new version using Studio Thinking. She hopes that the Studio Habits around-the-room activities will enrich her students' conversations about their work, provide broader contexts for whole-class gallery walks, and help students see how artmaking is developing their thinking (Gaub, 2017).

Understand Art Worlds: Domain and Communities

You walk into the museum . . . you go all the way through from the 14th century, the 15th century, the 16th century, the 17th century, the 18th century, the 19th century. All of that stuff is magnificent stuff. It's all good. We all like it. But you become acutely aware of your absence in the whole kind of historical timeline. We take it for granted that this is just the way art history has been structured. They are all Europeans, and when do other people start to come into the field?

—*Kerry James Marshall (Art21, 2008)*

Children need to form connections between themselves and "art worlds" (plural), rather than THE art world. There are many worlds of art and many ways of making art. Students may not intuitively connect what they do in art class with what professional artists do. Teachers must be explicit about these connections so that students recognize how other artists have used each Studio Habit of Mind, just as they do. This is why we have included connections to artists for each Studio Habit throughout this chapter.

Elementary art teachers carry the significant responsibility of introducing these worlds to their students—

not just fine art sold for high prices at Sotheby's auctions to private collectors and museums, but work made across all human history by folk artists, children and youth, graffiti artists, artists whose works are found in museums and books, artists from hundreds of years ago, and artists at work today, not only in the United States but all over the world. As Kerry James Marshall suggests above, there is the fine art world that, traditionally, is controlled by Western European males. Works by non-Europeans (and women) often do not make it into the most popular museums, and so we do not learn about them. As teachers introduce their students to works of art on every conceivable topic and by artists from every ethnicity, race, culture, and sub-culture, students begin to understand that they can make art about anything that interests them.

Art teachers can guide their students to make connections with subjects they're learning about in other classes as material for their own artwork—mathematical concepts, historical and political events, literary characters, scientific methods and discoveries, or interdisciplinary issues, such as climate change—all these can be explored through artmaking. The Studio Habit Understand Art Worlds has two related components: Domain and Communities. The Domain of art holds the artworks produced everywhere over the centuries. The Communities of art include, for example, those who make art, look at art, decide what art goes into a museum, write art criticism and art history, and teach art. As students develop the Studio Habit to Understand Art Worlds, they do so through experiencing works by other artists.

UNDERSTAND ART WORLDS: DOMAIN

Artists go to museums to get ideas. They learn from what other artists in other times and places have done. They use other artists' works for inspiration and ideas. It's not that they paint in the style of other artists but, rather, they react to other artists' works and ideas.

Students need to learn about the domain of art, too—so they can get ideas and so they can connect what they do with what professional artists do. They need to under-

---

Artist Connections — Understand Art Worlds: Domain

Katsushika Hokusai. When French Impressionists saw the woodblock prints made by the Japanese artist Katsushika Hokusai (such as *The Great Wave* [1832]), it changed how they painted. Hokusai's groundbreaking work in the early 1800s helped to set the stage for modern art. Claude Monet began to collect Japanese prints and designed a Japanese garden at his home in Giverny. The concept of "series" established by Hokusai is reflected in Monet's own painting series of haystacks and cathedrals. Edgar Degas was inspired by Hokusai's use of line and composition; Mary Cassatt and Henri de Toulouse-Lautrec made prints influenced by Hokusai. This is a good example of how artists learn from, take from, and react to the works of other artists (Farago, 2015).

Kehinde Wiley. Contemporary artist Kehinde Wiley makes portraits that reference and reinterpret classical portraits. For example, he reinterpreted Jacque-Louis David's 1871 portrait of *Count Potocki* by painting a muscular Black man wearing jeans and a red T-shirt, tipping his baseball hat while seated on spectacular white steed, gazing down at the viewer with slight annoyance. In speaking about his portraits, Wiley says,

> These paintings are referencing old European paintings that started this language, and I'm trying to use this language to make a point: The point is that anyone deserves to be celebrated on a massive scale of this type. And I hope that by exploding these paintings into such a large scale, we recognize the fragility of individual people . . . but also the possibilities of the individual. (McDonnell, 2017)

Wiley is another example of an artist borrowing from, using, and reacting against other artists.

TABLE 1.10. Understand Art Worlds: Domain

Ways to Talk about the Habit	I Can Statements
• Look at artworks from different times in history to open new possibilities in your own artworks. (with Observe) • Make connections with the art of other cultures to find personal meaning and inspiration. • Connect artworks with what you know about other disciplines, such as science, history, and literature. (with Engage & Persist)	• I CAN connect with other artists through their processes, techniques, stories, and ideas. • I CAN use others' art as a resource for my own work. • I CAN discover artists' work in my classroom, studios, art galleries, museums, and online.

Sample Questions

- Does your work remind you of any of the artists we've studied?
- Let's imagine how someone around during the Civil War [pick a period or place] would react to your artwork.
- Would you like to see work by other artists who were interested in [this idea or technique you're interested in or using]?
- Let me show you [this kind of work] that reminds me of what you're doing or thinking.

How Can Teachers Cultivate Understand Art Worlds: Domain?

- Show examples that cultivate appreciation for the people and institutions that create and support art, including artists, art teachers, curators, conservators, art critics and historians, patrons, museum educators, galleries, and studios.
- Connect contemporary artists' work with student work, and teach students how to identify personal connections to artists and artworks.
- Invite practicing artists—including parents and friends of students who work in traditional crafts—to the classroom to talk about their work.
- Establish relationships with arts institutions—museums, community organizations, art colleges, or art departments—and organize field trips.
- Teach children to locate artworks online to use as resources and inspiration. Tateshots, Art21, and the National Gallery of Art are good starting points.

stand that there is much more to art than the experiences they have in the art classroom. As students are introduced to a wide variety of art, their eyes are opened to art's possibilities—to all of the different styles and techniques and kinds of meaning and expression in art, to the many ways art serves as a form of activism (as in Picasso's *Guernica*, or in the work of Betye Saar, mentioned earlier). The goal is to get students to develop a lifelong relationship to the domain of art worlds (see Table 1.10).

UNDERSTAND ART WORLDS: COMMUNITIES

The Communities of art include those who make art, look at art, decide what art goes into museums, write art criticism and art history, and teach art. The concept also refers to how artists can form a community by developing ideas together; for example, consider the following:

- The community of writers, musicians, performers, and artists in the neighborhood of Harlem from 1910 to the mid-1930s that included such icons as Lois Mailou Jones, Romare Bearden, Augusta Savage, Jacob Lawrence, and Selma Burket
- The culture that developed at Black Mountain College in North Carolina from 1933 to 1957, where Josef and Anni Albers, Walter Gropius, Robert Motherwell, Cy Twombly, Robert Rauschenberg, Merce Cunningham, John Cage, Buckminster Fuller, Ruth Asawa, Willem and Elaine de Kooning, and Allen Ginsberg, among others, gathered, as Modernism developed in the United States

Elementary students can work in artistic communities in many ways. A pair-share during studio work with "What if?" questions or thinking routines results in a small collaborative community focused on inquiry. Other communities develop as students collaborate together to share ideas and technical skills or work directly together in small groups on artworks such as murals, animations, and films, as professional creators typically do. Students and teachers engage in back-and-forth discussions, similar to those of artists and their collaborators and assistants. Art teachers provide students with access to artistic communities whenever a contemporary artist comes into the classroom, or when students go on real and virtual field trips to art museums. Museum docents welcome students to collections and tell them that the artworks belong to all of them, as members of the public. Talking About Art plays a valuable role in developing Understanding Art Worlds: Communities, because students learn how to respond productively to others' artworks. Students come together to talk about art and share their viewpoints with one another, building artistic relationships in the class studio community (see Table 1.11).

❖ Connections to Other Disciplines

Children should be able to see connections between the things they think about when making art and the things professional artists think about—so, too, for all other school subjects. Children can learn to see connections between the nature study they do in a science lesson and how Darwin studied and meticulously classified beetles. It is helpful for children to recognize a connection between what they are being asked to do in school and what professionals do. This shows the extension of the habit of Understand Art Worlds: Domain into the world of science.

Children learn about how artists work together on projects and that not everything is created alone. They can come to this same understanding when thinking about other school subjects: rarely, for example, does

TABLE 1.11. Understand Art Worlds: Communities

Ways to Talk about the Habit	I Can Statements
• Belong to a group or groups of artists who have or had shared goals and interests. • Collaborate in learning groups or teams. • Listen and respond to peers, teachers, and visiting artists as a community of "critical friends."	• I CAN collaborate with my classmates to share skills and ideas for artmaking. • I CAN be heard by, learn from, and compromise with my classmates on works we make together. • I AM a member of my classroom artistic community. • I AM a member of the global artistic community of all artists who ever lived.

Sample Questions

- How are you working together?
- Can you summarize what your friend just said?
- Did your friend summarize all your ideas well enough?
- Who else in the room could help you with that?
- "Ask three, then me": When you have a question, ask each of your three tablemates. If no one can answer, raise your hand for my assistance.
- What would you say to or ask [the artist whose work we just saw]?

How Can Teachers Cultivate Understand Art Worlds: Communities?

- Reinforce clear expectations and norms for in-class collaborative work.
- Introduce students to various career paths within visual arts: curators, critics, conservators, patrons, educators, historians, lawmakers.
- Ask students to volunteer to be "consultants" on particular skills or areas of interest. When the teacher accepts them as consultants, they become available to students who need help in those areas.

Artist Connections — Understand Art Worlds: Communities

The Blue Rider Movement. The Blue Rider Movement in painting lasted only from 1911 to 1914 in Germany. The two best-known leaders of this school were Russian artist Wassily Kandinsky and German artist Franz Marc. This movement is an example of how artists worked together (though not on the same pieces) to develop a new way of painting. They wanted to create a spontaneous form of painting that expressed spiritual truths through combinations of colors and forms. They did not stick to realistic colors but used colors in ways that they felt conveyed a spiritual truth. Blue was considered the most spiritual color; "rider" referred to the fact that they were moving beyond. . . . These artists wrote about the principles of their new movement and were very aware each other's paintings.

Kara Walker. Kara Walker is a contemporary artist who created a monumental sculpture out of sugar in the old Domino sugar factory in Brooklyn, New York. She created this sculpture to demonstrate something about power—the power of the sugar industry, with sugar cane having been harvested by slaves. In the Art21 video *A Subtlety, or the Marvelous Sugar Baby* (2014), she shows us the kind of research about sugar and its role in society that she did before making the piece (an aspect of envisioning). But most relevant here is that you can see that creating this kind of massive structure cannot be done by one person but requires a team of assistants working in collaboration with the artist and guided by the artist's vision.

---

a scientific discovery spring full-blown from just one mind.

Classroom teachers can use the art world to help students understand other subjects. For example, they can talk to students about how social historical forces shape the choices museums make in collecting and displaying works (making some famous, excluding others). When students look at a painting of George Washington portraying him as a majestic man on a horse on a hill, they see how this reflected the powerful image that Americans wanted to create for themselves to the world. Artworks and artistic thinking can be used to illuminate ideas and approaches in every discipline.

❖ **IN THE CLASSROOM: *Art History GO!* with Samantha Kasle**

Prominent artists are featured in Samantha Kasle's art curriculum in Arlington, a suburb of Boston, Massachusetts. Samantha, in her third year of teaching, often visits art museums and galleries to find inspiration for lesson plans. She wants her students to care deeply about art (as she does) and to recognize well-known artists and artworks. She selects a different artist to inspire each of her units. For example, a 2nd-grade lesson featuring blind contour drawing is illustrated with the expressive line quality of works by Jean Michel Basquiat. Samantha introduces this artist as follows: "Basquiat combined styles of art from his heritage—his father was Haitian, his mother was from Puerto Rico—and he combined those art styles with different street art he saw growing up in New York City." She shows a brief video clip of Basquiat at work, and then students start their artmaking. Samantha circulates and demonstrates techniques with oil pastels, often making a connection to the artist: "When I make a mark like this it reminds me of Basquiat and his style, with really bold lines."

Basquiat joins other prominent artists in a game that Samantha designed called *Art History GO!* Based on the popular Pokemon GO game, in which players follow clues on their phones to find replicas of the popular characters, this game is first introduced during art class, and students are encouraged (on their own time) to find artworks that she has hidden around the school. Samantha designed one large bulletin board, far from the art room, that displays all four images along with brief artist biographies. She has hidden smaller versions of the same artworks in random locations around the school. She placed response cards in the display with questions for students to answer about each work:

- How does this work of art make you feel?
- What does this work of art remind you of?
- Draw a quick sketch of what comes to mind when you look at this artwork.

Students bring their response cards to art class and drop them in the *Art History GO!* jar. Samantha reads each one and adds them to the large bulletin board display so students can compare their own responses with those of their peers (see Figure 1.17).

Samantha also decided to use the game as an in-class activity for 3rd-graders. She chose four artists who had all previously been introduced as artist inspirations during class. Samantha tells students that people may have very different responses to the same artwork. She emphasizes the value of gaining new perspectives by listening to others about how they feel about an artwork. She's displayed the four artworks in the hallway across from the art room so she can monitor small groups of students as they fill out the response cards during art class.

As a result of these experiences, children are more alert to artist encounters outside of school. For example, when students saw artist Theo Jansen's *Strandbeest* on a TV show, they were delighted that something they had learned in school was important enough to be on TV.

Art History GO! is highly motivating because it capitalizes on popular and gaming cultures. Samantha knows that Pokemon will eventually fade as a motivation for children. For now, she leverages kids' fascination with the likes of Pokemon characters Pikachu, Jigglypuff, and Charizard as a way of motivating them to learn about accomplished artists. When these cute characters are no longer in style, she intends to redesign the game to incorporate whatever comes next in children's popular culture. Meanwhile her students eagerly enter into the domain of art to learn about different artists and join artist communities as they work and play together to understand art worlds.

FIGURE 1.17. Students fill out cards in response to artwork on the wall.

STUDIO HABIT CLUSTERS

Until now, we've described each of the Studio Habits individually. And teachers often introduce the Studio Habits to young children one at a time. But it is equally important to see that the process of artmaking rarely (if ever!) is so clearcut. One Studio Habit almost never functions on its own in authentic artistic practice.

Consider the example of Micah from earlier in the chapter. His teacher showed the class identity-themed artworks from practicing artists while students knew that they too would be creating identity-themed works. We can surmise that for Micah and the other students, Understand Art Worlds, Engage & Persist, and Express were all clustering together in a near simultaneous way during these Talking About Art discussions. Perhaps looking at a work of Barb Hunt [Understand Art Worlds] was inspiring to Micah [Engage & Persist] and helped him create an idea for his own work [Express]. Picking apart exactly where these three Studio Habits occurred would be difficult—they are clustering together. Later, as he thinks about how he will execute the facial hair on his figure, he considers what tools to use—permanent marker or a small brush. In this, he combines Develop Craft: Technique (what he knows about the art tools) with Envision (the picture he has in his mind for what he wants to create) in a cluster.

Because habits are used in pairs and clusters, and because artists slip quickly from one habit (e.g., Observe) to another (e.g., Express; Reflect: Evaluate), it might be difficult to pinpoint the habit you think you are seeing. Many habits can be seen in most art class activities. Trying to narrow a behavior down to one Studio Habit may not always be productive (though the conversations teachers have in discussing how these habits interact with each other can be productive for learning). Remember that there can be many habits operating at once.

There are numerous ways in which Studio Habits appear together in pairs or in clusters. Some groupings are more commonly practiced than others. It's good to notice the patterns of pairs and clusters that you see emerging in the culture of your classroom. Doing so allows teachers to see what combinations work well and what others to encourage. In Chapter 5, we'll consider further how the Studio Habits interact with one another in authentic artmaking.

STUDIO HABITS AS ENTRY POINTS

Most of us start by teaching the way we were taught or the way that *we* learn best. But students come in a whole range of flavors. Our teaching needs to adjust to that by using multiple entry points as we design curriculum. From the perspective of Studio Thinking, a lesson can begin from and/or emphasize any one or a group of habits, even though students will use many more habits during their creative process. But engaging students from the start requires close attention to the students you're teaching and consideration of the particular Studio Habits that may hook them. Here we consider two common ways to begin elementary art lessons.

❖ Starting with a Plan

One entry point we have seen teachers use is Envision. In lessons like these, students make thoughtful plans before embarking on the final work. Some students may need to plan their intentions before making any first marks of their final work [Envision]—much like Picasso's preparation-heavy approach as he created *Guernica,* discussed earlier. Similarly, Chris Jordan could not have constructed

his image of a human figure using two million water bottles, also discussed earlier, without envisioning and planning carefully how to configure them so that the "pixels" would yield the intended image.

❖ Starting with an Experiment

Not all students flourish with the preparation-filled, Envision-heavy approach of Picasso and Jordan; instead, they may respond actively to exploratory, experimental beginnings (Stretch & Explore). These students may prefer to work more like Jackson Pollock, creating best when they get messy and muck about with materials. Many artists fear the blank canvas. Surrealist painters sometimes used dice or spinners to select from a list of specified beginning actions; some splashed paint or smoke onto paper randomly and then responded to those marks. Some students may find such entry points helpful, resisting projects that ask them to plan work ahead of time and preferring low-stakes exploration. As described earlier, contemporary artist Julie Mehretu describes her "additive" process of working as one where she's not entirely sure how her plans will come together—she has to play and experiment.

IF YOU TYPICALLY use one of these entry points, we encourage you to think about shaking things up and seeing how starting with different Studio Habits (or Structures) pulls in students who may not be engaged by the approaches you generally use. Both ways we've described have value, and there are certainly many others. We suggest that you consider how emphasizing some Studio Habits at the beginning shapes the students' working process. Think about periodically altering the habit you ask students to start with so you can "catch more fish in your nets."

IN THE CLASSROOM: CATHERINE KARP'S 5TH-GRADERS PUT EVERYTHING TOGETHER

Bella, Grace, and Katie, 5th-graders in Catherine Karp's art classroom at the private Oak Meadow School in Littleton, Massachusetts, are model Studio Thinking users. Over several weeks, they work on their group assignment—a triptych that responds to a modern-day problem [Express]. The three girls quickly decide on a personally meaningful issue: climate change and its effects on animals in polar climates [Engage & Persist].

In a flurry of discussion and sketching on the kraft paper that covers all of the worktables [Envision], Grace folds a large paper into thirds for the triptych. She unfolds it and the three girls look at each other, recognizing a problem: the folds were uneven, leaving the middle section bigger than the two side sections.

> "No! Wait! That's fine," says Bella. "Because this is like our main area" [Reflect: Evaluate].
> "Yeah, you're right," replies Katie. "We almost like needed it like this" [Stretch & Explore].

Conversations move quickly as the girls decide on the subject matter. They choose to create an iceberg breaking apart in the Arctic. But the girls are clearly not interested in simply describing a meteorological phenomenon—they're most interested in showing the effects on animals, an emotionally laden topic [Express]. They briefly discuss what to include in their subject matter [Envision].

> "We have to be sure to include the sky somehow."
> "And the sun! Because the sun represents heat and it's too hot" [Express].
> "If we included a person, it would be easier to show that it's, like, a bad thing."
> "People are my least favorite animal."
> "Me, too."
> "They're killing our universe. That's why they're my least favorite."

The girls go to the computer to do some research on what might be the best animal to include, now that people have been excluded. After some searching, they decide an Arctic fox would be something they could draw (Katie spent much of 4th grade learning to draw horses and dogs, and foxes are similar) [Develop Craft: Technique], and emotionally evoking (It's so cute!) [Express]. They go back to the scratch paper on the table, and Katie begins trying her hand at drawing a fox. "It's just a sketch," reminds Bella, who is working on a draft of the sun, smudging the pencil markings of the rays and then erasing portions so that the rays look linear and penetrating [Stretch & Explore; Develop Craft: Technique]. "Do you like what I'm doing with the negative space in the sun?" she asks, to no one in particular [Reflect: Evaluate]. Katie is too engrossed in her fox to look up [Engage & Persist], but Grace, returning from offering suggestions to a nearby group [Reflect: Question & Explain; Evaluate; Understand Art Worlds: Communities], replies positively. Periodically, classmates meander over to ask a question, offer ideas, or get technical advice from one of the girls [Develop Craft: Technique]. Katie works steadily on her fox sketches [Engage & Persist]. "Oh, he looks more distressed now" [Express]. Bella observes what she has done

and asks what changed. "I made his lip more rounded. See? Instead of pointed. More sad" [Develop Craft: Technique; Express; Reflect: Question & Explain].

With sketching complete, Bella, Grace, and Katie set up the framework for their final piece, thinking about how all three of them will work at the same time [Envision]. They abandon the folded sheet of paper, instead choosing separate pages so they each can be working simultaneously. Grace and Bella work on the backgrounds of all panels of the triptych, while Katie is primarily responsible for the foxes [Understand Art Worlds: Communities]. They make detailed plans before beginning the final piece [Envision]. Bella, working on the leftmost panel, draws the iceberg and lines up with Grace's middle panel. She puts a dot where the two panels meet, so Grace is able to complete the bottommost portion of the iceberg while still making sure the panels will match [Understand Art Worlds: Communities; Envision]. Before Grace begins her work, the girls check that their pencils are of similar sharpness, so that no panel's lines are too thick or thin [Develop Craft: Technique; Understand Art Worlds: Communities]. They also make final subject matter decisions: with considerable drama, they decide to draw a baby fox on a detached piece of ice, floating away from his family back on the iceberg. Their reactions to this idea show how deeply emotional they want their piece to be [Express]. Indeed, the teary reactions of the 10-year-olds at such a prospect—a poor, orphaned fox—are heart-wrenching.

They start to work. Every so often, one of the three heads pops up from looking down, takes critical stock of what the other two are doing [Observe; Reflect: Evaluate], and then pops back down, sometimes after voicing a concern or compliment [Reflect: Evaluate; Understand Art Worlds: Communities]. Eventually, it's time to add color. Bella mulls over some possibilities: "Well, people associate warmer colors with melting . . . but people also associate blue with glaciers . . ." [Express]. Color choices are left at an impasse while Katie critiques her own drawings. She's skeptical that her fox is recognizable as a fox. Her workmates tell her that the context makes it clear—just as context can make a reading passage clear. On its own, maybe the fox could be a dog or a cat. But surrounded by the setting, it is certainly an Arctic fox [Reflect: Evaluate].

The time comes for difficult color and stylistic decisions. They decide to outline everything using a black marker like some pop art they had recently seen [Understand Art Worlds: Domain]. They spend considerable time choosing the color for the foxes. They think about white because it is the color of most of the images they saw in their research. But they decide that white is too similar to the colors of the surrounding snow and ice.

Then they draw silver on a scrap of white paper. While this looks best in Grace's opinion, they eventually decide it is also too similar to white [Observe; Reflect: Evaluate]. After much discussion and critical observation [Observe; Reflect: Evaluate], the girls eventually decide that bronze permanent marker will allow the foxes to adequately "pop" off the page [Express]. Katie applies color to the foxes, while Grace marks a scrap paper with each of the blue permanent markers to find just the right shade for the glacier she's working on [Observe; Reflect: Evaluate]. See their final result in Figure 1.18.

Readers may see additional evidence of Studio Habits being used here, because Katie, Grace, and Bella are thinking like artists, seamlessly integrating the Studio Habits as they work. They don't use Studio Habits serially, one at a time. They use them in pairs and clusters integrated so quickly that they seem to be used simultaneously. Perhaps this way of working resonates with what you have seen in your own studio classroom. Someone new to the classroom might just see your students working on a project. But through the lens of Studio Habits, you can see that students have internalized many ways of thinking. The Studio Habits of Mind come naturally to them—now, you can alert them to those habits so that they can use them more deliberately when challenges arise.

IN THE NEXT CHAPTER, we talk about how art teachers organize time, space, and interactions using the four Studio Structures.

FIGURE 1.18. Bella, Grace, and Katie observe their artwork, *The Melting Polar Ice Cap,* which is later exhibited at the art show.

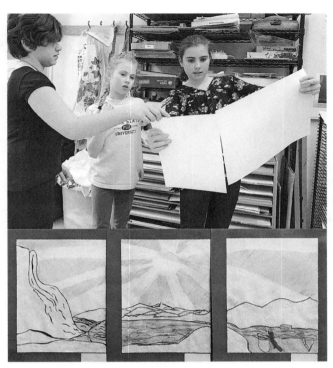

THINGS TO THINK ABOUT

1. Can you think of some Studio Habits that might go together because one leads a student on to the next one? Can you think of some habits that work in opposition to one another?

2. Look back to the various steps in a unit you taught recently and identify any Studio Habits you used. Which ones can you find, and which ones cluster or pair together? Are there any you never use? Why do you think this is? It may make sense not to use them in a particular lesson or unit, or it may be that you forgot and could add them, now that you are explicitly thinking about them.

3. Which of the Studio Habits have you found easier to teach, and which are more difficult? Why do you think that is?

4. When you make art, do *you* start by planning or exploring right on the page? Does your own style match how you introduce lessons to your students? Are there some students for whom this format works really well, and others who might flourish more with a different format? How can you honor multiple approaches in your classroom?

CHAPTER 2

Studio Structures

IN OUR ORIGINAL BOOK, *Studio Thinking* (Hetland et al., 2007), we described the four Studio Structures we saw in high school art classes: *Demonstration-Lecture, Students at Work, Critique,* and *Exhibition.* These structures represent ways that teachers organize time, space, and interactions in studio classrooms. The structures foster authentic artistic practices that help students think and act as artists. For this volume, we have renamed these structures in more child-friendly language, and we describe what they look like in the elementary classroom.

ADAPTING STUDIO STRUCTURES TO THE ELEMENTARY SCHOOL

To speak more directly to our elementary and middle school audience, we have renamed three of our original Studio Structures as shown in Table 2.1. Despite the name changes, the fundamental qualities of these structures remain the same for students at all grade levels.

We encourage teachers to use the flexibility of these structures to tailor instruction for various developmental levels. For instance, a Teacher Presents session for very young children is brief and concrete and includes scaffolding for the Students at Work session that follows. Older students can attend for longer periods and can use written reminders posted around the room as they work independently. Frequency, type, and depth of Talking About Art sessions also differ depending on the ages of the students and their familiarity with artmaking processes and terms.

Elementary and high school art programs usually vary in intensity. Time—always in demand and always insufficient—is an ever-present consideration in decisions made by elementary art teachers. Elementary students have art class once and, in rare situations, twice a week, while high school art students often have class daily throughout a term or year. In the high schools observed

TABLE 2.1 The Studio Structures for Elementary School

Structure	Characteristics
Teacher Presents (*High school equivalent:* Demonstration-Lecture)	• Group focus • Visual emphasis • Immediate relevance • Brevity • Connections
Students at Work (*High school equivalent:* Students at Work)	• Focus on thinking through making • Independent work • Ongoing assessment • Individualized interventions
Talking About Art (*High school equivalent:* Critique)	• Focus on student artworks • Reflective • Mainly verbal • Forward-looking • Varied formats
Showing Art (*High school equivalent:* Exhibition)	• Shows process and product • Varied formats • Involves students • Connects to "real world" art • Advocates for art

for our original research, classes were often 3 hours long. This is in stark contrast to the average elementary art class of 30–60 minutes—for a total of 20–35 hours in an entire school year! This great disparity in time between elementary and high schools often goes unacknowledged by administrators, although it certainly affects learning—including the quantity and quality of material that can be introduced, the classroom climate that can be cultivated, and the depth with which a teacher can assess a student's learning.

Because time is compressed in elementary art rooms, good teachers learn to use every second productively. Managing the passage from one structure to the next depends on routines and rituals—language and behavioral patterns that ease transitions and allow teachers to maximize efficiency and reduce lost learning time. Decisions about how to organize and structure each class become easier with experience, but even effective teachers continue to adjust the arrangement of structures throughout their careers, finding new efficiencies that empower students to think, create, and reflect on their artmaking experiences.

ZEROING IN ON EACH STUDIO STRUCTURE

In the next sections, we describe the four Studio Structures and how each contributes to student learning. We present the structures in the order in which they usually unfold in a classroom, but this order can of course be varied. In Chapter 3, Portraits of Practice, we'll visit classrooms that illuminate how these structures are embedded in practice.

❖ Teacher Presents

Teacher Presents is when teachers offer talk-aloud demonstrations and instruction to prepare students for what comes next, which is usually Students at Work. Teacher Presents typically opens the class to introduce the day's activities, highlight key concepts and skills to be used immediately, or feature an artist whose thinking and/or work connects with that of the students. This structure can also be used to bring the class together later on to re-orient or introduce next steps within a class, as shown in Figure 2.1.

Sometimes students actively participate during Teacher Presents. When teachers decide how interactive to make this structure, they need to consider the trade-off with time for Students at Work. An interactive approach to Teacher Presents could be a conversation, or a student

FIGURE 2.1. Samantha Kasle introduces an artist's work to her class.

might model a process alongside the teacher, assist in explaining a concept, or share a discovery made in his artwork that relates to the day's lesson. Teacher Presents should be kept brief, with clearly articulated goals to maximize student focus, since elementary students can typically listen for only 5–10 minutes before they need a chance to move or try something on their own.

Group Focus. Teacher Presents is a shared whole-group experience. As students enter the art classroom, they follow well-established routines for how and where to place themselves for the start of class. The lesson may announce a new project, outline next steps in an ongoing project, highlight a contemporary or historical artist whose work connects with students' ongoing work, introduce new concepts for students to explore, or re-teach a previous lesson that presented unexpected challenges.

Visual Emphasis. Visual information—images, materials, tools, and demonstrated processes—are central during Teacher Presents. Teachers carefully select and thoughtfully arrange visual prompts and manipulatives for easy student viewing and teacher demonstration.

Immediate Relevance. Teachers avoid vague references to future work during this structure, keeping the focus on the here-and-now of the immediate activities for that day's work. This heightens students' attention. Students are more likely to pay attention during Teacher Presents sessions when they sense that the information presented will be useful during Students at Work.

Brevity. Teacher Presents is brief and concise, providing sufficient information for students to get started with their work, but not going on so long that students lose attention. Teachers delay small-group and one-on-one instruction until the Students at Work structure. For multi-step projects, teachers may interrupt Students at Work for quick whole-group explanations of next steps.

Connections. Teachers reinforce and expand upon past learning by making explicit references to previous lessons. They also invite students to comment on connections that they notice. The question "Who remembers something similar that you did in 3rd grade?" activates students' memories for such links. The Studio Habits of Mind can become a familiar way to tie previous learning to new topics as they are introduced.

❖ Students at Work

Students at Work is at the heart of arts learning in the classroom. This is studio time, when students work independently. Here, students learn through making and in one-on-one and small-group conversations with teachers and peers. "Just-in-time" interventions from teachers are critical supports to student learning. As teachers circulate, commenting and asking probing questions, they also assess understanding (as in Figure 2.2). Careful setup of physical studio space helps students become independent learners, because the studio is organized with materials, tools, and visual references that are easily accessible and ready for use.

During Students at Work, teachers may see students applying Studio Habits singularly or, more often, in pairs or clusters of habits. This structure allows teachers to provide formative assessment consistently—giving them time to respond to individuals or small groups of students about their decisions and to point out Studio Habits that students use. As student and teacher observe an artwork together, they evaluate its progress and envision future steps. Teachers may also help students make connections between their own work and that of practicing artists. Students having trouble engaging or persisting may benefit from a "just right" tool demonstration, helping them to develop craft.

FIGURE 2.2. Catherine Karp talks with 5th-graders about their sketches.

Focus on Thinking Through Making. The authenticity of hands-on studio time is what distinguishes art class from most other subjects in school, allowing students to create personal meaning and develop agency. Thinking and making are intertwined in artmaking. For instance, 3rd-graders who observe techniques for clay surface decoration during Teacher Presents sessions can explore these new techniques during Students at Work. Through making, students expand their knowledge about what some medium can achieve and deepen their understanding of how other artists work with similar media and ideas.

Independent Work. Students work alongside peers in the community studio space, learning to access their work, tools, materials, and resources according to routines and guidelines set by their teacher. With this kind of teacher scaffolding, students can work independently. Students also can rely on one another as resources for additional information to reinforce skills, solidify understanding, and try out ideas. Teachers sometimes ask students to pause for a moment and speak to the whole class during this time, but these interventions are brief, direct, and infrequent. Some students come to art class with paraprofessionals or assistants, and these adults need guidance about ways to best support independent and meaningful learning.

Ongoing Assessment. Teachers circulate during Students at Work to observe, talk with, and assess students formatively. The focus here is on *process*—how students are making decisions—as they plan, carry out, and revise their artworks. Teachers listen as students reflect on their work, offering guidance, noting where challenges may lie, and tracking ways lessons can be revised. Ongoing assessment during Students at Work provides teachers with information about individual students' progress and about the effectiveness of their own instruction. It helps students recognize their strengths and areas for growth.

Individualized Interventions. Ongoing assessments help teachers make timely decisions and respond to student needs with individualized interventions. Because art teachers are acquainted with their students' unique working styles, abilities, attitudes, and interests, they can aim responses to address specific needs. New elementary art teachers need time to get to know all of their students well enough to tailor individual comments for each student. While they build and foster relationships, art teachers can work with classroom teachers and support staff to learn about their students and provide personalized learning.

❖ Talking About Art

Talking About Art brings students and teachers together as a community of artists to discuss ongoing and completed work. These reflection sessions help students learn to evaluate what is working and what is not—in their own art and in that of their peers (as shown in Figure 2.3). As they evaluate artwork temporarily posted for discussion, students use many Studio Habits—they observe, they interpret the expression in a piece, they envision how it could be revised, and, most notably, they reflect. With their own work, they also consider their process. Talking About Art is a social activity where commenting and active listening are essential for all students. Through looking, thinking, writing, drawing, and/or talking, students build community and develop the Studio Habits of Observe, Envision, Reflect, Express, and Understand Art Worlds.

During Talking About Art, teachers model age-appropriate ways to articulate observations of others' artworks and to ask about the stories and meanings behind the works. They may share sample responses, pushing students to go deeper and be more specific than surface-level responses such as "I like it" or "I think she did a good job." Students as young as prekindergarten can participate in

FIGURE 2.3. Students Eleanor and Grace discuss their in-progress artwork.

this process. Prompts for children at all ages can remind students that artists are always making decisions and that artworks are the result of thinking. Older children might focus on a particular set of artistic decisions, such as working with attachments in sculptures or varying brush strokes to suggest mood in paintings. Students can be encouraged to talk about a feeling inspired by a classmate's artwork or an interpretation of the artist's intended meaning. As students become comfortable with the routines of Talking About Art, teachers may offer greater latitude in choosing the kinds of comments, suggestions, or questions that will help students complete their work. (Look for examples of this in the teaching portraits in Chapter 3. Also see Appendix D for sets of sentence stems that can support students in constructing their comments.)

Focus on Student Artworks. Observation is at the center of Talking About Art. If the entire class participates, all other work is put aside so everyone focuses on carefully viewing designated student artworks. Teachers often choose to allot time for Talking About Art at the beginnings and endings of class or during an entire class set aside for this purpose. Teachers establish expectations for creating a safe community during Talking About Art and model ways of talking that facilitate helpful conversations. Though the focus is on student artworks, similar strategies can be used to look slowly and carefully at works by professional artists.

Reflective. When artworks are on display during Talking About Art, it may be the first time students have seen the pieces from a distance. As they describe their work, peers listen respectfully and respond with comments and questions about meaning, technique, expression, process, or other qualities of the work. As students hear what their peers and teacher have to say, they gain insights into their own work, often seeing connections missed previously, areas of strength, and areas for growth.

Mainly Verbal. Talking About Art is often conversational, but it can also involve writing on sticky notes or worksheets so that everyone participates. Teachers can teach students to be moderators, but they are always attentive to students who may lack confidence or who have limited conversational language skills so that they can support them in these sessions. For some students, Talking About Art requires stretching and exploring ways to communicate visual ideas through words or gestures. These sessions also support students in writing artist statements for exhibition.

Forward-Looking. Talking About Art can help students as they revise their works and embark on new ones. Students engage in the genuine artistic practice of giving and taking feedback to improve in-progress or future artworks. Talking About Art opens the door to possibilities with media and concepts that students may not have envisioned previously, and these sessions help them realize the impact that their own work has on others. Classmates can envision how they might approach similar work in the future or revise existing work based on new understanding.

Varied Formats. Talking About Art can be verbal, written, or even displayed through hand or facial expressions. Through written or oral discussions, students begin to envision next steps for revising and finishing their artworks. The goal is always to make time for students to reflect on their work through discussion or in private. Young children can learn "thinking routines" for pair- or small-group sharing at the end of class after completing cleanup. Students with solid writing skills (typically Grades 2 and higher) can leave an "exit ticket" at the end of class, add comments to an ongoing journal or sketchbook, or write artist statements, often following carefully worded prompts or sentence-starters from their teacher. (Examples of these can be found in Appendices B and C.) Some teachers institute classroom "gallery walks" to observe works in progress at the beginning, middle, or end of classes. Artworks can be displayed on tables or on classroom walls. Students can observe on their own, leaving responses on sticky notes or notes in envelopes set next to works, or the class can come together to listen as peers reflect on their process, decisions, and challenges.

TALKING ABOUT ART is a critical element of learning to think artistically, contributing to broader understanding of the visual arts and art worlds. Even when time is short, as it always is in elementary classrooms, it is important to make some time for conversation about artworks. Without it, students tend to think at more surface levels and develop less understanding. As students become familiar with the routines of Talking About Art, their comfort with sharing and responding to artwork grows. This structure supports the building of a learning community in the classroom and, through repeated practice, helps students internalize key concepts and art vocabulary as they learn to synthesize ideas.

❖ Showing Art

Showing Art completes the cycle of studio learning through presentation of students' artworks. Even with the youngest students, teachers introduce Showing Art as a way to convey messages and stories to one another, to families, and to the school community, through expression in the artworks themselves and in students' brief artist statements. Children become accustomed to seeing artwork hanging in hallways as they travel around their schools. During Students at Work and Talking About Art, students learn that not every piece can or should be exhibited and that they can have a role in choosing which pieces to select for exhibition.

Shows Process and Product. Showing Art is not only a way to show finished work but also a way to document learning and involve students in decisionmaking. Exhibitions of learning may display first drafts along with final works, and/or photographs of students as they worked, as well as student comments about decisions they made ("write what you were thinking in this photo"). Whether a whole-school annual art celebration in the gymnasium or a quiet shifting of artwork on bulletin boards in school hallways, exhibitions are powerful learning tools for children (see Figure 2.4).

Varied Formats. In elementary art programs, Showing Art may be teacher or student curated, informal or formal, temporary or permanent, physical or virtual. Depending on school size, available exhibition space, and teacher or volunteer time, any number of exhibitions is possible.

FIGURE 2.4. Student artworks are displayed throughout the San Francisco Friends School, along with peer comments on sticky notes.

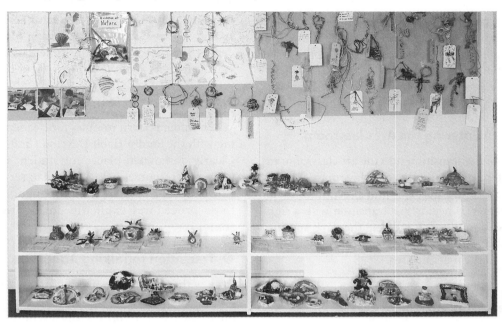

Involves Students. No matter the venue or format, we encourage involving students at every step of bringing work from the studio classroom to the public's eye. Students can work together to curate their work into a cohesive whole (see examples from Kitty Conde in Chapter 3), or they can participate in the process of installation and de-installation. Students can also serve to host formal exhibitions—creating publicity, writing letters to invite administrators and school board members, making programs, or giving speeches at the event. In this way, students begin to understand that artists not only *make* work but also *show* their work so that viewers can engage in conversations that works inspire.

Connects to "Real World" Art. Understand Art Worlds is evident whenever students show their work or attend exhibitions of students or professional artists. Throughout the elementary years, students and teachers exchange stories of exhibitions they have seen at galleries and museums, either as school field trips or with families. When a particularly relevant exhibition comes to town, art teachers highlight the artist and provide exhibition information so that families can attend. Such was the case with Theo Jansen's traveling *Strandbeest* exhibit, which was especially popular with young children. During Teacher Presents sessions, many teachers showed a video of Jansen moving his kinetic creatures across a beach (Exploratorium, 2018). Students told their families about this,

and many families made time to visit the exhibition. Students later reported back to their classes about their experiences with this unusual work.

Advocates for Art. Showing Art is a potent advocacy tool for an art program. When art teachers bring student artworks outside their classrooms, they create new audiences beyond the school and into the community. Exhibitions can be used to educate community members in and beyond the school about Studio Thinking and the artistic processes that led to the artworks displayed. This is an opportunity for teachers not only to showcase polished products but also to emphasize learning and the important thinking dispositions required in making art. Art teachers can design exhibits that explicitly highlight those Studio Habits that are demonstrated in students' artworks by asking students to include them in artist statements and student reflections, by speaking about them during exhibition receptions, or by directing viewers to ask student artists specific questions about Studio Habits used while making their work. As with any exhibition, communication and promotion go a long way toward building audiences and educating viewers. Art teachers who seize the opportunity to exhibit student artwork far and wide—even where the school board meets—make their art programs visible to the public and invite positive response from stakeholders who make decisions about the value of arts education in the school curriculum (see also Chapter 6).

MOVING FROM STRUCTURE TO STRUCTURE: TRANSITIONS

Transitions are potentially awkward moments when students move from place to place, switch activities, or have a few minutes of unstructured time. If not properly planned, transitions can eat up a lot of potential learning time. When art teachers create routines to better manage these moments, they gain more time for teaching.

❖ Transition to Entering the Art Classroom

Teachers facilitate the transition into the art classroom in many ways. Often, students enter the classroom silently, walk over to the meeting area, and find a seat. Julie Toole (featured in Chapter 3) begins this transition with a sign outside the classroom door to indicate the day's specific type of demonstration, allowing students to mentally prepare as they reach the meeting area.

❖ Transition into the Classroom for Art Teachers Working from a Cart

In some schools there is no art classroom, and the art teacher brings art materials on a cart to the regular classroom. To facilitate a quick transition, several students can be trained to unpack the cart and place materials in a designated spot, while the teacher sets up visuals for Teacher Presents. Some teachers give themselves time to facilitate communication with classroom teachers, aides, and individual students by beginning each class with the same activity or game, such as a student leader holding up that week's artwork and calling on peers to give comments about what they think is being expressed.

❖ Transition to Students at Work

Teachers should clearly indicate when it is time for students to begin their studio work. Students know the routines for setting up work areas and accessing materials independently. Their teacher uses this time to check in with individual students about ongoing work or concerns.

❖ Transition to Cleanup

When students learn routines for cleanup, they are engaging with the Studio Habit Develop Craft: Studio Practice. Clearly designated places for student work, materials, tools, and resources help students to set up and clean up efficiently, with or without class monitors. Teachers model these procedures explicitly during Teacher Presents sessions.

❖ Transition to Talking About Art

Even with limited time, Talking About Art is crucial in a Studio Thinking classroom. To save time, the focus can be on just one or two works. Many teachers preserve time for Talking About Art by cleaning up 2–5 minutes earlier than they would if cleanup were the final activity. Sometimes students move to the meeting area as they finish cleanup and find a classmate for a pair-share. As time permits, children may do more pair-shares while the rest of the class completes cleanup and before a brief whole-class reflection. Teachers use the final minutes of class to discuss a few works, review the day's understanding goal, highlight a new poster on the wall, or compliment the class on their demonstrated successes.

THINGS TO THINK ABOUT

1. Remember a time when your *Teacher Presents* session seemed too long and students lost focus. How could you have made the lesson more concise? What could you have prepared ahead of time to be more efficient?
2. Consider your typical *Students at Work* time. As you circulate, what questions seem to work best, and which leave students silent? What questions could you prepare ahead to use in the moment? Develop several that focus on each habit.
3. During *Talking About Art,* ask students to describe, without judgment, what they see so that they move beyond "I like it" or "that's really good." What questions help students talk about what they see? Make a list of alternative statements with and/or for them.
4. Think about how your classes use the structure *Showing Art.* How can students be more involved in that process? Could students curate what's shown? Help install? Decide what text to post so viewers understand what they're seeing? Can students speak at an art night to describe Studio Habits that they used?
5. Consider transition times in your classes. How can you train students to be more efficient in entering the room, getting set up, cleaned up, or leaving the room? How can a transition be used for learning, reflection, or observation?

PART II

Enacting Studio Thinking

CHAPTER 3

Portraits of Practice

IN THIS CHAPTER, we take you into elementary art classrooms where the Studio Thinking framework can be seen in action. You'll see, hear, smell, and feel these classrooms and experience what goes on there. We've painted a picture for you of what it's like to be in these rooms where students engage in authentic artmaking and practice artistic thinking. What does it look like when teachers consciously use the Studio Thinking framework in their teaching? Here, we take a glimpse into three examples.

"Let's Make Some Art"—Julie Toole

You're not far up the staircase of the Baker Demonstration School in Wilmette, Illinois, when you realize you're approaching a hub of activity: Julie Toole's art classroom. Through the glass windows in the staircase door a community recycling bin can be seen, filled with bottle caps, paper towel tubes, discarded board game pieces, and old yogurt containers collected to be transformed into art. A cardboard box sculpture the size of a tall child is nearby, painted in bright blue, orange, and green. From the back, you can't be sure of its purpose or what it represents. Perhaps it's a cardboard person?

As you approach the sculpture, you see it's not a cardboard person but a robot with his name—Bob—emblazoned across his chest in blue paint (see Figure 3.1). A conversation with Julie reveals Bob's creators: four 4th-grade boys who began by creating a robot head and then persisted in creating a whole being, some 3 or 4 feet tall. He stands easily and independently, is sturdy enough that he could withstand a light shaking without falling apart, and embodies a great deal of effort and original thought. As such, he served the requirement of a Wonderful Original Work (W.O.W.; Berry, 2007) for the four artists in this Teaching for Artistic Behavior (TAB) classroom (Douglas & Jaquith, 2009, 2018).

Julie's classroom spills out into the hallway, unable to contain all the materials, energy, and enthusiasm within its four walls. In addition to Bob and the recycling bin, the hallway contains display cases filled with other students' artwork and accompanying artist statements, including signs to educate school visitors about the artistic and thinking processes going on here.

A steady hum fills the room—the sound of constant chatter, the heat gun being used by impatient artists to dry the wet paint that they've applied to make rock art animals, and the Pandora station playing softly from the speakers. Periodically, the hum is interrupted with an outburst, a momentary lapse of self-control, as students make exclamations about their work or discoveries. "Yes! I figured out how to make the base of my Star Wars sculpture attach to the top!" or "This is so hard, but I want to keep going today," or "I'm going to make my tinfoil figure ice skate! Did you know my cousin ice skates in her backyard when it's cold?" Though written signs from teachers around the entire school tell of the rule, "No blurting," blurting seems unavoidable in the art room—a small price to pay for happy children filled with excitement and unbridled enthusiasm for creating.

Entering the art room door, two worktables come into view, and behind them is the painting studio and its four easels. One 2nd-grade girl has paintbrush in hand, complete with orange-dipped bristles that match the marks on the paper in front of her. She stands so she can periodically take a few steps over to get a better view for commenting on the work of her friends, who sit at the adjoining table. These girls are busy creating tinfoil sculptures with cloth outfits. "This one is the mom, and this one is her daughter." "Maybe I'll give him a white belt! . . . or a red belt! . . . or a black belt!" "This one's about to fail. Look at his head. I'll make a new one in a minute." The girl with the paintbrush is not the only one who is mobile. A group of three boys huddle at a table making a cardboard replica of Wrigley Field, and they receive frequent impromptu visits from children who are working on different projects but are impressed and interested in the progress on the baseball park. The artists and the other students give compliments, ask questions, and

FIGURE 3.1. Bob, a sculpture by David, Henry, Leo, and Theo.

FIGURE 3.2. Second-graders Julius, Felix, Noah, and Micah worked on a replica of Wrigley Field during the 2016 World Series.

offer suggestions. "Where's the scoreboard? You need a scoreboard." "What's going on over here?" "How are you going to attach that?"

A quick 360-degree spin around the room reveals deeply focused children. The room stimulates all of the senses. The walls are full, but there is some visual relief in the windows. Even there, however, a student has declared "Art is awesome!" in yellow window paint at the bottom of one pane. All signage is purposeful, educational, and aimed to inform careful craftsmanship and thoughtful work habits in each of the studios in the room, which currently include Drawing, Collage, Painting, 3D/Sculpture, and temporary studios for Rock Painting and Bookbinding. Though the class of 15 students works on a variety of artworks in a myriad of media, resources—available in books and signs made by peers and Julie—support children as they practice studio thinking independently or in small groups.

Julie notices one artist trying to attach a paper towel tube to Wrigley Field to hold the scoreboard. She suggests that the boys try a flange technique—cutting strips into the bottom of the tube so that they bend and can be glued down cleanly to the field. Because these are only 2nd-graders, they haven't yet been introduced to the technique in a start-of-class demonstration, but because they need it for their project, they focus their attention on Julie to learn it. They are bright-eyed and alert, because the new way of attaching has immediate relevance to their Wrigley Field sculpture (see Figure 3.2).

While she's demonstrating how to cut the card-board, a student at another table is having trouble using tape to create pants for his tinfoil figure. "I can't get this to stick," he says at regular speaking volume, seemingly to no one but himself. But because Julie seems to have eyes in the back of her head and an additional set of ears, she turns her head and replies, "Maybe try sticking the tape to itself instead of to the tinfoil." At the other side of the room, the boy nods and repositions his tape. Another problem solved.

MEETING JULIE

Julie (see Figure 3.3) has been teaching art to students in Grades 1–8 for 4 years at Baker, an independent school just north of Chicago. She sees her classes twice a week for 45 minutes. Families who choose Baker are committed to a progressive approach to education and are able to afford the independent school tuition, though many receive scholarships. Julie's background is in paint, collage, and mixed media, and she came to art education after teaching for several years as a special educator. Julie began her career using the Discipline Based Art Educa-

FIGURE 3.3. Julie Toole and Lola.

tion (DBAE) philosophy that was prevalent in art education in the 1990s. A decade ago while teaching at a Chicago public school, Julie felt frustrated with her practices. She wanted to give her students more freedom to express their own ideas and began to share ideas with other teachers who were using the Teaching for Artistic Behavior (TAB) choice-based concept.

Teaching for Artistic Behavior is a philosophical approach in which children are entrusted with the independence, time, space, and responsibility to make artistic decisions about their work. This includes both subject matter and media. Because students have much or full control of their artistic processes and products, every student's direction and outcome in art class is unique. Studio centers organized by media (e.g., drawing, painting, collage, fiber, sculpture) are designed for independent work, with accessible materials, tools, references, and directions. After presenting a lesson to the entire class, the teacher circulates throughout the room providing small-group and individual feedback and assistance. Signage, electronic resources, and peers also contribute to helping students generate and refine ideas, set up work spaces with appropriate materials, create and persist through work processes, and complete original artworks alone or in freely chosen collaborations.

In the art room, Julie signals cleanup by turning off the lights. The room goes dark, and the 2nd-grade artists begrudgingly finish their last scribbles and glue dabs, follow the procedures for cleaning up their materials, and put their projects in portfolios or 3-dimensional storage shelves on the side of the room until they're able to resume work in the next class. As they line up to leave, another class—5th-graders—appears in the hallway, eagerly awaiting their turn in the studio.

LOOKING AT JULIE'S CLASS THROUGH THE STUDIO STRUCTURES

❖ Teacher Presents

Students in Grades 2–5 know that when they arrive at the art room and line up in the hallway, they can look to the sign at the doorway to learn what activity awaits them when they enter (see Figure 3.4). Every other class meeting, an arrow is placed on "Studio Day," which means that they can get directly to work on their art when they arrive. Other days, they have a demonstration, a skill builder, or an artist inspiration. These sessions are 5–10 minutes in length and allow Julie to teach new skills [Develop Craft: Technique], talk about processes for imagining and creat-

FIGURE 3.4. Julie Toole's students know where to look as they arrive so that they know which routine to follow.

ing artwork [Express; Envision; Reflect], and show examples of works from well-known artists or older student artists from Baker [Observe; Understand Art Worlds].

Julie's curriculum includes a basic scope and sequence for introducing technical skills and established artists, but she allows her lessons to develop throughout the course of the year as student interests and needs emerge from her daily observations of Students at Work. Many of the demonstrations, skill builders, and artist inspirations are synchronized with the sequence in which studios are opened. At this point in the year, late October, the drawing, collage, painting, fiber, and 3D/sculpture studios are all open. Demonstrations for this week include more advanced techniques in the most recently opened studio, 3D/sculpture. Fifth-graders learn new techniques for cardboard attachments, prompted in part by a spark in interest because of the recent Cardboard Creativity Challenge (Imagination Foundation, 2017; see also Chapters 4 and 6) at Baker. Second-graders watch a refresher demonstration of a technique that they had learned in the previous year—tinfoil sculpture. Julie chose this for demonstration as its use had waned in the new school year, and she knows it's one of the easier ways for artists of this age to create the figures they envision. When she explains the process to the 2nd grade, she points to the chart she has created for the students' future reference and tells them how the creators of the Wrigley Field sculpture could

have chosen this technique as an alternative to the 2-dimensional paper for players that they created.

In the coming weeks, older students will learn or get refreshers on needle felting, a choice in the fiber studio, as Julie notices that use of this choice has also waned. In November, Julie plans to open another studio—clay—a long-awaited event about which she receives a daily peppering of questions. When it does open, she will use the beginning minutes of her class periods to show a series of demonstrations on techniques and material care, to lead skill building activities in coil or pinch pots, and to share artist inspirations from contemporary ceramicist sculptors. Throughout the year, Julie will continue to use Teacher Presents to show more advanced techniques in all the studios, open temporary studios such as puppetry or printmaking, and lead discussions about the work of student and professional artists.

> For the 5th-graders in the hallway, the arrow is placed on the "Demonstration" box. As Julie goes out to meet her students, there is a chorus of "Hello"s and some waving hands. "Good morning, friends!" says Julie. "Today we're going to head to the demonstration table when we come inside." This announcement is met with a brief but emotionally charged rebuttal. "But it's Wednesday! It's a studio day!" Their protest is indicative of the students' ownership and enjoyment of their work time and their desire to get in and get busy. Julie reminds them that their days have been switched because she was out of school last week, and the 10- and 11-year-olds enter the classroom and gather around the demonstration table.
>
> Today, Julie is demonstrating new techniques for attaching pieces of cardboard. She uses the examples of work by middle school artists at Baker to prompt discussion about what cardboard can do and what good craftsmanship looks like. Sculptures made entirely of cardboard by 6th-, 7th-, and 8th-graders depict porcupines, lip glosses, purses, and sailboats as part of their elective course in 3D. Julie begins with a short and simple observation activity prompted by a question, "What do you notice about these artists' works?" The students respond thoughtfully: "There are lots of details." "I can tell who made the pieces because of what they chose to make. What they made tells us about them." "That one looks like the character Wall-E."

By using their peers' work to observe, Julie emphasizes the point that all of her students are artists and that their creations are valued as art. By considering themselves artists, Julie's students begin to *see themselves as members of artistic communities* [Understand Art Worlds: Communities], able to create and critique works of art thoughtfully. Julie uses artworks by older students to encourage the 5th-graders to think critically about their own work and progress. The examples of artworks by students just a year or two older allow them to see tangible and reachable goals to develop craft by applying Engage & Persist throughout their work process. Julie continues speaking to the 5th-graders:

> "I want to challenge you to up your craftsmanship and to work on things over time. Look at the quality of these artworks. When I shake it, is anything coming off? Is it stable? Do I see duct tape everywhere? . . . I really want to challenge you to get to this level if you're going to use cardboard. You can do it." Julie follows this provocation by referencing one of the posters of "Cardboard Attachment Techniques" that is available in the studio. Student Ben volunteers to help, because he's used many of these techniques in his current sculpture of an airport. Julie and Ben use the middle school examples to show scoring—a technique used by a middle schooler to make the sail on a sailboat appear to be moving in the wind—flange, and L brace attachments, and how to make something movable, like the rivet used on a cardboard record player made by an older student.

Before students move onto studio time, Julie asks them to stop and envision what they're working on and what their first steps are.

> Looking around and seeing that no questions or comments remain, Julie signals the end of demonstration time. "Let's make some art."

❖ Students at Work

Julie's artists are familiar with the routines for working in studios for each medium, where studio practices and materials are kept consistent. When a studio opens, Julie shows each class a video she made of herself walking through the studio showing the proper place to store materials and how to care for them—aspects of Develop Craft: Studio Practice. Using a video ensures that each class gets the same message.

For in-the-minute questions and information during Students at Work time, students can find resources in the detailed and thoughtful signage that Julie provides. The painting studio has a particularly dense amount of signage. Posters on cleaning and caring for brushes and tech-

FIGURE 3.5. Julie Toole's students create signs for their own and their peers' reference. This sign shows the thicknesses and textures of different paintbrushes.

niques of painting are easily visible. A small poster in neon pink paint is also provided, but this one has messier, 3rd-grade handwriting. Julie explains that a student artist created and hung this sign to demonstrate the different strokes of various brushes in the paint studio (see Figure 3.5). Julie loves student-created signs and sees them as a way in which students take ownership as artists in their studio. Students also make signs to be helpful to their peers, many of whom are present or future collaborators, a part of Understand Art Worlds: Communities.

Because students work on different types of projects in the TAB classroom, Julie sorts their studio work into four categories: Skill Builders, Explorations and Practices, Take Homes, and W.O.W. pieces. Making clear the different ways that artists work is an important part of helping her students understand how artists authentically operate [Understand Art Worlds: Communities].

Skill Builders. Skill Builders are works students can choose that help them Develop Craft: Technique. This may be a drawing that challenges a student to incorporate perspective, or shading to achieve something envisioned, or a sewn doll's outfit as the artist gains experience with the sewing machine or practices threading a needle for hand sewing. Skill-building work may progress to a polished work (a W.O.W. piece), or it may be a one-class-long project. Because students freely choose their work, they must envision a plan for their projects, and these are often pieces that express an important message or personality trait of the artist.

> When Julie announces the start of work time, Noah and Quinn go to the worktable nearest the cart that is set up with materials for the temporary stu-

dio of rock painting—using rocks as canvases. Noah appears to be the expert: he shares that he's done rock painting in every class since the studio opened. "I've really persisted," he says. Quinn is not a novice, but she hasn't been as dedicated to the studio in recent weeks as her friend. They each inspect the collection of rocks, holding them up and feeling each in their hands, choosing just the right one. Noah flips through an instructional book to find an example of a panda rock and observes the picture of the final product provided and steps to make the panda. Quinn tells you about her piece because she knows that an adult can't understand the adolescent humor of the pictures on the rock without explanation—they are symbols from a television show. "I would say in this piece, I'm expressing, because these mean something to me." The pair continues to apply the paint markers to the rocks. Every so often Noah sighs loudly, frustrated by what he's marked on the rock, and hurriedly tries to remove the paint he's just applied. Quinn gets up and asks, "Where's the thing to dry these?" "I know! I'll show you. And I'll show you how to turn it on," replies Noah, jumping up. The two start and finish their rocks in today's class.

Explorations and Practices. Julie encourages explorations. She wants students to remember that artmaking is

playful and a source of novel ideas. Students are welcome to spend time inventing new tools or techniques or experimenting with ideas that are still only half-baked. By giving and encouraging time to stretch and explore, students engage in low-pressure activities that can lead to ideas for later Skill Builders or W.O.W. pieces.

Students aren't afraid to acknowledge that they spend time not totally dedicated to a polished artwork. As one girl, sitting quietly at a table, explains, "I'm just playing. I haven't used watercolors in a really long time, and so I'm just sort of reminding myself what they do."

Take Home. Because "kid culture" and personal relevance dominate student artwork, sometimes students take home creations immediately without saving them in portfolios. These include things like cards or gifts for someone, or games students create to play.

W.O.W. Piece. W.O.W. pieces are required artworks that show a high level of effort and time commitment. These are completed projects that use all the Studio Habits of Mind at various points and in various combinations. These pieces are the counterpoint to the more exploratory processes of Skill Builders and Explorations. A list of student-generated ideas is on the wall explaining how to tell a W.O.W. work from one that isn't (see Figure 3.6).

FIGURE 3.6. Students know what separates a time- and effort-intensive W.O.W. work from other types of artwork.

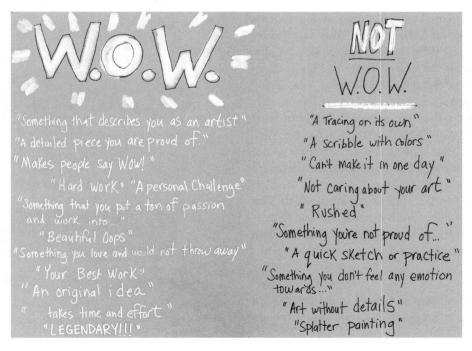

FIGURE 3.7. Ben's airport sculpture includes a hangar, runway, plane, attendants, and cargo trucks.

Many of the 5th-graders recently turned in a W.O.W. piece, but Ben is still working on his—a large-scale replica of an airport hangar, complete with many accessories (see Figure 3.7). Julie is particularly pleased that the sculpture shows Ben's progress in fine motor skills since she has been teaching him. Ben is also aware of his own progress, "I engaged in this and also I developed craft. I used to not be able to do stuff like this." He's worked steadily on this project every class period over the past couple of months, and his enthusiasm has traveled home. Ben's brother, Ryan, 2 years younger, also contributes pieces to the same sculpture during his art classes.

❖ Talking About Art

Every other class, Julie makes time at the end for students to present their work for 5–10 minutes. This happens on studio days when there is no demonstration, skill builder, or artist inspiration at the start of class. To keep track of students who have presented, Julie keeps a written log with the date for each student. Students do not share only finished pieces, but rather present all throughout their work process, whenever their turn is up on the log. This practice honors not just shiny, completed artworks but also the important thinking that happens while works are in progress.

Julie uses several techniques to get students to look critically at their own or at each other's artworks, a process that helps students understand how artists talk with one another, a component of Understand Art Worlds: Communities.

TAG. As explained in Chapter 1, TAG is an acronym for Tell–Ask–Give (Rog & Kropp, 2004). Julie uses this tech-

nique as a quick way to get students talking about art. First, artists Tell (T) the story of their artwork—why they made it, what it's made from, what was difficult about their process, or why they're proud of it. This allows students to reflect on any number of Studio Habits of Mind used in the work process, share how their pieces are personal expressions, acknowledge how they engaged and persisted or developed craft: technique, or discuss how what they had envisioned changed over time. Viewers then Ask (A) questions and Give (G) a combination of suggestions and compliments to the artist.

Critique Sandwich. Julie keeps various components of the *critique sandwich* magnetized on the whiteboard at the front of the class (see Figure 3.8). For younger students, Julie may construct the sandwich by leaving only the most basic ingredients on the board. For older students, she may prompt the artist with "What are you hungry for?" and encourage them to choose which types of feedback would be most useful for them at their current stage of the work process.

FIGURE 3.8. Julie Toole's critique sandwich lets the artists choose the types of responses they welcome from their peers.

Portfolio Cleanup. When we spoke to her, Julie didn't immediately list portfolio cleanup as a type of critique, but as she brings it up, she realizes that it provides students the opportunity for self-evaluation of their work. When portfolios start to get too full, Julie encourages students to take stock of what they have and what sort of process went into each. Pieces that are of W.O.W. quality should be submitted to Seesaw, an online portfolio for digital storage, while pieces that were for exploration or skill building can be taken home. Other pieces that were not fully developed or that students do not feel invested in can be donated to the collage paper piles or the Beautiful Oops bin (inspired by Saltzberg's 2010 book of the same name), where students who want a challenge can turn someone's "mistakes" into a finished artwork.

Gallery Walks. Gallery walks happen both inside the art room and in the adjacent hall, where Julie has a large bulletin board that serves as an art gallery. The aim of gallery walks changes based on Julie's focus. Sometimes students look around the room to observe artworks and write suggestions on sticky notes. Sometimes they move around the room with a worksheet noting artworks that exemplify particular Studio Habits of Mind. Viewing other students' artworks in and outside of the classroom gives young artists ideas that help them to express their personal visions in later works.

❖ Showing Art

As the 5th-graders leave the art studio, a new class waits for Julie in the hallway. These children are shorter, wigglier, friendlier, and a little more noisy. In just their seventh week ever of art class with Julie, these 1st-graders are still learning lots of basic techniques and skills. Julie explains to them that today they'll be taking their first trip to the gallery wall to look at the artworks there. They process out to an adjoining hallway, where a bulletin board is covered in 2-dimensional artworks by 1st- and 2nd-grade artists (see Figure 3.9). After a brief discussion about letting the art on the wall be inspirational to them as artwork viewers, the group goes over guidelines: Be respectful to the artists by not touching their works, and take time to read the artist statements next to the work. They then look at the gallery, finding something that inspires them that they can report back about later.

FIGURE 3.9. First-graders view the hallway gallery with their own and their peers' work.

The gallery is covered in inspired and inspiring works, along with age-appropriate ways for students to write about their artist statements. First-grader Oscar has contributed his art, and he writes, "Two people, me and Freja [his sister], walking on a sunny day." He also notes the underground world as a part of his work and hopes people notice (see Figures 3.10 and 3.11).

FIGURE 3.10. Oscar's collage.

After several minutes of observation and small-group discussion, the group resettles on the floor in front of the gallery. Julie asks what inspired them in the works, and one student quickly volunteers his appreciation for Lola's work, "because she uses really nice colors, and she's also a really nice friend." (Comments that mix "art criteria" with other rationales for approving of a work—"she's a really nice friend"—are common. It will take time for students to learn to focus exclusively on criteria about the works!) When the discussion ends, the students go back to the art room to make more art.

FIGURE 3.11. Julie Toole provides forms for students to complete artist statements.

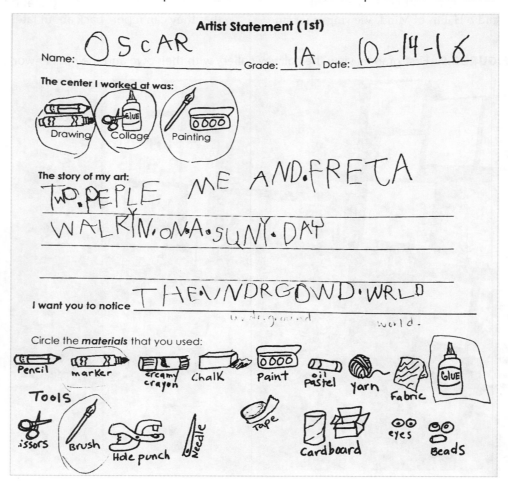

Hand, Mind, Heart, and Community—Celia Knight

It's a picturesque scene driving to the Gates School in Acton, Massachusetts. The town is quintessentially New England and nestles immediately west of the American Revolution's better known Boston suburbs of Lexington and Concord. There are several elementary schools in Acton, each just off the small town's main road, which, at this time of year, is surrounded by snowy tree branches amidst small coffee shops and old church buildings. Acton's Wikipedia page lists several awards, including Best Place to Live and recognition for STEM education.

Your walk from the parking lot into the building requires care to maneuver the icy pavement. Once buzzed into the secured front door, there is a rush of heat, so different from the cold air outside. The smell of cafeteria food and the hum of a game from the gymnasium greet you from the school's foyer. Walking a minute down an adjoining hallway takes you to Celia Knight's art classroom.

MEETING CELIA

Celia Knight (see Figure 3.12) has been the art teacher at the Gates School for 11 years. She has the support of a strong art department in her regional school district, and the group meets regularly to plan (see Chapter 4). Celia assigns projects to her students and uses Studio Habits, which are visible in many places around the room, to help reinforce thinking processes in making, viewing, and displaying artwork. Celia sees her students for 45 minutes once a week, but she also sees every class for another period per week for one-third of the year.

LOOKING AT CELIA'S CLASS THROUGH THE STUDIO STRUCTURES

◆ Teacher Presents

It is first thing in the morning, and Celia is prepared for a long day of teaching. Her computer is hooked up to the projector for the brainstorming activity the 4th-graders will undertake when they arrive, and the worktables have bins stocked with yarn and other weaving materials. She has already placed the students' works in progress at their spots to save time.

The class of 24 students arrives and all take their places on the rug at the front of the room for a dis-

cussion. Celia begins by acknowledging that weaving is difficult and some people find it tricky. "My Art Heart needs to stay focused on my artwork, so I don't give up. How can you engage and persist today while you weave?" she asks. As students volunteer answers, she types them onto a projected document so students can see and reference them as they work.

- Stop and think before adding next design
- Don't talk that much
- Only talk about weaving
- Help others if they're stuck
- Don't get discouraged
- Ask for help

Discussions like these are typically how Celia begins her classes—a mix of information about artistic techniques, Studio Habits, connections to art history, or lessons in looking at artwork. Celia refers to her "Art Heart" when

FIGURE 3.12. Celia Knight shows her threaded needle for weaving.

FIGURE 3.13. Celia Knight displays how each of the Studio Habits helps student artists use their artistic hands, heart, mind, and community.

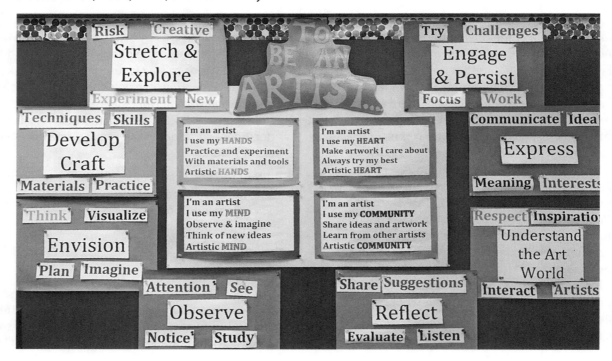

talking about Engage & Persist, which is common language for her students. Celia has sorted the Studio Habits into groupings that make sense for her, and she sings a song about these to the tune of the French folk song "Frère Jacques." For Celia, "Artistic Hands" include Develop Craft and Stretch & Explore; "Artistic Heart" is comprised of Engage & Persist and Express; "Artistic Mind" is made of Envision and Observe; and "Artistic Community" contains Understand Art Worlds and Reflect (see Figure 3.13).

In the next class period, the 4th-graders are replaced by 5th-graders. These students are working on an intensive project in which they are each building a sculpture with a moving element powered by a solar panel (see Figure 3.14). Celia quickly transitions to this class—plugs in the glue guns, takes out the toolboxes, and pulls out large boxes of sculptures from underneath some worktables—transforming the room into an art makerspace.

Class begins with a discussion—Celia is preparing her students for Talking About Art with the aim of improving their work process. She describes the format of today's partner critique, which will happen at their worktables once students get their pieces. The display on the projector says that stu-

FIGURE 3.14. Vanna and Abigail connect elements of their sculptures, leaving a spot in which to insert the solar panel.

FIGURE 3.15. Celia Knight shows guidelines for partner critiques.

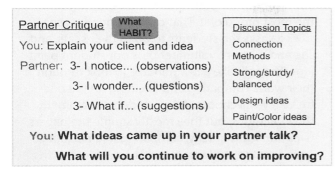

dents will give each other three comments about their work for each of three types of statements:

- I notice . . .
- I wonder . . .
- What if . . . ?

She also includes some of the topics they might choose to talk about, which are closely related to the assignment: connection methods, balance concerns, design ideas, and paint/color choices (see Figure 3.15).

"Before we do anything today, we're going to have a partner critique. What Studio Habits do you think are involved in a partner critique—when you talk to your partner about your artwork?" Students are used to talking about the Studio Habits, and displays with definitions and examples are at the front of the room for reference.

The first student begins, "It's Understand Art Worlds because you're sharing your artwork with the world."

"So this is how artists talk in the art world?" interprets Celia. "Okay."

Another student volunteers, "It's Observe because you're looking closely."

"Like an 'I Notice . . .' statement," says Celia.

A final student replies, "It's Reflect."

"Yes, you're making an evaluation, an argument about how it should or shouldn't look."

Celia acknowledges that while Talking About Art in this way is primarily a Reflect activity, it also involves many of the other Studio Habits, depending on how you choose to look at it. By acknowledging all the different ways of thinking that are present in an activity like this one, Celia emphasizes that interacting with art is a complex process.

◆ Students at Work

Following partner critiques, the 5th-graders will be using potentially dangerous hand tools like saws and hammers, working with finicky panel attachments, and using many materials, so Celia has recruited reinforcements: Several volunteers are in the room with her, including parents and a retired science teacher. She assigns each a task: The science teacher helps attach and test the solar panels, while the parents distribute and monitor use of tools.

Students were asked to think of a client and invent something for them. Some students create objects that they think would be useful for celebrities—Advait envisions a flying car that holds an indoor basketball court for Michael Jordan. Other students make objects for more personal clients, like the girl who creates a moving Rubik's cube for her mathematically inclined brother.

Glancing around the room, you can see various emotions on display. Some students are having trouble getting their sculptures to stand; some feel a little anxious, trying to both do their best and finish in what they know is inevitably not enough time in art class; others gleefully hold their panels up to the light to watch them work. Celia makes an announcement, "I hear a lot of great things. I don't hear people talking about things that don't matter [to our work]. I hear people asking each other for help and questions, so that's great."

Over several weeks, students continue work on their sculptures, carefully observing problems, offering each other help, and reflecting on what did and didn't work so that they can improve. The unit culminates in a trip outdoors on a sunny day so everyone can see each other's sculptures in motion and take videos. Students then spend time reflecting on their process, resulting in 1-minute films created on iPads that incorporate their thoughts on their artistic process and product. They take videos and still photos of their processes and product and add spoken and written words (see Figure 3.16).

◆ Talking About Art

After lunch, Celia sees her 1st-grade class. Today they aren't making art, which is rare. Instead Celia uses the Talking About Art structure as she leads the class in three activities that call on the habits of Observe and Reflect.

The class proceeds to the rug and sits down for a discussion and preview of the day's events. Celia

FIGURE 3.16. Still images from 5th-grader Alex's iPad presentation. While demonstrating his tape attachment, he says, "I used Engage & Persist and Stretch & Explore by trying out different ways to stick my cardboard pieces together. First, I tried hot glue but it didn't work. Then I tried using a stick to connect them, but that didn't work. Then I used duct tape, and it worked. That is how I used Engage & Persist and Stretch & Explore."

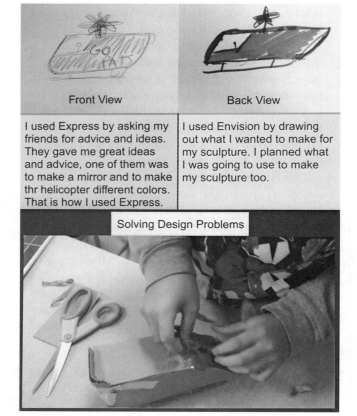

begins, "Today, we're going to think about a question: How do I choose my best work? We're going to look at all the paintings we've made over the past few weeks. You have four paintings. You're going to look through and pick which is your best work. What are some of the things you're going to look for that painters do?"

"Art mind," says one child.

"What do you mean by that?" asks Celia.

"Like, what's in your mind. So your idea."

"Okay, so you could choose which one of your ideas that you like the best. What else would make it your best work? What else do painters do?"

"Lots of mixed colors," volunteers another student.

"Okay, colors, maybe brushstrokes, too," replies Celia. "I'm also going to add that it might just be your favorite. It's your best work, because you're the most proud of it. That can be a good reason."

Celia asks the students to go to their seats, and she and a parent volunteer pass out student paintings. They all take a few minutes to look through their work, comparing and deciding on the one that they will choose. A few students chat about their decisions, but they mostly shuffle the papers back and forth quietly, comparing and deciding. Celia asks the students to put their choices to the side of their desk, and she collects those paintings that weren't chosen, leaving the "best work." Meanwhile, the parent distributes bingo cards and markers (see Figure 3.17). Once everything is settled, Celia explains the rules of the game—using a website that allows her to add a bank of words that are then chosen at random, she calls out various colors and brushstrokes. When she calls a particular color ("orange!") or brushstroke ("dotted line!"), students who see that in their painting mark off the box. While playing the game, students search their work carefully, hoping to find whatever color or stroke has been called. They continue until someone gets five in a row and calls out "Bingo!" and the winner receives a high five from Celia.

FIGURE 3.17. A bingo card of colors and brushstrokes.

Color	Brushstroke	Color	Brushstroke	Color
purple	dotted	red	wavy	mint
grey	wiggly	yellow	straight	teal
brown	thin	orange	thick	pink
black	bumpy	blue	curvy	maroon
white	zig-zag	green	twirly	peach

After about 25 minutes, students are ready to move on from the game, and Celia passes out some artist statement templates and models how to complete them. Using one student's work as an example, she counts the number of colors and brushstrokes and tells the students that they can complete the sentence stems using "kid spelling" and not worry too much about what's correct. At the art show, these forms will accompany the works that each student chose as their best work. Student Johann completes his form. "I used 5 different colors in my painting. I used 6 different brushstrokes in my painting. I used overpainting to make pink. I like the way I made Mewtwo" (see Figure 3.18). (Johann's entries on the form are underlined.)

❖ Showing Art

The year at Gates culminates in a schoolwide art show that takes over the gymnasium (see Figure 3.19). Celia, students, and volunteers set up the displays on a Thursday in preparation for the night event that parents attend. In

FIGURE 3.18. First-grader Johann counts the number of colors he used in his work, a depiction of a Pokemon character.

FIGURE 3.19. Art displays transform the gymnasium.

FIGURE 3.20. Student artist Amelia received a letter of feedback from an older student, Ellie: "I love your [painting]! It's so colorful and pretty! I also like how you decorated the frame. My class also did a [painting]! I called mine "broken glass" because the middle looks like broken glass. I really like your title."

addition to the visual arts displays, the music teacher leads families in folk dancing activities in the cafeteria. The following school day, Celia doesn't teach her typical schedule but instead meets with each class in the school for 20 minutes in the gymnasium so that everyone has a chance to see the art show. She has the support of the classroom teachers and administration to make this possible. Celia uses several strategies for incorporating the exhibition into her program.

Art Buddies. Celia directs students' viewing experiences by assigning each child an "Art Buddy" (older students are paired with younger students). During the time while viewing the works on display, students search for the work of their buddies and respond to these works on a form. The next week in art class, students receive the completed form about their own artwork (see Figure 3.20). Celia also makes the forms available when parents visit, and some choose to complete forms for their own or other children.

FIGURE 3.21. Fifth-grader Elise's artwork and artist statement are displayed alongside the listing of learning goals created by Celia Knight.

The Forest of Copper Trees

I studied Pierre Auguste Renoir. The artwork that inspired me was a painting of a man with his dogs in the forest. I wanted to paint a forest, too, so I painted one and then turned it into fantasy. Colorful leaves, copper trees, and a majestic deer stand tall on the canvas. I used blending in the sky and grass. I used over painting on the trees. They started as red brown to dark brown to gold to copper. I used brushwork on the spots on the deer. I used envision to vision before I painted what it would look like. I also used observe to observe what Renoir's painting was like. This is my painting, The Forest of Copper Trees, and I hope you enjoyed looking at it!

UNIT: 5th Grade Art History Inspiration

Big Ideas:
- Artists are inspired by the work and lives of other artists.

Essential Questions:
- What is inspiration?
- What inspires you?
- What is the difference between inspiration and imitation?
- What aspects of an artist's work or life could inspire you? (Ideas, Techniques, Life, Work, Subject Matter)

Skills:
- Learn about an artist's life and work and create a painting inspired by your research.
- Understand difference between inspiration and imitation.
- Apply previously learned painting skills in a finished painting (mixing, blending, overpainting, brushwork).
- Use sketchbook for compiling research and planning sketches.

Art History Connection:
Students will research the life and work of an artist and use their research to inspire an original painting.

Assessment:
Title & Artist Statement
- How did the artist's work inspire your painting?
- Describe the idea behind your painting.
- How did you use painting techniques such as mixing, blending, overpainting, & brushwork?

Educating Parents About Art. At every exhibit in the show, Celia posts signs to document and emphasize what is being taught in art class (see Figure 3.21). She uses various ways of getting this message across—standards, Studio Habits, connections to art history—to reach (and impress) as many parents as possible.

Using Student Words to Educate Parents About Art. In addition to creating these postings, artist statements and other reflections are displayed with student work. Hearing from students about what they're learning can be more powerful than hearing explanations by adults. Second-graders created mini-booklets that required them to question and explain their process of creating a clay animal (see Figure 3.22). Celia uses the opportunity of the art exhibition to advocate that at the Gates School, art-making is about thinking.

FIGURE 3.22. Second-grader Zoe's elephant sculpture is displayed alongside a book that describes how it was created.

"I Have Something That Might Work Better for You"—Kitty Conde

Walking the 15 minutes from the nearby L Subway stop to the Ravenswood Elementary School in Chicago, Illinois, you pass a patchwork of low-income housing units interspersed with cupcakeries, coffee shops, and art studios in old factory buildings.

As art teacher Catherine "Kitty" Conde explains, the neighborhood has gone through socioeconomic changes in the 25 years since she first started teaching art at the preK–8 school. She recounts that when she began, 99% of the student body was living in poverty, but now that percentage is down to 49%. Kitty says this almost wistfully, as she loves to teach students most in need. Over her years at the school, Kitty has worn a number of hats—art teacher, parent, and neighbor living across the street for several years. If you're looking for information about Ravenswood, she's probably the best person to ask.

The electronic sign on the school's front lawn advertises dates of upcoming progress reports and the Arts Showcase; in the school itself, children can be found preparing works for the showcase in their visual arts, dance, and theater classes. The art room sits in the center of the school, through the main door and up the staircase that you observe as you enter the school. Kitty's voice can be heard from inside the room, and middle schoolers are spilling outside into the hallway painting murals on canvases that later will be put up around the school as part of the yearly class Kitty teaches on public art. Some students are actively painting, others are looking back and forth to compare their pencil sketches with what they've already painted, and others are reading or discussing a handful of sticky notes—responses they received earlier in the class during a whole-class critique activity. Artmaking is thoughtful here—students are not just creating but acting fully like artists: they reflect on their work, discuss feedback, and think together about their work's context.

The art room is jam-packed. Large paint bottles with 1990s graphics, which have obviously been refilled many times over the years, are stacked on shelves covered with makeshift cloth curtains. Signs cover the walls—how to attach different materials to each other, definitions of the Studio Habits, and ways to cool down when you get angry—aiming to make students as independent as possible. The building is old and its materials are well loved, but signs of aesthetic care (like neatly color-coded and organized oil pastels, sitting in bowls) and provocations to inspire artwork (thoughtfully placed ceramic skeleton heads and a gigantic amethyst) can be seen on various shelves.

Eventually, the students pack up to leave, and Kitty's schedule on the whiteboard denotes a lunch break. But Kitty doesn't seem to "break"—ever. As the other two arts teachers enter Kitty's room for a meeting, she multitasks—filling a barrel with water for the kindergartners who will try watercolors later that afternoon (and aren't tall enough to reach the sink!), collecting work from tables from the last class and putting it into the class storage bin, checking email on her phone, and munching on a few crackers.

MEETING KITTY

It takes only a short conversation with Kitty to know that she breathes and sleeps Ravenswood (see Figure 3.23). When she's not teaching her hectic schedule, she's running to meetings about how to bring more teaching artists or grant money to the school or to appointments with classroom teachers to plan integrated units. Her days are long, and her classes are large (e.g., nearly 30 kindergartners), but Kitty keeps a consistent attitude of patience and enjoyment for what she's doing in her weekly 1-hour classes. As principal Nate Manean notes, "Kitty is eter-

FIGURE 3.23. Kitty Conde and Aiden discuss his artwork.

nally curious; not only curious for her own professional development, but curious about the world of kids." Kitty's curiosity means that her teaching is always evolving.

In 2001, after years of teaching on a cart, Kitty finally transitioned to having her own classroom. It was also at this time that she branched out to incorporate more choice in her teaching. She wanted to allow her students freedom to pursue individual interests while simultaneously pushing them to do their best work. Several years later, while writing her master's thesis on autonomy in the middle school art room, she learned about Teaching for Artistic Behavior (Douglas & Jaquith, 2009) and the Writers Workshop model in language arts (Calkins & Mermelstein, 2003). She found similarities in both that helped her think about her teaching. She also sees the schools of Reggio Emilia, Italy, as an influence on her practice (Krechevsky, Mardell, Rivard, & Wilson, 2013). Kitty regularly engages with the rich art education community in the Chicago area, attending professional development workshops with local nonprofits and museums.

Currently, Kitty's room is set up into studios—drawing, painting, collage, construction, clay, fashion and textiles, and technology—and she opens these to students gradually throughout the year. Sometimes she embeds assignment-based structures, but she always maintains a high level of choice in her studios. For instance, Kitty noticed that when sculpture materials are made available, "[the students] want to hot glue everything to everything." Wanting to slow them down and ensure that they think, she began the "transformation challenge." In this assignment, students choose one object from the sculpture area (a toilet paper cardboard tube or an old water bottle or something else) and envision it in three different contexts. They make three different plans for what it could be, stretching and exploring beyond their original idea. Before they choose one to create, they do some research using the Internet on materials needed and about other related artworks that might exist. She creates a checklist so students can progress independently through their process. At other times, students are free to design independent work using materials from the various studios.

The lunchtime meeting with the arts teachers is wrapping up, and principal Nate Manean pops his head in to talk to the teachers.

"I used my favorite habit today," he says.

Kitty laughs. "What's that?"

"Stretch & Explore."

"That's my favorite, too."

"I'm trying it with adults. My Assistant Principal and I realized we were in a rut thinking about this particular situation, and so we decided we needed to stretch and explore and try different ways of thinking about how to work with this person."

"Did it work?"

Nate pauses. "TBD," he says, and then ducks back out.

As an arts magnet school (a program Kitty helped implement several years ago to get extra funding for arts programming at the school), arts integration is central at Ravenswood. *Studio Thinking* (Hetland et al., 2007) was one of four books that all Ravenswood teachers could choose to read and discuss in a book club during professional development time. Clearly Nate has been taking care to integrate what he's reading into his school community.

LOOKING AT KITTY'S CLASS THROUGH THE STUDIO STRUCTURES

❖ Teacher Presents

Lunch is over and 2nd-graders enter the room, moving to spots at several worktables. Kitty has their class's box of work out so that when the time comes, they can find their in-progress works. Sketchbooks hold "envisionings" of plans created prior to beginning these final works for the showcase. Kitty starts class, explaining how important it is to reference sketchbooks. "The reason your sketchbooks are important is that you need to have your . . . ," she pauses and raises her eyebrows in anticipation, ". . . ENVISIONING in front of you." At the sound of "envisioning," the students cue in—they scratch their chins, look up, and make a "hmmm" sound. Envisioning is part of the vernacular of the art room, and the students' previously choreographed responses help draw attention to it.

As Kitty explains, she uses the exact names of the Studio Habits so children hear them consistently and remember them better. Young children learn new words every day—she doesn't find any of the Studio Habits words to be beyond what her students can learn to use in their vocabulary.

"We're working on our showcase pieces. It might be time for some of you to ask for feedback on some of your pieces. Bella told me that she was done, and so I was like, 'Cool, let's give it a PQS.' How does a PQS help us?"

"A PQS is an 'I like it' and why," volunteers a student.

"Yeah. It's a Praise (P), a Question (Q), and a Suggestion (S)" (EL Education, 2017), Kitty says, holding up the form that they use for completing the activity. "Okay, so give me a good reason why you like this piece," she says, holding up Bella's painting of a nature scene.

"I like how on top she put, like . . . it kind of looks like sponges," says one student.

"Oh, so like there's a textured mix of colors up there?" says Kitty. Then she calls on another student.

"I like it because it looks like the branch is over like a hurricane of color, and the leaves are falling."

Kitty moves on, "Okay, so we've done our Praise (P). How about a Question (Q)?"

"Why are the peapods colored?"

Kitty looks at Bella, aware that there are no peapods intended to be in the picture. "Okay, so Bella, people are seeing peapods."

"How did you come up with this painting?" asks another student.

"I have an answer for that!" says Bella. "I looked in an art ideas book."

"Oh? Look up at the 'Where Do Artists Get Ideas?' wall. Some artists gets their ideas from books," says Kitty.

Because Kitty's students often design their own projects, sources for ideas are explicitly taught and discussed.

Above the whiteboard at the front of the room, Kitty has created a large graphic that displays some of the many sources of ideas artists use (see Figure 3.24). Because she refers to it regularly, students naturally ask each other how they got their ideas for their work, and students have the words they need to describe how they came up with their ideas.

"Does anyone have any Suggestions (S) for Bella?" asks Kitty.

A student responds, "Maybe you could go over the peapods darker."

Kitty interprets, "Oh, so you think if she goes over these shapes that she has darker, it might solve the problem? They might not look like peapods anymore?"

Kitty concludes the modeling of a PQS by asking Bella her next steps. "You got some suggestions and compliments. Do you want to go back in and change anything?"

Bella replies honestly, "Not really."

Kitty laughs. "Yeah, sometimes, not really. The paint's dry. And that's okay. Maybe these suggestions will help you with your next work. But if you're looking for some more ways to engage, you could try expanding this into a series." Kitty completes her Teacher Presents time by showing some of her own artworks and how she chose to expand her idea into multiple pieces as part of a series, an idea she suggests frequently as students prepare their works for the showcase.

FIGURE 3.24. Kitty Conde's wall includes a list of different sources of inspiration for choosing art topics.

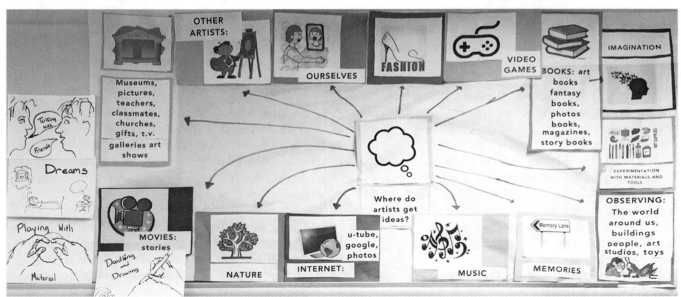

Teacher Presents time in Kitty's room is sometimes about artistic techniques, but it is also often about other areas of engaging with art—how to give and get good feedback, how to prepare artwork for display, how to be a good collaborator. This time is used to prepare for students to be independent during their Students at Work time. Kitty's students are just that—they individually and independently decide when they are ready for a PQS in their work and find someone to work with. Because they make choices about media, the students also set up their own workstations—even kindergartners get their own containers for paint water and practice what to do to clean up when they spill that water.

❖ **Students at Work**

It's time to get to work. Those who have works in progress get them from the class bin, while Kitty speaks to a student in the far corner of the room. Joshua heads for some paper. He walks with determination—he has a plan. He takes the paper and a pencil and goes back to his easel. In one swoop, he whips off his T-shirt and is left in his undershirt. A few of his peers glance at him and at Kitty, wondering about her response. But she's busy helping another student, and everyone goes back to work. Joshua places the paper on top of the shirt and begins to move his marker back and forth on the paper. The shirt is textured, and he's hoping to capture its pattern onto the paper.

First the paper rips. He switches to pencil, and the pencil breaks. And then the paper rips some more. Joshua appears unphased, though his tablemates stop to look up at him every so often. Finally, someone figures out what he's doing, "Oh! I did that once. With a coin." Joshua finally stops and nods his head. "Yeah. I thought my shirt was kind of funny, so I thought maybe I could do that. I saw someone do it before." Joshua is determined to keep trying his idea, and Kitty arrives with a just-in-time intervention before any frustration can emerge. She looks at Joshua and his bare arms and ripped paper and realizes what's happening. "Hey, I have something that might work better for you." She opens a drawer and grabs some texture plates. "These are texture plates. I think you're going to love these. Close your eyes and feel them. They're hard, but your shirt is really soft, so I don't think that's going to work out. See, this one has polka dots. . . ." Joshua notices one looks like dragon scales. "Oh yeah. Hey, Gael?" Kitty calls across the room. "You might like these. Joshua noticed they

FIGURE 3.25. Gael works on his drawing of a dragon up-close.

look like dragon scales." Kitty has also now helped interest Gael, who is busy at work on a close-up drawing of a dragon in marker (see Figure 3.25).

Meanwhile, at another table, Aiden is systematically exploring a painting of an octopus. "This was an experiment. I used watercolors and salt . . . I put all this blue salt to see if it falls into a ball and becomes hard. Blue is my favorite color. I also put salt on it to soak up the color. It gave it a sort of bumpy effect. . . . And look what's on the back. The colors show through right after I put the salt on. Because watercolor . . . can sink through paper very fast, in a blink." Aiden realizes that his tablemates and you are a rapt audience. "I have an octopus as a pet. At home, in a big tank."

"Really??" someone asks.

He smiles. "Naw." But then he immediately gets serious. "This is an extinct giant octopus. People are killing them. They even killed a baby. It's extinct."

"Where did you get this idea?" asks a nearby student.

"I was thinking about my grandma. She's dead, and so is this giant octopus. This is like an underwater heaven."

Kitty's students are not short on ideas. Their natural inclination is aided by how methodically she teaches them to find sources for inspiration. In addition to the chart of ideas, Kitty teaches several other strategies to students.

Wheel of Choices. Kitty and one of her previous student teachers once came up with a wheel of choices to help students engage and persist. Following a lesson that didn't go as her student teacher had hoped, Kitty helped her brainstorm some of the reasons why. She and the student teacher went through the problems they noticed—some students were lost, others intimidated, others would do better with a more social assignment—and then they created the wheel to help individualize instruction and provide ways to get more students to engage (see Table 3.1).

Using Previous Work to Inform New Work. Students are getting ready to display work in the Arts Showcase, and those who finish their artworks may have a hard time starting pieces from scratch with brand new ideas. Kitty encourages them to stretch and explore to expand their original ideas into new artworks. As mentioned earlier, one way she does this is by talking about artwork in a series. On the board, Kitty displays her own artwork of a pastoral scene, along with several smaller artworks that represent parts of the series—one is a close-up of just one portion of the scene, another is blurred and more abstract. As students finish their works, she encourages them to

think about how they can change their idea for a new work. Posters on the wall are displayed for student reference (see Figures 3.26 and 3.27).

❖ Talking About Art

The 2nd-grade class has left, and a combined 5th- and 6th-grade class is now busy at work. Some are making art, while others are talking and writing in pairs as they fill out PQS's. One student, Vincent, has just chosen a black background on which to mat his work (see Figure 3.28). He feels the sections where the black ink fills the postcards and eagerly reflects on his work:

> "We watched this slideshow where people that dyed ink drawings did it on lots of materials. I thought these postcards were the ones that

TABLE 3.1. Options on Kitty Conde's Wheel of Choices

Gallery Walk	To give students ideas when they aren't sure what to do next, Kitty encourages taking a break to look at what others are working on.
Ideas Chart	The chart that hangs at the front of the room gives examples of where ideas come from.
Go Back to Envisioning Sheet	Nearly all works begin with a sketch or plan, and revisiting that first step, acknowledging what changed and why, can help students think about what comes next.
Break It Down	Some students benefit from a checklist, and Kitty often helps individual students make them, or she creates one herself for projects that all students are working on.
Look at Artists/ Do Some Research	The Internet and the class library provide additional inspiration beyond the class gallery walk. During Teacher Presents time, Kitty explicitly teaches how to search for what you want on the Internet.
Make a List	Sketchbooks of "seed ideas"—ideas to be explored later when more time is available—give students a place to keep possible ideas and narrow their choices.
PQS (Praise, Question, Suggestions)	This thinking routine provides a structured way for students to ask for feedback.
Think About the Story	Sometimes students are stuck in the trees instead of seeing the whole forest. To help them, Kitty encourages them to set the scene for their artwork and tell a story about what's going on within it.

FIGURE 3.26. Kitty Conde displays a reference poster of ideas for expanding a work into a series.

FIGURE 3.27. Kitty Conde and her students think about how they can build on work they've already done.

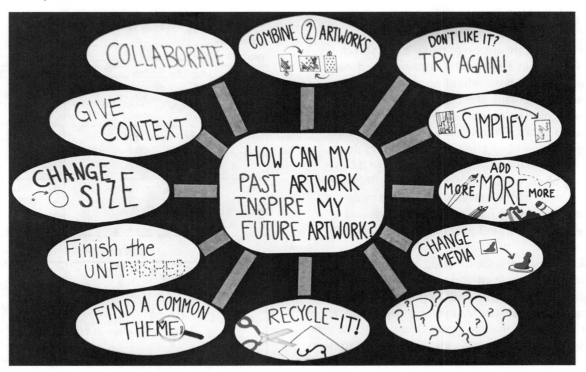

FIGURE 3.28. Vincent shows off his textured ink postcards that express "devastation."

stuck out to me the most. Ms. Kitty agreed that ink would look really good on these things, because I really like adding a lot of texture. . . . I knew I wanted to do one big topic, but different postcards. These are all very dreadful. . . . I wanted to make them devastating . . . like this is a city being attacked or something. This is a lonely girl alone in the fields by herself. . . .'"

Vincent explains that he worked for about four classes on the work. There is nothing random about his decisions about where and how to lay down ink.

"This card on the top, she's in the desert. So I just painted the ink on to make it feel sort of dry and plain. Here on the bottom, I used ink with a stick. I drew what I wanted and then went over it in ink. But I left part of it blank, so then I could just scribble that part around to make texture. This one here is dripped . . . since the picture's black and white, and I thought it would be like, really old, I tried to make it like a really blurry picture, like on a little TV. This one here looks a little newer, since color is newer. But this is a very bad, dreadful picture, so I blew the ink around a lot and made it a mess."

For Kitty's students, the meaning and decisionmaking embedded within their artworks are things to talk about during all four Studio Structures. By giving them resources for doing so, and constantly modeling how to talk about one's art and how to give and get feedback, Kitty sets them up to talk about their art independently during Students at Work time.

One table over, Mila and Ethan are talking and filling out PQS forms to give each other feedback on their artworks. Mila has painted two panels of a mountain scene, and Ethan is telling her his Praise.

"I like how that has detail of the ocean and the forest and how you kind of set the scene wherever it is. Like, I know exactly where it is with the ocean and the icy mountains. I don't have to look at it for a long time to know. I know right away."

"Okay," says Mila. She pauses to interpret the information and add it to the form (see Figure 3.29). "So . . . you understand the work?"

"Yes," says Ethan. "I want to know what that is," he continues, pointing to a spot on one of the pages. "And what are those black things that are falling?"

"Ms. Kitty asked the same thing!" says Mila. "[They] are pine trees, but they look like they're falling off the side of the mountain, but they're not. That why I put that [line of horizon] there."

"What's up here? Is that like, white sky? When you go outside, you don't see the white sky. Even if the sun is out."

"That's not the sun; it was a mistake. I went to go get white paint, and then my paint brush had yellow on it still, so it came out yellow."

FIGURE 3.29. Mila fills out her PQS (Praise, Question, Suggestion) worksheet, interpreting her feedback from Ethan.

PQS WORKSHEET		
YOUR NAME Mila		
PARTNER'S NAME Ethan		
	What did you hear?	How was it helpful?
PRAISE	I could under stand my artwork	That people know the reason just by looking at it
QUESTION	are the tree falling off the mountins	Conect the tree line to the mounting
SUGGESTION	add clould and snow	to make it look like a cold breeze
NEXT STEPS		
☆ add clouds an snow ☆ connect the tree line to the mountin		

"So I think you should add more greyness or clouds then."

"Like this?" asks Mila, pointing to the other panel of her work.

"Yeah."

As class ends, Kitty comments on the group's work. "I like that you guys see each other as artists. And you've taken me out the picture. I like that."

A glance around the room reveals that students are regularly engaged in Talking About Art. As explained earlier, Kitty uses her time during Teacher Presents to model the process of PQS forms and explicitly teaches how to get, give, and make use of responses from others so that it is an ongoing process.

◆ Showing Art

All students put their work in the Arts Showcase, which happens simultaneously with report card pickup so that parents are already in the building. All students make individual and group decisions about how their work will be displayed.

Preparation for the Showcase. Third-graders arrive, and Kitty uses Teacher Presents time to talk about signs that an artwork is complete and ready to be showcased, and how to mat a finished work.

"How do you know when you're done with an artwork?" asks Kitty.

"If other people think it's good, and you think it's good," says Griffin.

"Okay, feedback from others. How should you feel about it?"

Griffin continues, "If you think it's really good, it's a showcase."

"So I'm proud of it?" Kitty interprets.

"Yeah, like Kiran and his box art," Griffin replies, referencing a student's work.

"What else would help us know we're finished?"

"When you put your best work into it, and you know it's the best you can do," says Megan.

"So it has a lot of craftsmanship, I took a lot of time to make it my best," responds Kitty.

Joy volunteers, "When you know it's finished, you look at it, and see something in the art, not just colors."

"Let's talk about that. . . . Let's look at the Studio Thinking board. Is it something you express? Do you mean you've expressed an idea?"

"Yeah, like people know what it is."

Rebecca has another idea, "You know it's completed when you look at it, and you say, 'Hey, this looks like my envisioning but even better,' and it has everything from your envisioning."

"I just want to say something about what you're saying," says Kitty. "You're talking about having a conversation in your head. We call that self-talk. So when you're proud of something you tell yourself, 'This feels right. This feels good.' Does anyone have an evil person in your head? Someone who says 'You're bad. You're wrong?' Who has that? At our house, we call her Becky. We don't like her. . . . So today, tell Becky to be quiet. 'Be quiet on this, Becky.' Give yourself some positive self-talk."

Kitty prepares to release students to get to work and draws their attention to other showcase-level work reminders. "Think about the idea you're trying to express. Think about your craftsmanship. Think about your envisioning. Get feedback from each other."

When the 3rd-graders return for their next art class, many pieces are further along, and Kitty reviews how to select a color to mat a work for the showcase. "So you have to look closely at your work and think. Do you want a color in the painting, or do you want something that's a contrast? So Eduardo's series here, he felt black was the main color, and he wanted to highlight that, so it's matted on black. Oliver thought he wanted orange, but he played around with it, and he realized yellow was better. So you have to make some decisions. Do you want to emphasize a color that's there a lot? Or do you want to bring out a color that's only in there a little? Or do you want to do something totally different and make it pop?"

As students complete their work, they circulate around the room showing off their pieces and getting and giving comments and suggestions. They then go to Kitty, who is at the paper cutter—she reviews artwork, and if she doesn't have suggestions (or the student chooses not to take her suggestions), they have a discussion about which color to use as a mat.

Curation. In recent years, Kitty has become increasingly curious about how the presentation of artwork influences the making of the artwork, and she also encourages her students to consider this question.

Through a scheduling imperfection, a handful of Kitty's classes meet with her twice per week instead of once.

Kitty makes use of some of this extra time by adding curation activities, although all classes may curate some. She uses a variety of strategies to help this process:

- Create assignments with curation in mind—Kitty recalls an assignment in which each student created part of a city after studying architecture. While all students created their own works, in the end, they had to find themes from which to create a cohesive display.
- Practice looking for themes—Even kindergartners have discussions about sorting artworks in multiple ways (realistic/abstract) so that when it comes time to display work, they can create logical ways to do so.
- Reconceptualize artist statements—Fourth-graders create 3-dimensional artist statements on a poster board with more information than is typically seen in an artist statement. These include background research, actual materials that were used, sources of inspiration for the piece, and other pieces of information so that all that went into the piece (physically, mentally, and emotionally) is apparent to the viewer.
- Make public art—As mentioned earlier, Kitty runs a public art class every year as a middle school elective. Students consider from the very start who will view their art, when, why, and the purpose it will serve within its context.

- Explore the display space—Kitty sometimes photographs the area where the showcase will be on display so that multiple plans can be drawn on printouts as students organize and look for thematic groupings of their work.

Even the youngest of Kitty's students participate in curation. She recalls a kindergarten class where the students realized how their works could show various vertical levels. It began from a Ninja Turtle tunnel, which they situated low to the ground. The class realized they had many artworks that were air-bound, like birds and flying creatures, and these were placed higher on the wall. One student's sewn clouds were hung from the ceiling. Kitty asked them whether they were sure the viewer would understand what was going on. In response, they decided to add a tall building and a tree, which would show the vertical growth from the roots (and the tunnel) to the sky (and the flying creatures).

By participating in this curation process, students engage with the Studio Habits. They must carefully observe each other's artworks, interpret what they express, think about display and how to work with each other to do so [Understand Art Worlds], and envision how the artworks will look in the display space. At Ravenswood Elementary School, curation brings the artistic process full circle, tying together activities from the four Studio Structures with the Studio Habits of Mind to deepen student awareness of artistic practice.

THINGS TO THINK ABOUT

1. Julie, Celia, and Kitty all use systematic language to talk about the Studio Habits. What do you see as benefits of this practice? Recall a recent lesson you taught: Were there any missed opportunities to use Studio Habit names and language? How can you combine systematic language with corresponding visual classroom displays?
2. Celia almost always talks about the Studio Habits that will be used that day during Teacher Presents, and she displays Studio Habit language in signs and posters. Could your students tell you which Studio Habits they're using at any given time? How can you model talking about artistic thinking to get them there?
3. Julie's students all display enthusiastic engagement during Students at Work time. How can you create more opportunities for students to put personal meaning into their work and thus increase intrinsic motivation to engage and persist with their learning?
4. Julie has lots of ways for her students to engage in Talking About Art. What are some of the ways you've tried in your classroom? What scaffolding techniques can you use to support students in becoming independent with this process, as Kitty does with PQS partners?
5. Consider public art exhibitions when your students are Showing Art. Kitty's students are involved in curating and sharing comprehensive and informative artist statements. Celia provides signs to help visitors understand what is being learned. How could visitors to your exhibitions learn about artistic thinking?

CHAPTER 4

Portraits of Planning

TEACHERS have a lot to juggle—implementing local, state, and national curricular frameworks and standards, participating in school initiatives, planning public exhibitions, communicating with parents, reading and addressing individualized education plans, being an arts advocate to the school and greater community, opening stubborn milk containers at lunch duty, and, don't forget, teaching sometimes hundreds of students. How do teachers balance these demands and plan for success? What are their goals and priorities for students progressing through an elementary art program? How do teachers plan, alone and in groups? In this chapter, we present four stories.

What Does It Mean to Make Art?—Nicole Gsell

Nicole Gsell is a 3rd-year art teacher of students in preschool–Grade 7 at the public Henderson Inclusion School in urban Dorchester, Massachusetts (see her self-portrait in Figure 4.1). Her students are from diverse ethnic, linguistic, and ability backgrounds. Because Henderson is an inclusion school, children with disabilities learn in general education classrooms alongside their typical peers. Her classes include students with various special needs—physical, emotional, and intellectual challenges. Nicole's teaching practices are influenced by her experiences as a practicing artist and her need to differentiate instruction for her diverse group of students.

SETTING UP A YEAR-LONG TRAJECTORY

For Nicole, an illustrator (illustrator of this book's posters and cover, in fact!), art is always about telling stories. This belief plays a big role in how she plans at all levels—from a year-long throughline, or overarching goal, to unit and lesson plans to day-to-day interactions in her classroom. She believes art is about your voice and the stories it can tell.

The year-long question *How can art help us to tell a story?* is one Nicole uses every year, although it manifests differently across grade levels and classes of students. She

FIGURE 4.1. Nicole Gsell's self-portrait in clay and paint.

separates sections of the school year based on how she, as an artist, thinks about the storytelling/artmaking process (see Table 4.1). In the following text we share some of her thoughts for the forthcoming school year that she had planned in August.

❖ September

In her notes, Nicole writes about September: "Developing our inclination." This first month of school is about nurturing the desire to make art and includes lots of exploration activities and opportunities for personal meaning-making. By frontloading the first month of school with chances for students to discover what they like (and don't like), Nicole is aiming to instill intrinsic motivation for artmaking in her students (which we discuss in Chapter 5). In her list of ideas for this month, Nicole has brainstormed a phone selfie project, in which students use a template of a phone and their own media choices to create an artistic portrait of themselves. This gets students thinking about what represents them and what is personally engaging as they choose their style and props. Other classes may work toward this goal by creating "heart maps," in which 2-dimensional space is filled with meaningful subject matter, or hobby cubes, in which each side of the cube tells a different story about the artist.

❖ October

From there, Nicole and her students tackle the next question. Now that we want to make art, and we know how to make that exciting, what do we need to do so? This is an important month for learning tools and techniques and studio procedures [Develop Craft]. But in the spirit of keeping her diverse student body interested and engaged in their process, Nicole embeds choices within this month. After attending a conference session by Cynthia Gaub about "Around the Room" activities, Nicole was inspired to implement these as students learned new techniques that interested them (see Chapter 1 and Appendix A for more descriptions of this approach). During the month of October, students have flexible assignments in which they design settings (such as real or imagined landscapes, maps, or skyscraper cityscapes) while experimenting with a required number of techniques and tools for drawing, painting, and collage. During this first half of the year, students are working with only 2-dimensional materials.

❖ November and December

By this time of the year, Nicole has planned for students to have intrinsic motivation to make art [Engage & Per-

TABLE 4.1. Year-Long Throughline: How Can Art Help Us Tell a Story?

Month(s)	Storytelling Connection	Studio Habit Focus	Essential Question
September	Getting to know ourselves and each other	Engage & Persist Stretch & Explore	What drives us to make art?
October	Setting the stage	Develop Craft Observe Stretch & Explore	What skills do we need to tell our story?
November and December	Introducing your characters	Engage & Persist Envision Express Reflect	What represents my voice in my art?
January and February	Action and expression	Develop Craft Engage & Persist Envision Express	How do I bring my story to life?
March–June	Big projects	Reflect Understand Art Worlds	How do we tell our story from beginning to end?

sist], to have the skills needed to use tools in the art studio [Develop Craft], and to have begun thinking about evocative settings where stories take place [Express]. The next step is to fill these settings with characters. While the earlier part of the year has been spent in mostly shorter, exploratory projects, character creation is a more involved and polished process and requires deeper engagement and more dogged persistence. For younger students, this may involve challenges to create characters based on a prompt and using a limited set of materials; they might create an imaginary friend, the people inside a snow globe, robots, or insects [Express; Develop Craft; Stretch & Explore]. Older students spend time working on realistic and fantastical drawing skills for creating still lifes, characters, or self-portraits. Because these artworks require more time, Nicole also emphasizes the reflection process, as students both explain and evaluate their work one-on-one with Nicole during Students at Work or as a group during Talking About Art time.

◆ January and February

Nicole prepares for the long New England winter by making exciting 3-dimensional materials available after the students' return from winter vacation. Students learn techniques for using these materials (such as polymer clay and wire sculpting) while thinking about how to convey action and expression, which Nicole sees as a natural extension of character creation. To practice ways of bringing stories to life, older students create Claymation movies or other computer animations [Envision; Express]. Younger students explore ways to show excitement in an ordinary object with a zoomed-in still picture, creating works inspired by Georgia O'Keeffe [Understand Art Worlds: Domain]. Nicole has also brainstormed collaborative projects in which students work in small groups and create characters who interact to tell a story. The goal in these months is to really bring all the pieces together—setting, characters, action, and expression.

◆ March, April, May, and June

Nicole leaves the last part of the year open, knowing it will take the form of a large project that encompasses the entire storytelling process—from idea generation to final presentation. She uses some of her time over the February vacation week to think about what might interest each particular grade and class. In previous years, Nicole didn't begin her final unit until April or May, but now she plans to begin earlier because of the difficulty of engaging student attention in the final weeks of school as the weather warms.

While Nicole always holds to her yearly focus on storytelling, each year has its own flavor. Some students tackle this topic with a focus on imaginative stories like fantasy and fairy tales, while others take an interest in stories from a personal point of view, creating journals or portraits of families and friends; another lens is performative storytelling, which includes artworks like costumes, murals, and animation. Nicole determines what might be appropriate for each of her classes by noticing popular culture themes emerging during free draw activities, informal surveying (What's everyone's favorite movie right now?), and lunchtime conversations with students.

Nicole recalls the Superfood unit of last year's 3rd-graders. "Superfoods" are food-based superheroes inspired by Nicole's own artworks in college (which are discussed more in the section below). Here, we trace the steps of the projects in that unit to see how they align with the generic storytelling process she's addressed throughout the year.

In the Superfoods unit, students take accessible subject matter (foods) and combine it with fantasy and superpowers, which are so developmentally relevant to students in Grade 3. Students begin by developing interest and setting the stage (as in the focus of lessons in September and October) by looking at other food-based art and brainstorming ideas for future artwork. Nicole shows artworks from the movie adaptation of the children's book *Cloudy with a Chance of Meatballs* (Barrett, 1978), including the Tacodile Supreme, who emerges from the water like a crocodile but whose mouth is a giant taco, as well as showing the characters from the *VeggieTales* TV program [Understand Art Worlds: Domain]. As students begin to form their ideas in response to the artworks they've viewed, Nicole asks them to brainstorm a list of their 10 favorite foods, because one of these will become the main character in a cast that each student creates. Nicole teaches techniques for anthropomorphizing foods (first try making the character with the face IN the food, then try putting the eyes and ears OUTSIDE the food) [Develop Craft: Technique], and students sketch various versions of their main characters (What if you give him legs? Arms? How many arms, do you think? What if you give him wheels?) [Envision; Stretch & Explore]. Students choose one of their sketches to develop further and create a trading card for the character, sometimes endowing it with a name or a superpower, similar to the character creation process that took place in November and December. From there, students branch off to create more characters and set them into action (see Figure 4.2). Some students create a sidekick (Taco Man's sidekick might be Guacamole Boy, or a character called Spaghetti-tron might have Lil' Parmesan as a sidekick), while others use their least favorite foods to create a villain or team of villains. Many students stick with a trading card, expanding it into a game and trading duplicated copies with other classmates, while others recreate their characters in the newly available 3-dimensional media choices. Students turn these stories into comics, claymation videos, dioramas, or other expressive forms.

EMBEDDING STUDIO HABITS

When first describing her planning process, Nicole doesn't mention the Studio Habits. But when questioned, she readily tells us which ones are most emphasized in each section of the year. This is because Nicole's graduate training emphasized planning with the Studio Habits, and she has developed the lens to see the Studio Habits hiding in plain sight. So while they are not first on her mind, she

FIGURE 4.2. Carrot Guy went through several revisions by a student before he was able to stand upright.

trusts that by planning authentic art experiences, she will easily be able to focus on those Studio Habits that are embedded within what she and her students are working on. She also makes extensive visual maps that help her look at the year through different lenses, including that of Studio Thinking, as shown in Figure 4.3.

PLANNING FOR SPECIAL LEARNERS

Inclusion is embedded in the fabric of the day-to-day for students and teachers at the Henderson school, and the art room is no different. Some of the strategies Nicole plans with are described below. Nicole has not trained formally to work with special needs learners, but she confers regularly with classroom teachers and therapists at her school for assistance.

❖ Encouraging Productive Breaks

Nicole takes breaks in her work as an artist, and she thinks her students need that opportunity as well. It helps students to engage productively to know that they can take a break and switch gears to something else when they need to. Sometimes breaks take the form of quick energizers—art jobs like sharpening pencils or checking the bulletin board displays for any falling or about-to-fall artwork—and sometimes they are more substantial changes like switching to work on a different piece.

During the Superfoods project, she recalls a student who had trouble transitioning to make his character in 3 dimensions. She encouraged him to play around with different drawing materials, and that's how he eventually settled. He used the new drawing materials to expand his character in 2 dimensions instead. As Nicole puts it, "I'm not trying to torture you here. I want this to be a place where you can make mistakes and have tools [for engaging]. The tool here is to go do something totally different for awhile."

For the most part, students in this school are used to individual children working differently. But Nicole says she does have students question why some are allowed a different path. "I had a student with anger management problems, and he came in and knew exactly what he wanted to do. He said, 'I'm going to collage onto a shoebox.' And I said that was fine." When some students asked why they couldn't do the same, Nicole explained that this is how he needed to work in order to engage—and told the ones who were asking that they already were engaged. She uses an accommodation story, "If you couldn't walk, I'd give you a wheelchair. This person needs a different way to get into this project, so he has what he needs."

FIGURE 4.3. Nicole Gsell uses visual mapping to help herself make sense of her plans.

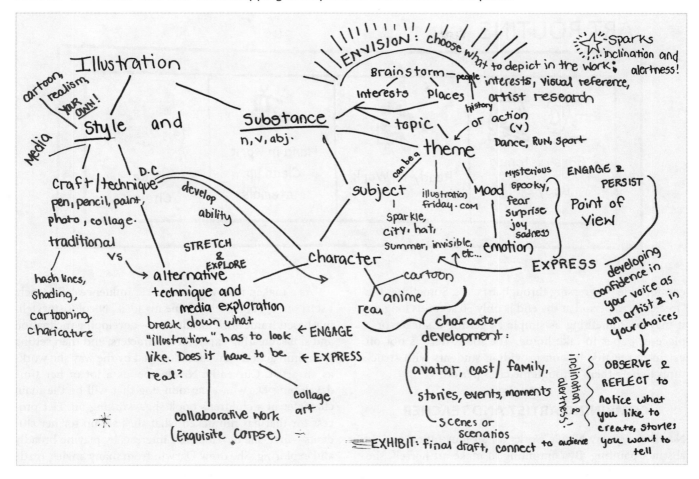

◆ Focusing on Strengths

Nicole is not interested in what her students can't do—she focuses on what they can do. Some of her students volunteer themselves as teaching assistant experts, which she encourages. If a student declares she's really great at threading needles, she becomes an extra pair of hands to help others thread. The focus on strengths is a particularly helpful approach for those students with challenges. "I had a student who used to [meltdown] when there were only 5 minutes left. He'd throw pencils and [panic]. I said, 'I'm going to give you a timer and when it goes off, 10 minutes before the end of class, you can let everyone know we have 5 minutes until cleanup.' So now we have a timekeeper." Every class has different needs—in another class, one visually impaired student with a sensitivity to noise has become the noise monitor. Nicole turns accommodations into privileges, making everyone a valued art community member.

◆ Offering Cameras as Accommodation

Because Nicole has students who may not have the manual dexterity to create art using traditional means, she and paraprofessionals help students use cameras for photography. In the selfie project described from September, some students take photos of themselves and edit using software. Those unable to draw easily may instead make or find props to photograph for expressive reasons.

◆ Providing Signage

In addition to these strategies, Nicole uses the standard fare of accommodations that is common in school environments. She creates lots of signage for reminders on how to use different materials in words, pictures, and Braille, and she makes sure her nonverbal students have art symbols on their communication boards. Figure 4.4 shows a sign some of Nicole's students use in order to feel

FIGURE 4.4. An accommodation checklist Nicole Gsell uses for some of her students.

ART ROUTINE

comfortable progressing through art class. Sometimes the "free choice" period at the end is only 30 seconds long, or it may be something as simple as getting a sticker or a piece of paper to take home. The focus here is not on extrinsic rewards but on providing students with structures to help them through the class period.

COMBINING ARTIST AND TEACHER

Nearly every day Nicole works on an illustration and/or abstract painting. By continuing to make art herself, she remains constantly engaged in what it feels like to do so, and this helps her to better relate to her students and to develop design assignments that capture how she works as an artist. She also always creates artwork for the assignments she gives, either ahead of time or alongside the students as they work. "Some teachers maybe don't have to, but I have to get my hands on it . . . if I'm not personally invested, the lesson doesn't work." Nicole's own artmaking is her way to prepare to teach.

Sometimes, ideas for assignments come from her previous or ongoing artworks—this was the case with the Superfoods assignment. In college, Nicole designed a team of drawn egg-based characters (they had "super powerful protein power") that battled sugary cupcakes and other treats. It was this experience that helped Nicole develop the project and relate to some of the struggles students experience along the way. She's able to scaffold steps of the process appropriately to mimic the storytelling process and address meaningful student questions during Students at Work time, because she's been there. She also creates trading cards of her own characters to trade with her student artists (see Figure 4.5).

"As a maker, my own process . . . influences all I teach. I start out big and then I refine my idea." Nicole's storytelling-based framework for the year—developing inclination and skills, creating expressive characters, and then setting them into action—are all influenced by the way she works as an artist. Currently, Nicole spends a lot of her time developing Darwin, a cartoon dog that will be the main character in a children's book she's working on. Her process for that has mimicked what she's set up for her students—first, she develops her interests by playing broadly and exploring. She drew Darwin from many angles, made him in different media, and wrote his life story. She then further developed her characters—Darwin belongs to a human girl who has a sister—and she thought about the different qualities of the world he lived in, delving into his setting. Now, she centers on expressing stories with Darwin. He and his owner go to the beach and to birthday parties, and Darwin helps his owner through the typical friendship troubles experienced by young girls.

As Nicole explains her work process, she pulls out a series of her own abstract work—paint, collage, and sewn elements on canvas—all left at a temporary stopping point. "Sometimes, a piece needs a break. I have to work on something else for awhile." This acknowledgment of the complexity of the artistic creation process is part of how Nicole helps her students, some of whom may become frustrated easily and can benefit from taking breaks and/or working on multiple projects at once.

Nicole's planning process reminds us that art education should be about what it is like to make art authentically. By remaining true to the process she uses as an artist and creating a place where everyone is valued, she is able to create accessible and genuine experiences for her students.

FIGURE 4.5. Nicole Gsell makes trading cards of her own egg characters to exchange with students.

Planning a Year in a Choice-Based Class—Wynita Harmon

Wynita Harmon, art teacher at Huffman Elementary School in Plano, Texas, inspires her students to act and think as artists, not only in art class but everywhere they go (see Figure 4.6). "I hope that my teaching leads students to have creative and innovative minds that can easily adapt and work through challenges they may encoun-

FIGURE 4.6. Wynita Harmon addresses her class.

ter in life, as well as the tools and knowledge to express themselves creatively in every environment they encounter," she tells us. This belief is visible in the priorities she establishes, the activities she designs, and the special events she coordinates throughout the school year.

With 12 years' art teaching experience, eight of them at Huffman, Wynita has entered the stage of mid-career educator. She anticipates the ebb and flow of the school year and balances district expectations with her own spin on arts learning. Like Julie Toole at Baker Demonstration School (described in Chapter 3), Wynita is a TAB teacher, designing studio centers to teach for artistic behavior in her classroom. She plans with *Understanding by Design* (Wiggins & McTighe, 2005), the curriculum model that is used by her district. Since she sees each class for 50 minutes once a week, she plans so that every minute is productive.

THE BIG PICTURE

Wynita starts her planning with a simple map of the year in her mind, a sequence that remains fairly consistent from year to year. Like many experienced TAB teachers, she estimates when studio centers will open and expects that the year's concentrations will progress in three chunks: from media explorations to a focus on artistic

TABLE 4.2. Wynita's Planning Cycles: Concentrations, Big Ideas, and Studio Habits

Fall Planning Cycle (Plan in August) *Exploration Concentration*		**Winter Planning Cycle** (Plan over winter break) *Expression Concentration*		**Spring Planning Cycle** (Plan over spring break) *Exhibition Concentration*	
Big Ideas	**Studio Habits**	**Big Ideas**	**Studio Habits**	**Big Ideas**	**Studio Habits**
Art Olympics Artists Get Ideas Portraits	Stretch & Explore Envision Observe Develop Craft: Studio Practice	Mood Friendship Identity Artists' Exhibit	Develop Craft: Technique Engage & Persist Reflect: Question & Explain	Movement Nature Spring	Observe Reflect: Evaluate Understand Art Worlds
Studio Centers		**Studio Centers**		**Studio Centers**	
Drawing Painting Collage Technology		Drawing Painting Collage Technology Clay Sculpture		Drawing Painting Collage Technology Clay Sculpture Sewing Printmaking Mixed media	

expression to exhibition. Table 4.2 shows how Wynita develops these broad areas of concentration with *big ideas* (themes Wynita develops and makes available to her students), Studio Habits of Mind (selected for connections to big ideas and concentrations) that are emphasized in whole-class discussions and responses to individual students, and TAB studio centers (material centers that are available for student use).

Wynita does not outline specifics for the entire year in advance. Instead, she divides the year into planning cycles so that she can adjust the curriculum as the year progresses. In August, she plans lessons for the entire fall, when she teaches the Exploration concentration. During the winter break, she reviews student progress in each class and plans for January through early March, when she teaches the Expression concentration. She also plans during winter break for the spring art show—the Exhibition concentration. Spring break provides time to look forward to the remaining months of school and plan for meeting objectives that were not addressed earlier in the year.

◆ Year-Long Organizing Principles

Studio Centers. Wynita begins the year with a strong emphasis on drawing by introducing or reviewing specific techniques to help students Develop Craft. TAB classrooms are organized around studio centers, areas in the room dedicated to specific media—drawing, collage, painting, technology, clay, sculpture, and fibers—and each includes materials, tools, resources, and instructions. Wynita follows a typical TAB order for opening centers: drawing, collage, and painting centers open immediately in the fall, followed soon by technology. Students have full access to materials, tools, and resources after the teacher introduces each center. During the fall, students practice techniques and care for materials within each of the available centers. In early winter, clay and sculpture join as temporary studios that rotate between grades because of issues tied to space and firing. As the exhibition approaches in the spring, printmaking, sewing, and mixed media studio centers open, giving students a full range of media choices.

Studio Habits. Wynita introduces or reintroduces each of the Studio Habits to Grades 1–5 during the first 2 months of school. She does one or more at a time during Teacher Presents sessions. Wynita explains each Studio Habit using grade-level appropriate language to acquaint students with precise terms to describe their thinking. The introduction and repetition of terms builds student awareness of when, why, and how they might be using a particular Studio Habit. As the year progresses, Wynita emphasizes Studio Habits that correspond with the big ideas and areas of concentration (refer to Table 4.2).

Big Ideas. Wynita uses *big ideas*—broad concepts that frame understandings—to connect media with guided explorations. As explained by author Grant Wiggins (2010), "An idea is 'big' if it helps us make sense of lots of confusing experiences and seemingly isolated facts. It's like the picture that connects the dots or a simple rule of thumb in a complex field." It is through the context of big ideas that Huffman students find meaning and build understandings with art media and Studio Thinking. Wynita introduces one big idea every few weeks and often combines it with clusters of Studio Habits.

❖ Concentrations

Fall. The fall concentration of Exploration means a discovery approach for the beginning of the school year. Wynita pairs explorations of media with the Studio Habits Envision, Stretch & Explore, Observe, and Develop Craft, which help students practice skills in the drawing, painting, and collage centers. As Wynita writes in her blog:

> [Stretch & Explore] focuses on learning to reach beyond one's capacities, explore ideas and thoughts, as well as embracing the opportunity to learn from mistakes. . . . Although kindergarteners had choice with their ideas, I limited their media by placing charcoal pencils, crayons, oil pastels, and stamps at four tables and let them rotate to explore each material. It was fun to watch some students get new paper for each medium and some used the different medi[a] on the same paper, which created mixed media art. I was proud that some went beyond their capacity and ventured off into new subjects that they typically did not create and tried new things. (Harmon, 2016)

Wynita also emphasizes Develop Craft: Studio Practice early in the year to establish expectations for students for how to set up their workspaces, care for media and tools,

and clean up the studio centers for the incoming class. When Wynita observes students demonstrating mastery of Studio Practice, she introduces the Studio Habit Envision. She describes this introduction in her blog:

> Before we start, I remind students about where they can get ideas from (surroundings, memories, emotions, nature, life, family, studying artists' styles, etc.). We do this by closing our eyes and reflecting on our own artistic practices and what we want to be inspired by for the day. Some students come prepared with their own personal sketches or notebooks with ideas. It is great to see them thinking about art time outside of school. (Harmon, 2016)

Winter. In late winter, Wynita introduces additional media, broadening the studio offerings. With more complex techniques and concepts, students can now create more expressive work in preparation for the spring art show. Throughout the year Wynita incorporates artist inspirations and includes many modern and contemporary artists, particularly during the concentration on expression. She selects artists to highlight such as Banksy, Pablo Picasso, Amedeo Modigliani, Melissa McCracken, Jim Dine, and Henri Matisse, all for their expressive qualities. As she shows videos of these artists at work, Wynita points out ways they are using particular Studio Habits so that students can begin to see similarities between professional artists' uses of these habits and their own work processes.

Spring. The spring term culminates in a schoolwide celebration of learning, including an art exhibit that opens in April and remains up until the end of the year in May. This event is firmly planted in the school culture: an annual Fine Arts Night showcases both the art and music programs. Wynita has established Exhibition as a curricular concentration; students are heavily involved in planning and preparing for this event. During the winter break, she reviews her notes from the previous year to plan lesson activities. Students maintain paper portfolios to collect artwork for the art show and select an exhibition piece from their portfolio or create a new piece. Parents assist Wynita with matting and labeling the artwork. The display, organized by grade levels, includes written artist statements and corresponding Texas Essential Knowledge and Skills for Fine Arts standards.

The Studio Habits Observe, Reflect, and Understand Art Worlds are closely connected with the Exhibition concentration. Wynita supports students as they select and prepare their work for exhibition, including organizing table critiques and helping with selection, mounting, and writing artist statements. The exhibit provides a new learning space where students build understandings about the purposes and benefits of exhibition. The final event during the exhibition concentration is when upper grades visit the Dallas Museum of Art to view other artists' work. This opportunity places exhibition in the context of the discourse about art, and students begin to recognize that they are part of the worldwide community of artists.

A LOOK AT WYNITA'S PLANNER

Some art teachers plan on their laptops, some in a sketchbook, and others, like Wynita, prefer an old-school three-ring binder. Every August, she customizes a new planner for the approaching school year. At this point in her career, she knows the sequences and connections inside and out, so she does not always specify them in her planner. Her planner also includes day-to-day information that is useful for her, like schedules and notes about preparation for particular classes. This year she is organizing her lessons in a week-to-week calendar, by grade level. Her organizing priorities are listed as headings across the

top of each grid: Grade, Big Idea, Objectives/Standards, Demo/Mini-Lesson, Resources/Videos, SHoM/Vocabulary, and Notes/Special Prep. Each of these categories identifies components of the lessons she needs to research and prepare. Let's see how Studio Thinking fits into Wynita's organizing priorities and planning routines.

◆ Grade Levels

The left column of the planner lists each grade in the order in which it is scheduled during each day of the week. Six different classes come daily to the Huffman art studio, one of each grade level. Wynita has only 5 minutes between classes with five grade-level changes. As a TAB teacher, Wynita's studio centers remain consistent from class to class and grade to grade, which smooths these quick transitions. Though more sophisticated materials may appear for older students, the room does not require a major turnover after each class departs. Only kindergarten classes have a substantially different curriculum, with their own big ideas and predetermined media separate from the studio centers. Table 4.3 shows a page from Wynita's planner.

TABLE 4.3. Wynita's Plan Book

Grade	Big Idea	Objectives / Standards	Demo / Mini-Lesson	Resources / Videos	SHoM / Vocabulary	Notes / Special Prep
2	Artists' exhibit	**117.108.b.4.A** Support reasons for preferences in personal artworks **117.108.b.4.C** Compile collections of artwork	Mounting artwork	Virtual museum	*Observe* *Reflect* *Understand Art Worlds* Exhibit Mount	
1	Artists' exhibit	**NCAS VA:Pr5.1.1a** Ask and answer questions such as where, when, why, and how artwork should be prepared for presentation	Artful thinking (strategies for Talking About Art) Titling artwork	Virtual museum	*Reflect* *Understand Art Worlds* Exhibit Mount Museum	

TABLE 4.3. Wynita's Plan Book *(continued)*

Grade	Big Idea	Objectives / Standards	Demo / Mini-Lesson	Resources / Videos	SHoM / Vocabulary	Notes / Special Prep
K	Friend-ship	**117.102.b.3.C** (b) Identify the uses of art in everyday life **117.102.b.4.A** Express ideas about personal artworks	**Essential Questions:** • What are friends for? • Who are your friends? • How should we treat our friends?	N/A	*Express* Friendship Mixed media	Cut paper
3	Artists' exhibit	**TEKS 117.111.b.4.B** Use methods such as oral response or artist statements to identify main ideas **NCAS VA:Pr5.1.3a** Identify exhibit space and prepare works of art including artists' statements for presentation	Mounting strategies Titles	Virtual museum	*Observe* *Reflect* *Understand Art Worlds* Exhibit Mount	Construction paper Artist statement labels
4	Artists' exhibit	**TEKS Gr 4 117.114.b.4.C** Compile collections of personal artworks for purposes of self-assessment or exhibition **117.114.b.3.C** Connect art to career opportunities **NCAS VA:Cr3.1.4a** Revise artwork in progress on the basis of insights gained through peer discussion	Artful thinking Titles Mounting art	Virtual museum	*Observe* *Reflect* *Understand Art Worlds* Exhibit Mount	Construction paper Artist statement labels
5	Artists' exhibit	**117.117.b.4.C** Compile collections of personal artworks for purposes of self-assessment or exhibition	Artful thinking Titles Mounting art	Virtual museum	*Observe* *Reflect* *Understand Art Worlds* Exhibit Mount	Construction paper Artist statement labels

❖ Objectives/Standards

After she identifies a big idea, Wynita looks to state and national standards to find core knowledge and skills for each grade. Plano teachers are required to cite the Texas state standards (Texas Essential Knowledge and Skills, or TEKS [Texas Education Agency, 2013]) for all lessons. TEKS for Fine Arts includes end-of-year benchmarks in four areas: foundations in organization and perception, creative expression, historical and cultural relevance, and critical evaluation and response. At each grade level, a dozen visual arts standards specify skills and concepts that target learning about media, expression, visual literacy, and response to artworks.

Wynita and her art colleagues also look to the National Core Arts Standards (NCAS) to identify additional skills. Criteria in the NCAS address many more of the artistic and thinking behaviors that develop in art classes, including Studio Habits (State Education Agency Directors of Art Education, 2015). (See Appendix F for a reference chart of how the NCAS and Studio Habits overlap.)

For each big idea, Wynita writes I CAN statements on the whiteboard for every grade as goals in language and form that are familiar for students. The I CAN statements are derived from the standards and matched with one or more Studio Habits:

K. I CAN build skills in creating art with primary colors and identify them. [Develop Craft: Technique]

1. I CAN build a variety of skills necessary for using a variety of materials to produce drawings, paintings, and collages. [Develop Craft: Technique]

2. I CAN express ideas and feelings in personal artwork and practice skills necessary for producing drawings, paintings, and collages. [Express]

3. I CAN elaborate on an imaginative idea, use knowledge of art media, resources, and technology to investigate personal ideas. [Envision]

4. I CAN generalize and conceptualize artistic ideas and work. [Envision]

5. I CAN develop and communicate ideas for life experiences (school, family, self, peers) and imagination for artwork inspiration. [Envision]

❖ Demo Lessons

Individual lessons and demonstrations introduce activities that target understanding goals and skills identified in the standards. The demonstration or mini-lesson often introduces a Studio Habit, big idea, or challenge, breaking down big ideas into manageable chunks for teaching and learning. For example, under the kindergarten big idea of Friendship, one lesson focuses on three essential questions to explore the concept of relationships:

• What are friends for?
• Who are your friends?
• How should we treat our friends?

On a different day, 2nd-graders consider how they stretch and explore at studio centers. The big idea here is Exploration, and the lesson addresses different ways that artists Develop Craft: Technique in the media of their choosing. In table groups, students discuss the essential question *Why do artists practice?* to connect the cluster of Studio Habits of Stretch & Explore, Develop Craft: Technique, and Engage & Persist. As the year progresses, the Studio Habits are revisited often in the context of each mini-lesson, so they become familiar concepts.

On occasion Wynita extends lessons with challenging assignments to prompt students to test their skills and understandings, often opening up the challenges as a choice to all students in Grades 1–5. Children in elementary and middle school grades enjoy a twist on familiar routines and rise to meet challenges that appeal to them. For example, the Oops Challenge (inspired by *Beautiful Oops!* [Saltzberg, 2010]) invites students to purposely make a mistake and then elevate that mistake into art. The Global Cardboard Challenge was initiated by the Imagination Foundation (2017; see also Chapters 3 and 6). This challenge invites students to envision and create a sculpture or structure made entirely of cardboard. Later, some students choose to participate in the Scrap Challenge, which encourages students to envision artworks made from found objects.

❖ Resources/Videos

The Resources/Videos section of Wynita's planner includes links to websites, artists, or videos that provide supplemental information for the lesson. Under her own YouTube channel, *Art Is Life,* Wynita has a collection of videos that she has made or collected to demonstrate processes or techniques. A student who either missed a studio demonstration or needs a refresher can watch the relevant video before getting started.

❖ Studio Habits/Vocabulary and Notes/ Special Prep

The Studio Habits, along with other art-related terms to introduce or review, are listed in the SHoM/Vocabulary column. The last column in Wynita's planner, Notes/

Special Prep, identifies additional materials and special arrangements that are not part of the regular daily preparation.

WYNITA ENJOYS a great deal of freedom in her planning. Currently the only district requirements are that she cite TEKS in her lesson plans and follow the principles in *Understanding by Design* (Wiggins & McTighe, 2005). Like all teachers, her plans serve as a guide to the weeks ahead and remind her of important concepts to highlight during instruction. Though she does not list assessment practices in the planner, she follows simple assessment routines to track student learning and inform planning for subsequent weeks.

ASSESSMENT

Plano students in Grades K–2 maintain classroom portfolio collections representative of their work in all subjects throughout the year. Instead of grading, portfolios go through a review process to document student understanding and growth. In art class, children maintain 2-dimensional portfolios that provide Wynita with information about each student's progress so she can target areas for instruction. To monitor their understandings, Wynita developed a routine for exit tickets at the end of each class. These sticky note reflections are displayed on a reflection board in the hallway. Students select one of the four NCAS anchor standards—*Create, Present, Respond, Connect*—and follow prompts for each category.

Creating
- I learned . . .
- I liked . . .
- I explored . . .
- I created . . .
- I experimented . . .

Presenting
- Interpret your work:
- Explain why you created your art:
- Discuss the materials you used:

Responding
- Describe how your art shows your life:
- Talk about the subject of your art:
- Explain why you created your art:

Connecting
- Tell the purpose of your artwork:
- Compare your artwork to art outside of school or to a famous artist:
- Did your community inspire your art?
- Did society, culture, or history inspire your art?

EMERGENT EVENTS AND THEMES

Flexibility in planning leaves room for Wynita to connect ideas that may unexpectedly surface between planning cycles. Emergent curriculum often comes from students' interests, current events, and popular culture, connecting learning with students' lives. This year, the first week of school arrived just as the Summer Olympics were winding down. Art Olympics was an appropriate opening lesson, under the concentration of Exploration, though it would have been less relevant in a non-Olympic year. Just a few weeks later, on Dot Day, students recognized the Studio Habit Stretch & Explore in the children's book *The Dot* (Reynolds, 2003). Dot Day is an event observed in elementary schools around the world—all Plano elementary students participate—to celebrate creativity and literacy through an offering of activities by the Reynolds Center for Teaching, Learning & Creativity.

During the fall of 2016, when the Mannequin Challenge became popular, Wynita saw a connection between people frozen in poses and gesture drawing. When the trend started to appear on television, she knew that many of her students would notice. This prompted a drawing session for all, with 2-minute poses by half of the class while the other half drew their classmates, practicing the habit Observe. As a result of this emergent lesson, students began to understand how visual culture informs art and that ideas for art can be found in everyday life.

Trends can enter the school from outside or grow from within an individual class. Sometimes a child arrives with an idea that is more exciting than the lesson the teacher planned—like the day a group of children collaborated on a mixed media fish collage. Being able to shift gears in the moment to acknowledge an emergent idea is a TAB core principle. Themes can also emerge from the community or from adults in the school (see Figure 4.7). Wynita incorporates several schoolwide initiatives into her curriculum, such as when her school participated in the Be Like Brit campaign for Haiti (The Be Like Brit Foundation, 2017). In this social activism effort, students created art and cards to send to the Brit's Home Orphanage in Haiti to spread good will while raising awareness in the Huffman school community. Mid-year, a STEAM initiative brought the school community together to examine the ways that art connects science, technology, engineering, and math. Huffman students joined this districtwide effort to highlight integrated learning through the arts. And in the spring when an art teacher colleague asked Wynita if her students would collaborate with the high school by drawing monsters for the older students to design and sew, she agreed immediately so Huffman students could be part of this collective effort. Most of these

FIGURE 4.7. Students share their hopes on a community-themed bulletin board.

activities could not have been foreseen in August when planning for the year began. Because of the flexibility in Wynita's TAB curriculum, she can adjust her schedule to include emergent topics so learning opportunities mirror real-world events.

FLEXIBILITY AND BALANCE

Sometimes beginning teachers see an experienced teacher like Wynita Harmon and recognize that her style of planning would work for them. They admire the open, flexible model without extensive individual lesson plans. However, Wynita did not begin her career in this way. Like most, she built up her curriculum through trial and error, gradually finding the cornerstones—such as Studio Thinking and TAB—that would ground her planning around the throughline of artistic behaviors. Each teacher discovers his or her own path by stretching and exploring, developing her craft, and reflecting on the year just past.

In some school districts, art teachers are provided with curricular frameworks that outline goals, themes, and activities for the entire year. As we were writing this book, the art teachers in Plano had just begun a department study group to examine Studio Thinking in elementary art programs. Plano Art Coordinator Laura Grundler comments, "Our vision is about how we infuse the Studio Habits of Mind, big ideas, and artful thinking (Project Zero, n.d. a) into our planning process. We want a balance of divergent thinking and skill. Finding that balance is where the Studio Habits come into play—teaching kids to have that persistence and be able to envision ideas" (personal communication, May 25, 2017). Plano teachers continue to align their curricula to the TEKS standards and highlight specific essential questions and big ideas. Assessments reflect essential understandings, and each teacher can design his or her own assessments as well as individual lesson plans. With these new curricular initiatives, Plano art teachers continue to enjoy a great amount of flexibility—an excellent fit for Wynita's TAB art program.

Working Together on Scope and Sequence—
Caren Andrews and Jennifer Stuart

At the San Francisco Friends School (SFFS), Caren Andrews and Jennifer Stuart are a dynamic team (see Figures 4.8 and 4.9). They collaborate on every aspect of the visual arts curriculum to design sequential, comprehensive learning experiences for their K–8 students. Closer examination reveals deeply intertwined structures that support Caren and Jennifer's beliefs about understanding, learning, and character development. The core values of the SFFS community echo in the opening description of the Visual Arts Program Overview from 2016–2017:

> We are a community of artists developing our minds through a reflective practice of the arts. We are joyful and playful in our approach, valuing intuition and inventiveness. At the same time, we are focused and reflective, taking note of our growth and understanding that practice is at the core of our work together. One of the central tenets that drives and guides our program is the idea that every child is a creative child, full of potential.

Caren has been at SFFS since its inception, 16 years ago, and teaches Grades K–4 and 7–8. Jennifer joined the faculty 7 years later, working with Grades 5–8. Classes meet for 45 minutes twice a week throughout the year. Their schedules include time for a weekly planning meeting with each other and a second planning meeting to connect with the music and drama teachers.

Jennifer and Caren's partnership started in 2007 when SFFS was expanding its middle school. Jennifer gave Caren a copy of *Studio Thinking* (Hetland et al., 2007), suggesting that they could use the ideas presented there and adapt them for a K–8 visual arts program. As practicing artists, the Studio Thinking framework resonated with them. Later, Caren introduced Jennifer to Arts-Based Research, an approach written about extensively by Julia Marshall (Marshall & D'Adamo, 2011). These are only two examples of Caren and Jennifer's collaborative approach, which—paired with their attitudes as lifelong learners—has helped to provide the roots of their program.

CURRICULAR SCOPE AND SEQUENCE

San Francisco Friends School reflects Quaker values, incorporating social-emotional learning into all curricula, with common language and practices that extend to the art program. Caren and Jennifer set up course

FIGURE 4.8. Caren Andrews talks with her students about their ideas.

FIGURE 4.9. Jennifer Stuart reflects on her teaching practice.

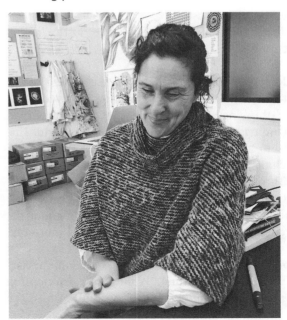

throughlines, or goals, that catalyze their planning (Blythe et al., 1998), blending Studio Thinking into essential questions for the year. With these overarching purposes in place, the art teachers look at students' skills to provide a balance of media and techniques at each grade level. National and state standards do not guide the SFFS visual arts curriculum. As Caren explains, "Once Jennifer and I invested the time to coordinate scope and sequence, where we do 2D and 3D and layer in 4D work, and what materials we are going to commit to, then for the rest of it, the dominoes fall." A brief description of each curricular element follows.

❖ Quaker Beliefs

The Quaker values of Integrity, Simplicity, and Community are important to Caren and Jennifer's planning. Year-long goals (throughlines) reflect artistic integrity through simple questions. The program introduces the discipline of art to kindergartners and builds on basic concepts in each sequential year. The school has intentionally sparse classroom spaces, and the environment is warm and friendly. Community service is integrated throughout the art program, with many opportunities for student activism through art.

❖ Throughlines

Planning begins each year with the throughlines for the entire art program. The throughlines ask students to consider the following:

1. What is art? What is an artist?
2. How am I an artist?
3. What is the relationship between art, justice, and action?

These deceptively simple (actually, quite complex!) questions are posted in Caren and Jen's classrooms to guide students' thinking and actions as they construct broad understandings about their own places in the world. This is central to the purpose of throughlines, as described in the Teaching for Understanding framework (Blythe et al., 1998). Throughlines help students develop disciplinary understandings—big takeaway messages. Because students and teachers revisit throughlines throughout the year, students gradually construct richer and more systematic responses to these questions.

A core value of Quaker education is community service. The third throughline, *What is the relationship between art, justice, and action?* asks children to make connections among three ideas. Social justice is embedded in every aspect of SFFS and is visible throughout the school in words and actions by both teachers and students, seen in classroom signage, and revealed in the many exhibits throughout the school. Belief in the relationship among these three concepts is central to the school's mission and also permeates the art program through the teachers' perspectives, their choices of artist exemplars, and the specific units of study selected. For example, in an elective unit called "The Space Between: Art, Justice, and Action," students connect their artmaking directly with community action. In this issues-based elective, students examine social justice themes. In a second elective, "From Pop Ups to Museums," students make art to educate the public and raise funds for social causes by selling their work.

❖ Essential Questions

After the year's throughlines are established, Jennifer and Caren start to map out the scope and sequence for each grade. They begin by identifying two to four essential questions for each grade level. These goals begin by looking at art and the ways artists work, gradually moving toward deeper understandings about the artist's role in society as a community's voice. The curriculum outline, described in Table 4.4, lists the throughlines and grade-level essential questions. Next in the planning process, Caren and Jennifer turn to the Studio Habits of Mind to design an inclusive curriculum that highlights thinking and making skills that are central to artistic practice.

❖ Studio Thinking

The Studio Habits of Mind surface throughout the year in the throughlines and essential questions, often inferred and sometimes directly referenced in a unit or lesson plan. If you look closely at the essential questions for each grade level (refer to Table 4.4), you will see that the Studio Habits of Mind are embedded in each essential question. Sometimes habits are explicitly named ("Why do artists observe their own process and their work?") and, at other times, they are embedded in language ("What is artistic voice?" [Express]). A habit may work alone to anchor an essential question, or it may be clustered with others, as in the Grade 2 question "How do artists observe the world?" Here, Observe joins Understand Art Worlds to recognize communities and domains of knowledge beyond the classroom. Jennifer and Caren follow the studio structures for their classes, with Teacher Presents and Students at Work segments during each class. Students reflect

TABLE 4.4. San Francisco Friends School Visual Arts Curriculum

Throughlines (all grades)

1. What is art? What is an artist?
2. How am I an artist?
3. What is the relationship between art, justice, and action?

Grade	Essential Questions
K	• Why do we make art? • How can we stretch and explore in art class?
1	• What do artists do when they make mistakes? • Why do artists plan their work? • How do artists decide when an artwork is finished? • In what ways are we artists and writers?
2	• How do artists see? • How do artists observe the world? • Why do artists observe their own process and their work?
3	• What is artistic voice? • How do artists develop their techniques? • Why do artists express their ideas?
4	• How do artists stretch themselves and take risks? • What are the ways we can stretch and explore as artists? • Why do artists affect their communities?
5	• What do I stand for and what stands for me? • How do artists communicate?
6	• What and who do I stand for? • How do artists help form communities?
7–8	• How do I deepen my practice in the arts? • How do I serve my community in the arts? • Why are the arts important to a life well lived?

throughout the process in their arts-based reflection notebooks, and each unit concludes with Talking About Art sessions and Showing Art activities and exhibitions.

◆ Social-Emotional Learning

SFFS uses Responsive Classroom (Center for Responsive Schools, 2016) to design safe learning environments that teach self-monitoring skills to children. During the first 6 weeks of school, students practice routines to facilitate learning for the rest of the year. Jennifer and Caren work with students to establish studio norms and prepare documentation systems for the year. These include arts-based inquiry notebooks for each unit of study and processfolios to maintain artifacts of the process—plans, sketches, and other items that lead up to finished artworks.

CAPACITIES FOR LEARNING

The Visual Arts Program Overview at SFFS states: "Art provides a way for students to construct meaning and an understanding of the world around them." Over the years, Caren and Jennifer have observed shifts in their students' capacities to learn, as have many K–12 educators. Within one grade level, students' abilities and attitudes span enormous ranges, and the SFFS art teachers make an effort to engage and honor all students by meeting them at their individual levels.

Teachers cannot assume that all students come to school ready to challenge themselves with deep learning. This is acknowledged in the essential questions, which taken together form a cumulative outline of basic understandings about art and artists, and which gradually introduce new concepts at each grade level. In their weekly meetings, Jennifer and Caren discuss groups and individual students to target key thinking, social-emotional skills, and technical skills to provide students with the tools they need to access the curriculum.

CURRICULUM MAPPING

During their weekly meetings, Jennifer and Caren discuss and map out their plans, starting big and working through various lenses to detail each lesson. They each design a curriculum map that meets their needs, filling it in as the year progresses. Caren likes to refer to her map as the "swim lanes" for the grades she teaches—each row designates a grade level, showing the curricular progression over the year (see Figure 4.10). Jennifer's map uses two pages per grade to detail more elements of the curriculum (see Figure 4.11).

FIGURE 4.10. Caren Andrews describes each grade's curriculum in monthly progressions that she calls "swim lanes"—that is, the row of units through which each grade "swims."

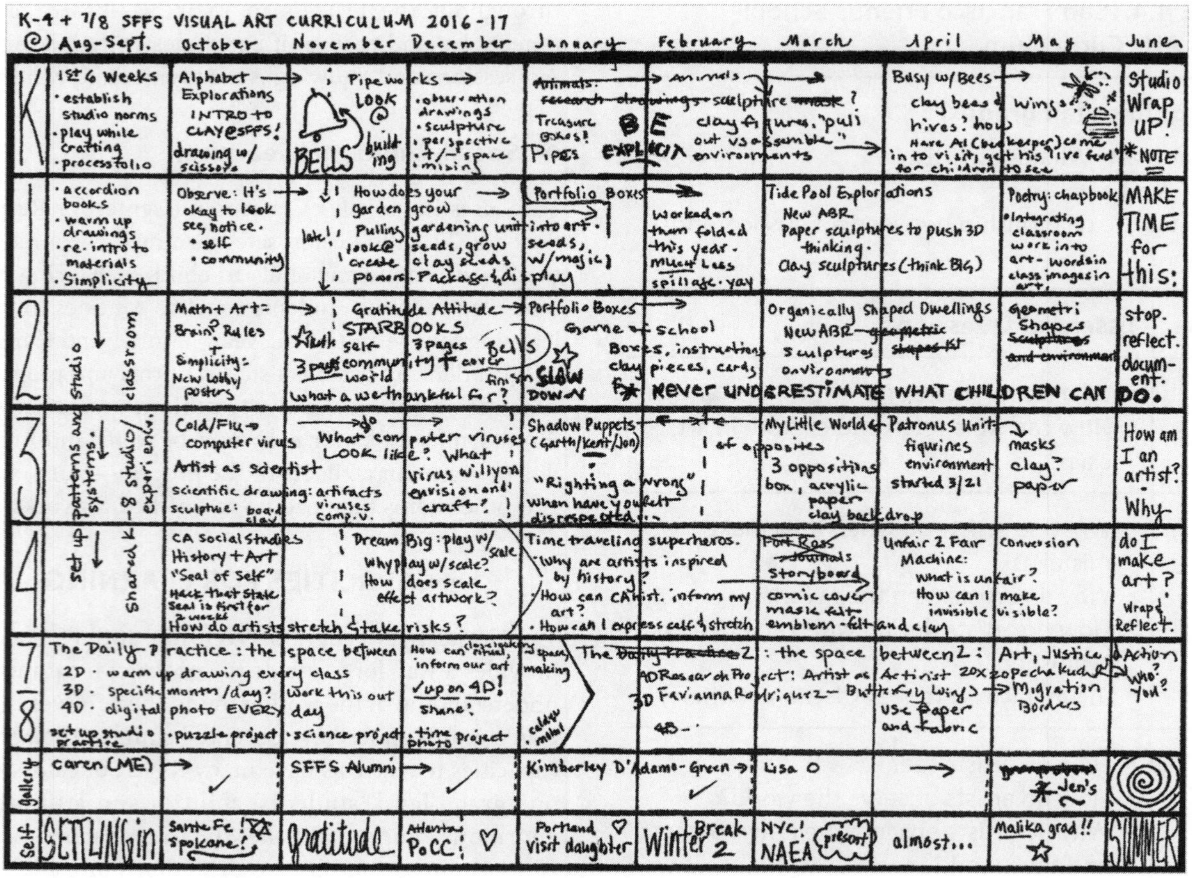

FIGURE 4.11. Jennifer Stuart's map for 5th grade identifies throughlines, essential questions, media, habits/skills, and social justice.

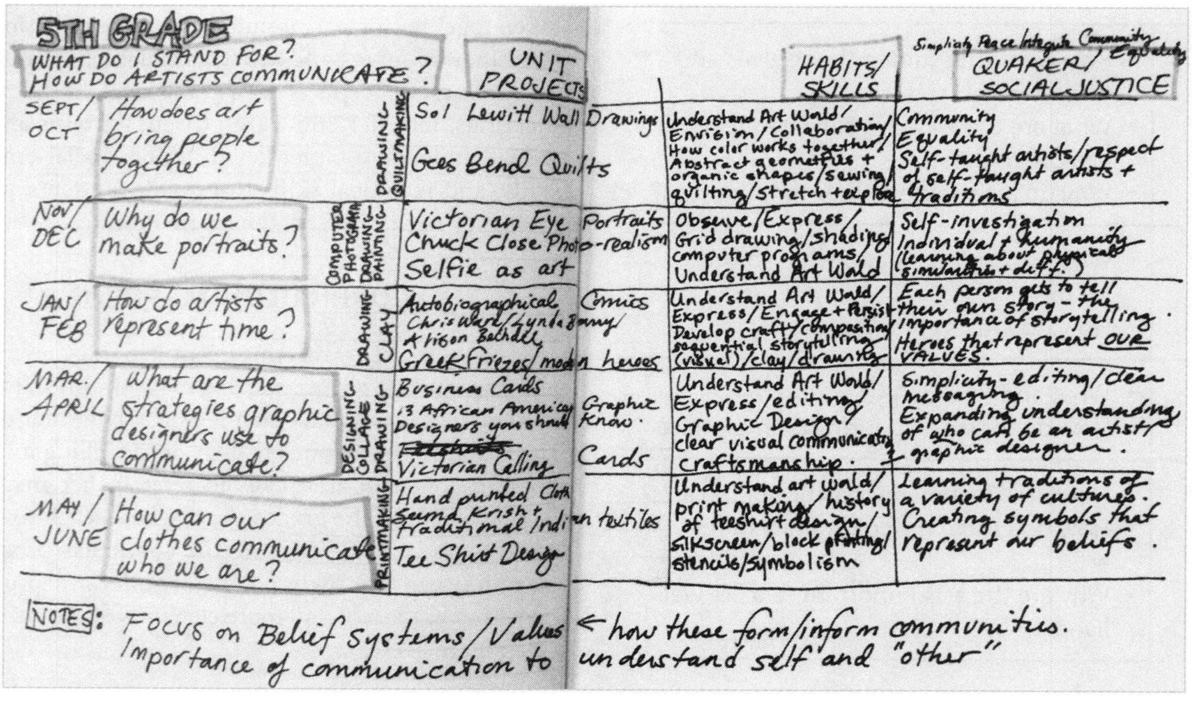

INDIVIDUAL UNITS AND LESSONS

❖ Grade 5 Portrait Unit (Jennifer)

In Jennifer's second major unit, her 5th-grade students learn about various forms of portraiture. First, students practice drawing eyes before observing their own eyes. That leads to drawings inspired by Georgian miniature eye portraits that feature a detailed eye surrounded by a border. The unit continues with Chuck Close's photo-realist works as artistic inspiration. Students choose a photograph of someone they admire, draw a grid on the photo and on their paper, and with pencil, replicate the image. Next, students look at portraits by Vik Muñiz and Ana Mendieta to create "materials based" collaged portraits. The unit concludes with a contemporary look at portraiture, "Selfie as Art."

The progression reveals how the experiences Jennifer designs develop students' appreciation of the essential questions. "What do I stand for and what stands for me?" is developed from close looking at facial elements (eyes), which evolves into a Georgian-style eye portrait that expresses something students "stand for" (value). "How do artists communicate?" is revealed through students' experiences with the various forms—the observational drawings, the Georgian eye portraits, photo-realism, and pop-culture selfies.

❖ A Pipe Journey Kindergarten Unit (Caren)

While 5th-graders learn about portraiture, kindergartners in Caren's classroom explore their school to understand something about buildings, integrating art with engineering, science, and math. The father of one of the kindergarten teachers was a pipe-fitter; the connection to his story engages the children, and the building focus narrows to become a study of pipes, which are also connectors (see Figure 4.12). Children practice close observation

FIGURE 4.12. Caren Andrews's unit plan illustrates concepts, understanding goals, and Studio Habits of Mind for a 6-week kindergarten unit, Pipeworks.

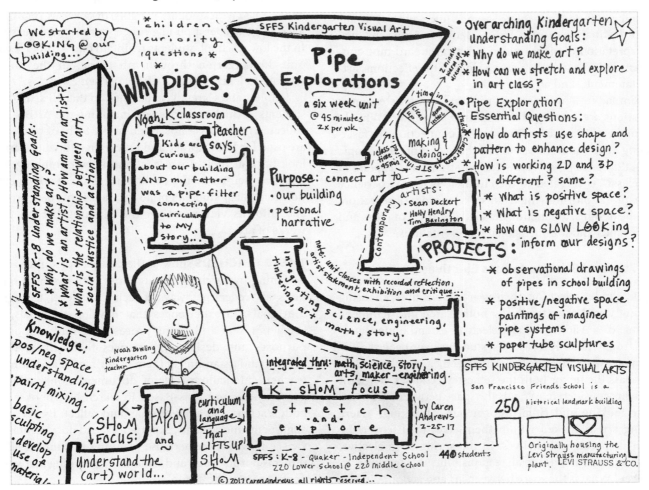

FIGURE 4.13. A kindergarten student observes positive and negative space in her artwork as she paints the background around pipes.

with photographs of pipes to prepare to sketch their pipe designs, considering shapes and patterns. The sketches inform large, detailed line drawings with pipes transporting imaginary fluids (chocolate, orange juice, glitter) to unseen destinations (as in Figure 4.13). A 3-dimensional interpretation of pipes follows, with cardboard tube constructions. The unit comes to a close with reflections, artist statements, and an exhibition.

Similar to Jennifer's unit, the kindergarten's essential questions are developed through the pipe unit. "Why do we make art?" is exemplified by the connections to fascinating people and stories and by the evolution of the topic of buildings to pipes. "How can we stretch and explore in art class?" is revealed to the children as they experience an exploration—moving from story, to close observation, to pipe designs, to fanciful, detailed drawings of pipes and their fluids and 3-dimensional representations.

❖ 7th- and 8th-Grade Arts Electives

Upper grades select four, half-year arts electives, choosing among visual arts (taught by both Caren and Jennifer), drama, or music. Visual arts electives extend understandings from Grades K–6, as most students have been at SFFS for many years. In "The Space Between," a visual arts elective class theme for both the semesters' courses, fall-term students considered "What is the space between? How can close looking and ritual inform our artmaking?" Here young artists looked within themselves to discover the liminal spaces in their lives. In the spring-term elective, students examined social responsibility by working to answer "What is the space between art and action?" In one

elective, "Wearable Art," students asked "What does how we adorn our bodies say about who we are?" In that class, young artists looked at a variety of different ways to express themselves by reflecting on what people put on their bodies—from tattoos, to henna, to clothes, hats, and jewelry. The explorations and projects investigated the unexpected ways in which humans have adorned their bodies in order to express beliefs and values, or to make a statement.

STUDENT DOCUMENTATION

Students maintain a record of artifacts that document their learning as they take ownership of their growth as artists. Student documentation, starting with Arts-Based Research Notebooks (ABRNs) are housed—along with sketches, plans, writing, and artwork—in processfolios that connect the many types of learning throughout the year (see also Appendix E).

Arts-Based Research Notebooks (Marshall & D'Adamo, 2011) are where students explore and expand on their ideas through observation and inquiry. Students expand their artistry to include inquiry and scientific thinking with and through the arts. ABRNs can be elaborate artist books, filled with students' insights, discoveries, maps, and ideas to go deeper around a concept or essential question. In the lower school, students maintain one ABRN for each unit, kindergarten through 4th grade. In the middle school, students craft one ARBN per semester.

Jennifer and Caren have planned so that all artifacts of students' artmaking processes, including the ARBNs, are collected in processfolios, often in the form of boxes that are used for both storage and reflection. Students learn to look back at their process, connect their thinking, and improve their craft. The explicit use of these documentation tools help students build awareness of their process and informs viewers about the thinking behind their works of art.

THESE TEACHERS show us the power of planning. From designing overarching throughlines with essential questions as "feeder" pathways at each grade level, to aligned unit goals, to experiences that develop the goals, the teachers reveal a planning process that finds important purposes and designs experiences that help students achieve understanding of them over time. In addition, the teachers' meticulous uses of documentation, including processfolios and Arts-Based Research Notebooks, help both teachers and students plan and reflect. By revealing alignment among goals, experiences, and documentation, we see how the teachers use planning to connect all art projects purposefully and build understanding across students' years at the school.

District-Level Planning and Professional Development— Elementary Art Teachers of Acton-Boxborough, Massachusetts

The elementary art teachers in the Acton-Boxborough school district in Massachusetts are a professional and fun bunch. They convene regularly as a group, about monthly, during schoolwide early release days. As they enter their central meeting spot, the classroom of Celia Knight (see Chapter 3), elementary teachers Eileen Barnett, Anne Kress, Heidi Kupferman, and Beth Warner chat about typical art teacher "stuff" with their department chair and high school art teacher, Diana Adams Woodruff (see Figure 4.14). After friendly greetings, snacks, and casual conversations about strategies for reducing paper towel use and speeding up purchase orders, the group gets down to business. During these meetings, the group is revisiting department documents that were initially written a few years ago. All of these documents use Studio Habits of Mind as a framework.

CREATING COHESIVENESS

Diana explains that about 5 years ago, all school departments were revisiting curricular documents. The art team had professional development days to work on curriculum and redefine learning goals. The group knew that they needed more flexibility than other departments, like math, which they described as having a particularly prescriptive curriculum. Each teacher wanted the freedom to continue using favorite lessons, or to have time to continue school traditions, or to integrate with classroom teachers in their particular sites. At the same time, middle school art teachers hoped that creating a more formal curriculum would mean that students arrived at the district middle school from their various elementary schools with a consistent set of skills on which they could build.

❖ Common Units

The teachers built a happy compromise between standardization and freedom. They created three common units per grade, one each in drawing, painting, and sculpture. This matches the way most of the teachers plan their units, by media, which are then embedded with essential questions, connections to the greater art worlds, and the Massachusetts Art Curriculum Framework. Table 4.5 depicts the common unit for Grade 1 Sculpture. All other units in each grade are created by each teacher individually.

FIGURE 4.14. Acton-Boxborough teachers—Beth Warner, Heidi Kupferman, Celia Knight, Anne Kress, Eileen Barnett, and Diana Adams Woodruff—meet to talk about Studio Habits.

TABLE 4.5. Grade 1 Common Unit (Sculpture)

Big Ideas

- Sculpture is different from other art forms.
- Artists make both temporary and permanent sculpture.
- Artists explore materials by making temporary sculptures.

Essential Questions

- What is the difference between 3-dimensional and 2-dimensional artwork?
- What can you learn by exploring materials?
- Why would an artist choose to make a temporary sculpture?
- Why would an artist choose to make a permanent sculpture?

Skills

- Experiment with different sculpture materials, such as paper, wood, clay, wire, and repurposed materials.
- Practice process: choose, manipulate, arrange, and join
- Understand the difference between temporary and permanent sculpture.
- Describe making your sculpture.

Vocabulary

- 2-dimensional/3-dimensional, 2D/3D
- Shape vs. form
- Temporary/permanent
- Balance
- Choose, manipulate, arrange, join

Art History Connection

- Look at and discuss suggested artworks: *Lincoln Memorial* and *Concord Minuteman* [statue by] Daniel Chester French; [sculptors] Deborah Butterfield, Kitty Wales, Patrick Doughtery, [and] Andy Goldsworthy; [and] Sand Castle Competitions.
- Where have you seen a temporary sculpture? (sand, ice, snow, playdough, nests . . .)
- Where have you seen a permanent sculpture? (statues)

Assessment

- Teacher/student discussions, using prompt:
  Prompt: How did you make your sculpture? (Process)
- Pair-show-and-tell of permanent sculpture, using prompt:
  Prompt: How did you make that part of your sculpture? (Pointing)

Standards (Mass Arts Curriculum Frameworks: http://www.doe.mass.edu/frameworks/arts/1099.pdf)

1.1 Use a variety of materials and media.
1.2 Create artwork in a variety of 2-dimensional (2D) and 3-dimensional (3D) media.
1.3 Learn and use appropriate vocabulary related to methods, materials, and techniques
1.4 Learn to take care of materials and tools and to use them safely.
2.4 For shape and form, explore the use of shapes and forms in 2D and 3D works.
3.3 Create 2D and 3D artwork from memory or imagination to tell a story or embody an idea or fantasy.
5.1 In the course of making and viewing art, learn ways of discussing it.
5.2 Classify artworks into general categories.
6.1 When viewing examples of visual arts, ask and answer questions about sculptures.

❖ Grade-Level Learning Goals

When teachers met several years ago to plan goals and curriculum, they split into smaller working groups, each tackling student learning goals from a different framework. Once they reconvened, they decided Studio Habits of Mind felt most appropriate for their needs. The group shares how important it is that students be able to talk about what they're learning and how the density and comprehensiveness of the National Standards seemed difficult to embed into an elementary school vernacular.

Diana: You can't realistically address everything in the National Standards, but you can in the Studio Habits of Mind. It has applicability to [the students] . . . I think you have to be able to articulate [what you're learning]. [If the students] are not able to articulate the process of what they're doing, not just technically, they can't talk *really* about it. If you can't talk about it, you can't have an understanding of [art's] importance.

Celia: It's advocacy. If kids use the language, others know. We know, but lots of people don't. So they're sharing that so much thinking is going into an artwork, and it's not just "pretty."

Beth: Also, making the kids aware. They do it, and they may not know it. They were nodding their heads [when the teacher talks], but they have to be made aware [within the context of their work].

Anne: I think there are certain students who won't be able to verbalize it. They're not verbal about what they do. And I can recognize that clearly. I have a 4th-grade boy right now, and he exemplifies the habits of mind, he really does, but he doesn't talk much at all. So I say, "so and so, do you know you are practicing Engage & Persist—you weren't chatting; you solved problems" and all I'll get is a grin from him. I hope I'm helping him identify it. He doesn't have to think about it that way, but I want him to know that he's doing it.

Eileen: It's so important to do that individually, like Anne said. You do it as a class sometimes, but when you do it one-on-one, it's much more meaningful. When you say it to them one-on-one, you can have a conversation.

The district's entire K–12 art department summarizes student learning goals using Studio Habits, as shown in Table 4.6. The group created broad learning targets that matched their interpretation of each Studio Habit and that could be addressed by students of every age.

TABLE 4.6. Acton-Boxborough Art Department: K–12 Learning Goals

Develop Craft	Students practice and apply artistic techniques using selected tools and materials.
Engage [&] Persist	Students understand that artmaking involves problem-solving, practice, and perseverance.
Envision	Students visualize and plan as part of their artmaking.
Express	Students create artworks that convey ideas, feelings, and personal meanings.
Observe	Students look at the world around them and consider aesthetic possibilities and ideas.
Reflect	Students contemplate and articulate ideas about their artmaking and the artmaking of others.
Stretch [&] Explore	Students experiment, take risks, and explore ideas in their artmaking.
Understand Art World[s]	Students learn about art history and current art practices and share their artwork with the broader community.

TABLE 4.7. Acton-Boxborough Art Department: Grade 4 Learning Goals and Criteria

Develop Craft: Students practice and apply artistic techniques using selected tools and materials.

- Students demonstrate the ability to create shape and space in an observation drawing.
- Students demonstrate an understanding of color and brushwork in transparent paint.
- Students demonstrate an understanding of coil technique in constructing a clay vessel.
- Students demonstrate an understanding of the elements of art and design (focus: line, shape, color, texture, space).
- Students demonstrate and practice good craftsmanship.

Engage & Persist: Students understand that artmaking involves problem-solving, practice, and perseverance.

- Students understand that they may encounter difficulties in the process of artmaking and will need to access artistic knowledge to work to a solution.
- Students demonstrate focused practice of unit skills.
- Students demonstrate the ability to stay focused and concentrate on the task at hand.

Envision: Students visualize and plan as part of their artmaking.

- Students demonstrate an understanding that there is a thought process before and during artmaking (visualize, plan, implement).

Express: Students create artworks that convey ideas, feelings, and personal meanings.

- Students demonstrate the ability to communicate ideas in artwork based on personal interests.

Observe: Students look at the world around them and consider aesthetic possibilities and ideas.

- Students "re-present" their observations in artwork.
- Students apply knowledge gained from reflecting on their own working process.

Reflect: Students contemplate and articulate ideas about their artmaking and the artmaking of others.

- Students demonstrate the ability to write a reflection about an artwork.
- Students demonstrate the ability to discuss an artwork.
- Students demonstrate the ability to assess their own artwork.

Stretch & Explore: Students experiment, take risks, and explore ideas in their artmaking.

- Students are willing to apply new techniques, processes, and media.
- Students are willing to consider multiple options.

Understand Art Worlds: Students learn about art history and current art practices and share their artwork with the broader community.

- Students understand that part of artmaking is sharing their artwork.
- Students demonstrate the ability to interact appropriately when sharing artwork.
- Students understand that art is created in a cultural context.

Then the K–6 teachers created more detailed goals by grade to help them think about how young students demonstrate each of the Studio Habits in developmentally appropriate ways. These are living documents that the teachers continue to revisit and discuss, making changes as needed. As the teachers realized during one of their meetings, the variation that exists across grades is minimal within each Studio Habit, and they mentally bookmark that for possible further analysis. Table 4.7 shows Grade 4 criteria for each of the eight learning goals.

❖ Learning Goal Strategies

The learning goals articulate the thinking and behaviors that teachers nurture in their elementary students. The teachers have created documents filled with strategies to support students, and they've shared these strategies with one another to facilitate Studio Thinking. Initially these documents were broken down for younger students (K–2) and older students (3–6), but eventually most were merged for strategies that could be used in all grades with slight developmental adaptations.

The teachers spent several hours in meetings going over their lists for each of the eight Studio Habit learning goals. This was a chance to remember forgotten strategies and share new ones that weren't yet on the list. As Diana remarks, "We aren't the same people we were when we wrote these," making note of all the new additions and changes. These lists are similar to those provided in Chapter 1. Table 4.8 is adapted from the Engage & Persist document created by the Acton-Boxborough teachers. The fruitful discussions about whether a certain strategy worked best for one habit or for another, along with hearing the practices of others, make these meetings not just an administrative chore, but a chance for teachers to learn from each other and develop professionally.

PROFESSIONAL DEVELOPMENT

The time these teachers have to meet, despite their busy schedules, is extremely important. Because art teachers are often the only artists in their school buildings, having the chance to meet with others who are in the same role allows teachers opportunities to talk and think through important issues, from mundane conversations about paper-towel use to larger programwide learning goals. This is an important professional support needed by all specialist teachers.

As the Acton-Boxborough teachers discuss strategies for using Studio Habits of Mind in their learning goals,

TABLE 4.8. Acton-Boxborough: Engage & Persist Strategies

- Provide choice to pique student interests.
- Encourage breaks between focus time.
- Reinforce not rushing.
- Recognize/acknowledge persistence in students.
- Talk about not giving up.
- Brainstorm strategies to help persistence: What do you do if you are frustrated?
- Arrange for partner talk about how each persisted.
- Display a poster: What do you do if you are stuck?
- Point out that mistakes are possibilities and part of the learning process
- Ask: What needs to change to solve your problem? To meet your vision, expectation?
- Provide an exit ticket: How did you persist today?
- Have students share out about how they persisted today.

they end up sharing questions, stories, challenges, and strengths from their teaching. They engage in shared inquiry focused on the Studio Habits, though sometimes these habits become the jumping off point from which other conversations emerge.

As they begin to discuss Reflect, Diana shares something she observed while visiting Anne's room. With just a couple of minutes left, Anne posted a few art postcards and asked 3rd-graders to think about which ones might belong together and why. The teachers then talk about whether this was an activity that asks students to reflect or to observe. They wonder at first, and then realize that it's both. When teachers discuss activities through the lenses of the habits, they see that multiple habits are usually involved, and they gain clarity about the meanings of each habit.

Later, the group considers Stretch & Explore and inadvertently stumbles into a conversation about skills, inclination, and alertness—the three elements of each habit. Visitor Jill Hogan notices the wording of the learning goals "Students are willing to apply new techniques, processes, and media" and "Students are willing to consider multiple options," which are focused on attitudes (willingness) over skills, unlike some other learning goals. The group then considers how perhaps some Studio Habits are more likely to be first examined through a skill lens (such as Develop Craft: Technique) while others turn up first through an inclination or alertness lens (such as

Stretch & Explore). The conversation was messy and perhaps led to more confusion than clarity, but resolution isn't always what matters. Opportunities to talk with other art teachers open up possibilities to reflect on, and that's the point. Meeting with like-minded individuals who share similar settings and challenges allows for a depth of analysis and connection that art teachers can't always find with classroom teachers or other specialists.

THE ELEMENTARY ART TEACHERS in Acton-Boxborough model dedication to teaching with Studio Thinking in mind, while having the opportunity to meet and grow as individuals and as a group. Their story shows how they implement traditional means of organizing curriculum—by artistic media and themes—with the Studio Habits of Mind as ways to assess students' artistic thinking.

THINGS TO THINK ABOUT

1. Think about all the things you consider as you plan (some of these might include state or national standards, your district curriculum, Studio Habits of Mind, Studio Structures, thematic content, or classroom integration). How do you prioritize these considerations and why? How might you change them to better suit your personal values as a teacher?

2. If you're more visual, try writing out all the things you consider as you plan and how they interact. If you're more verbal, try drawing a picture map to show what you consider and how those things interact. Are there any new relationships that appear for you when you use your nontypical approach?

3. Nicole makes systematic accommodations for some of her learners. What accommodations do you use in your classroom, and in what areas do you want to accommodate students better? Who can help you do this?

4. Wynita leaves flexibility in her planning to account for trends in student interests and popular culture. Look at the flexibility you leave yourself in your own process. Is it enough to create relevance for your students? What's one trend going on right now that you could incorporate meaningfully in your classroom?

5. The core Quaker values of Caren and Jennifer's school trickle down to all elements of their planning and teaching. What are your school's articulated values? How do those manifest in the art program?

6. Teachers in Acton-Boxborough regularly share ideas as a team. Who are your resources for sharing and learning new ideas? If you don't have thinking partners in your school or district, are there others you could connect with in your area or on social media or "meet" over distance media (Skype)? Are there artists with whom you talk about your own artwork who might be glad to think with you about curricular issues? Is there a small group of people with whom you'd like to read and discuss this book?

PART III

Evaluating
and
Sharing

CHAPTER 5

Assessment

Methodologies used to evaluate works or procedures in other fields may be useful in the arts, but often are not.

—*Council of Arts Accrediting Associations (2007, p. 7)*

In this chapter, we confront the vexing problem of assessment in the visual arts. As the quotation above suggests, art educators in colleges and universities wrestle with ways to assess in art, just as elementary art teachers do. Should teachers assess product or process? Which products? Which processes?

What and how we assess demonstrates the values of teachers, administrators, and entire societies. When choosing what to measure, we must select those things that we value as most important. In turn, what we choose to assess ends up being further valued, as the expression "we treasure what we measure" encapsulates. In creating processes for assessment, our values need to lead; values come first. So, we need to determine what values are held by members of the field of art education.

Our perspective holds that art education's most valuable product is all students' abilities to think like artists. It is this, the *artistic thinking process,* that we treasure as most valuable and that we must assess. We don't believe that artistic thinking can be revealed by looking only at a set of technical skills, a final artwork, or even a portfolio of artworks. Rather, understanding artistic thinking requires that we look at the sources for a student's motivation and his or her capacity to use the full panoply of Studio Habits of Mind in an integrated manner. Thus, we advocate for assessing students' thinking by using all of the Studio Habits of Mind as assessment lenses.

QUALITY ASSESSMENT

Our focus here is on formative assessment (ongoing and in-process). That is because we believe that the goal of assessment is to benefit learning and teaching, and that is what formative assessment does. Formative assessment helps students understand their own growth, helps parents understand what their children are learning, and helps administrators recognize the important thinking dispositions that students are gaining through art classes.

Inevitably, some readers will want to know about summative assessment—that is, assessment that "adds up" to a final judgment and is usually captured in a grade. We are not convinced that summative assessment is necessary, nor that it benefits anyone. On the other hand, we see several ways in which it can harm students and teachers—by convincing students not to bother with art because they learn early on that "they aren't good at it"; by demoralizing teachers who strive to engage every child in artistic inquiry; and by forcing teachers to succumb to assessing only what is easy to see (technical skill and/or knowledge of art history or vocabulary) at the expense of assessing important qualities of artistic thinking. We challenge those who insist on summative assessment in art to persuade us that its benefits outweigh its potential harm. At this point, we are unconvinced.

❖ What Is Formative Assessment?

Formative assessment involves gathering information about students through observation, documenting that information, interpreting it, and communicating conclusions to various audiences. Many art teachers already do much of this. They *gather information* as they observe students' work (noticing what students make from moment to moment), talk with students and ask them to reflect and write artist statements (listening to what students say and reading what they write), and attend to how students respond in class (watching what students do). Often, teachers also *document* at least some of the information they are gathering with photos, videos, notes, lists, or charts. Next comes *interpreting* these observations to describe students' thinking—that happens when teachers and students combine the clues they've gathered into communicable understandings of a student's current phase of learning. Finally, the assessment is *communicated* to various audiences.

❖ Guidelines for Quality Assessment

In this section we describe what we believe to be the most important guidelines teachers can turn to when designing quality assessment (Blythe et al., 1998; Wiske, 1998). These are intended to *nurture learning* (formative assessment) rather than make a final judgment (summative assessment).

Make Learning Intentions Visible. Students need to know what they are supposed to be learning. They know this when teachers post learning goals in the classroom and facilitate discussions about student work in reference to these goals. Goals are often tied to standards and posted visibly as overarching, unit- and lesson-level goals or district benchmarks, or as other organizational charts, messages, and formats that teachers design. When teachers make learning intentions visible and refer to them often, students gain additional language for talking about their own thinking process, which bolsters metacognition.

Assess Qualitatively. Artistic thinking is poorly measured by paper and pencil tests yielding numeric scores. Teachers need to assess qualitatively based on what they observe as students make and talk about their art and the art of others. When students are involved in formative assessment practices, they develop abilities for judging quality autonomously. Teachers facilitate an ongoing discussion about what artists do and how they do it so that, like professional artists, students talk to their friends about their work, write artist statements for their exhibited work [Talking About Art], and co-curate exhibitions [Showing Art]. As students learn to evaluate works, including works by established artists, they begin to notice what qualities satisfy other viewers, what could be different, and what makes others think and wonder. Public discussion about students' work—in class or when art is exhibited [Showing Art]—reinforces students' understanding that what they make and think matters to others, and, therefore, that its quality is important.

Assess Works in Process. Assessing final works alone is insufficient: only some qualities of artistic thinking are revealed in the end product. To focus art assessment on student thinking, teachers need to assess students in the process of making, viewing, and discussing artworks. They need to consider how students make decisions, revise, and evaluate; how they engage, persist, explore, and reflect; how they make connections to art by other artists; and how they imagine and select among possible solutions. None of these qualities can be directly seen in a finished painting, sculpture, or any other final work.

Assess Continuously. Teachers need to think about assessment as something that is constantly ongoing. Opportunities for gathering evidence for assessment happen through nonstop observation, both when students are present and before and after classes. Teachers observe most during Students at Work and Talking About Art sessions, because these are the times when students are actively constructing and revealing their thinking. Teachers turn these observations into assessment when they pull their interpretations together into tentative hypotheses and action plans to communicate to the student or others. Continuous formative assessment also helps teachers examine their teaching practices and curriculum. Teachers can use information from assessment as checks on what makes sense to students and what needs to be changed.

Assess Longitudinally. Teachers need to strive to check students' thinking repeatedly over time to understand their growth. Art teachers often see students for several years—they have the opportunity to look for change over the long term. Assessment of students' thinking over time—by continually observing and interpreting their talk, actions, and artworks in progress—is what is needed to assess improvement in artistic thinking. Comparing works and approaches that students make over time reveals how seeds planted in previous years grow and begin to bear fruit. Some teachers do this by reviewing collections of student work, including reviewing reflections and photos from each school year that they keep in online or hard copy portfolios (see Appendices C and E).

Manage Assessment Strategically. Most elementary art teachers, teaching hundreds of students a week, cannot carry out assessment as frequently or as rigorously as they might like—there simply isn't enough time. However, teachers can work on their own or in groups to analyze a single student in depth, as we do in the examples provided in this chapter. Looking closely at a few students on a regular basis builds teachers' assessment muscles so that they learn to identify quality in the immediacy of classroom teaching. We encourage teachers not to approach assessment as "one size fits all." Some students may require greater attention through assessment than others, and that's okay. And for all students, when teachers see something noteworthy, it's helpful to jot it down, because these insights fade quickly. (For examples of how teachers have managed documentation and interpretation for assessment, see Appendix E.)

Use Assessment to Advocate—These Are Your Values! Assessing formatively serves as a powerful advocacy tool to the rest of the school and the wider community, because such assessment highlights the *thinking and understanding* that occur in the arts. It is important that teachers use the information gathered through their ongoing assessments to talk about the benefits of art education with their school and with the greater community (see also Chapter 6).

◆ Seeing Studio Habits of Mind: Kelly's Waterfall

To show how groups of teachers might use the Studio Thinking framework in a back-and-forth conversation to assess a student's thinking, we focus on a 5th-grader, Kelly. Diane Jaquith was Kelly's teacher for 5 years (K–4), and Diane collected samples of her work throughout that time. During her years in elementary school, Kelly preferred 2-dimensional work with nature themes, often exploring color, patterns, and textures [Develop Craft: Technique]. Now in 5th grade, Kelly looks back with Diane on her painting of a waterfall from 4th grade (see Figure 5.1). In the following passage, Kelly's comments are shown in italics. Interspersed are reflections by Lois Hetland and Diane as they examined the transcript of Diane's and Kelly's conversation. Lois and Diane explore what the Studio Habits reveal about what Kelly had (and had not) been doing, and what a teacher might do (or might have done) to support her artistic growth. At first Diane and Lois simply identify Studio Habits that Kelly had been using. The dialogue then shifts to understanding Kelly's work through using Studio Habits as lenses.

Kelly: [I chose to paint this because] *my friends were all doing landscapes, I think. My dad owns a boat so . . . I remember once seeing a waterfall* [Envision from Observe]. *Also, my brother once painted a waterfall and he gave me tips on it* [Understand Art Worlds: Communities]. *I had this image of a waterfall in my*

FIGURE 5.1. Kelly's painting of a waterfall.

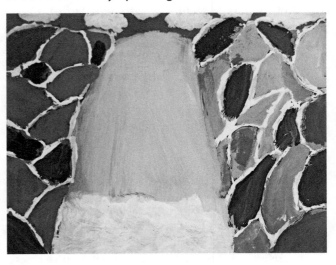

brain [Envision], *and I really wanted to paint it* [Engage of Engage & Persist]. *Whenever I got into painting* [Develop Craft: Technique], *I really liked to stick with that* [Engage & Persist]. *When I paint I like to give it more of a texture* [Envision], *and that's what I did at the bottom of the waterfall. I like how the texture makes it like . . . gives it more of . . . like you'd know what the water would look like* [Express].

Diane: Once Kelly decided on her idea, she always stayed with it, often for many weeks [Engage & Persist]. In this painting it sounds like Kelly was going for "frothiness" as a texture in the water.

Lois: Is that Express? She was trying to express the idea of "frothiness"?

Kelly: *When I made the bottom of the waterfall more of a lumpy texture, it was more how the water is going separate ways. It wasn't all straight down like it was at the top of the waterfall when it went straight down, and at the bottom it went all crazy* [Reflect: Question & Explain].

Diane: She has a picture in her head about what it's supposed to look like, and she keeps going back to that [Envision; Reflect: Evaluate] and adjusting [Express].

Lois: In this case, she's using Express to help her match what she envisions.

Diane: Yes, she wants to express her concept of what a waterfall should look like.

Kelly: *I really like the way I changed the color of the rocks* [Reflect: Evaluate] *because not all the rocks—if you look at a waterfall* [Observe; Envision]—*around it they* *are not all the same color. So I tried to change the color* [Develop Craft: Technique]. *I started mixing, and I started to put the lines in between to show the different rocks* [Develop Craft: Technique; Envision; Express]. *I had a lot of mistakes in this one, but I fixed them all* [Stretch & Explore].

Lois: I'm thinking about Kelly's memory of looking at a waterfall with her family [Observe]. The rocks were not all the same color, and she was dissatisfied with her painting [Reflect: Evaluate], because it didn't match her memory [Envision] of reality [Observe], and it was reality that she wanted to express.

Diane: She said that the rocks are all different colors in a waterfall in nature [Envision]. She wanted to capture that naturalism [Express].

Lois: If she were observing in the moment, she'd see more colors [Observe]. Her memory seems likely to be less rich than the actual observation would be.

Kelly: *When I first made this I just painted the rocks without the lines, in all the same color. And then I decided to put lines in them, and the color started changing* [Observe; Reflect: Evaluate; Develop Craft: Technique to Express]. *And that was a mistake* [Stretch & Explore] *because it looked weird* [Reflect: Evaluate], *and I said, "I'll just make all the rocks different colors"* [Stretch & Explore]. *Then the colors started going into the waterfall* [Observe], *and I painted over them. I painted over the waterfall* [Stretch & Explore], *I think, every class I had to redo it* [Engage & Persist], *because they were all different colors* [Reflect: Evaluate]. *I like that way* [Reflect: Evaluate], *because it shows how the waterfall was different colors* [Envision]. [Although her waterfall had several different shades and tints of blue, this is difficult to see in the black-and-white reproduction.]

Lois: She responded to the problem of the rock colors bleeding into the waterfall—that's Stretch & Explore.

Diane: Explain to me how that's Stretch & Explore.

Lois: Stretch & Explore includes making errors and learning from them. Here she noticed a "mistake," something she did not plan. She made something out of this mistake—the varying colors of the waterfall. Stretch & Explore allowed her to capitalize on that error rather than just try to undo it. She repainted the waterfall in response to her mistake, rather than sticking to her original idea and being frustrated. She took a flexible artistic approach.

Diane: You haven't convinced me yet. I would have said that Kelly used Engage & Persist through the error and Develop Craft: Technique to fix it.

Lois: We can look at Kelly's behavior—changing how she tackles the rocks, and see it from many sides, or through many Studio Habits: Stretch & Explore, Engage & Persist, Develop Craft: Technique, maybe more—they're all involved, and it's all happening so quickly—it's a cluster [as introduced in Chapter 1]. Sometimes it's not worth pinning down an exact Studio Habit for a particular behavior, because so many are involved.

Diane: Can you explain "clusters"?

Lois: Here's what I mean. As artists work, they move quickly around their artistic thinking dispositions—if they're observing, they don't just observe, they go from one habit to another—observing, envisioning, developing craft, expressing, stretching and exploring, understanding art worlds, observing again, and so forth. That movement is a pathway or a trail or a flow. Each habit works as a launching pad for the next one in an ongoing process—which *is* Studio Thinking. But sometimes, the pathway has a small collection of habits that work together as a group. We call those clusters. That's when two or more habits keep echoing one another. For example, because Express is the *meaning* of what we make, and we use craft as the *vocabulary for conveying that meaning,* artists often bounce back and forth between Express and Develop Craft: Technique. So if I see a child working on an idea, I might suggest a variety of ways to convey that with materials—play with color, or the hardness of the pencils, or composition/placement [Develop Craft: Technique], for example, to make it say what she wants it to say [Express]. That's a cluster pair of Express and Develop Craft: Technique. But if I see the same child enamored with a material, say cardboard, I might suggest playing with it [Stretch & Explore] to see what she can do to make new techniques [Develop Craft: Technique], and then think about [Reflect: Question & Explain] what those different effects might convey [Express]. So, there, we've got a cluster of Stretch & Explore with Develop Craft: Technique, Reflect: Question & Explain, and Express. Clusters don't have any specific number of habits in them—it can be two or eight.

This kind of extended conversation around a single piece of work builds teachers' abilities to pay close attention and notice how students are thinking when they are in the classroom. It's not that teachers should do that with every student—that's not possible with so many. The point is to build up familiarity with the different Studio Habits. That's why it's good to write a weekly reflection or to have a monthly thinking group with other teachers where you look at student work together.

ASSESSMENT AND MOTIVATION

In this section, we propose an approach to formative assessment that is based on what we value in arts education. The goal of quality arts education is for all students to develop well-rounded, artistic minds appropriate to their developmental level. This means that what is taught—the curriculum—needs to allow opportunities for students to use all of the habits, and to do so with skill (*Can* they do it?), inclination to use them (*Will* they do it?), and alertness about when to deploy them (Do they know *when* and *why* to do it?). Students need to use the habits seamlessly so that they flow into one another, as they do for professional artists. For example, Understanding Art Worlds gives students ideas from other artists, which helps them to engage. Engaging drives persisting, and they might look at more work from other artists, and round and round—a cluster. In another cluster of habits, Observe can lead to developing craft as a student aims to replicate something in the real world—and back to Observe, Develop Craft: Technique, Observe. And artists reflect to clarify and improve what they are doing, and that clusters with any of the other habits. To teach students how to think like artists, teachers deliberately slow down this integrated process, showing how one habit leads to another, or how developing one habit leads to developing strength in another.

In a Studio Thinking classroom, the teacher's role is to keep students sufficiently motivated so that they will engage in artmaking and develop all the habits. The best way to do this, in our view, is to build on students' strengths, since focusing on weaknesses may cause students to disengage. We propose motivation, the source of student engagement and follow-through, as the initial focus of formative assessment. Conversations about learning and assessment have gone on far too long without considering motivation as a (perhaps, *the*) primary factor.

There is a long-standing debate between teachers who say, "But he tried so hard—we need to give credit for that effort!" and others who say, "You can't give an A just because a student tried hard. What about the quality of the work?" We urge you to avoid this trap. Do what you must to assign the grades that are required, and do that in ways that are as helpful to the child as possible. Then, spend your real energy focusing on how to motivate the child to learn.

First, become aware of the student's motivation. Is the student motivated at all, or disengaged? If motivated, is the motivation extrinsic (i.e., assignments are completed because they are assigned) or intrinsic (i.e., assignments

FIGURE 5.2. Motivation is the engine of all genuine learning.

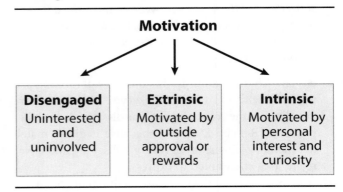

are completed because of the student's interest)? (See Figure 5.2.)

Beginning with an honest assessment of a student's source of motivation might be unsettling. A student you pick as intrinsically motivated might not look like a strong student to an outside observer, because that student is messy or fidgety. A girl who can't seem to stop working at cleanup time may not be defiant but, rather, just highly engaged in her work. A student you pick out as extrinsically motivated might look strong to that outside observer, because he is compliant and neat. While that student may be easy to have in your classroom, we worry that he's unlikely to become an artistic thinker when the carrots and sticks are gone.

Thinking in this way, by beginning with sources of motivation, is a shift that we believe is crucially important to taking learning seriously in art classrooms. Motivation is the engine of all genuine learning. Without it, nothing important happens. Nothing "sticks." When intrinsically motivated, students are open to integrating artistic behaviors into their daily endeavors and can develop Studio Habits of Mind as resources for lifelong artistic thinking—whether they become artists or not. Intrinsic motivation helps students develop the full complement of Studio Habits, which then leads them to make high-quality products and, most importantly, to think like artists. Below we describe differentiated assessment and teaching strategies to use once you have identified students as either disengaged, extrinsically engaged, or intrinsically engaged.

◆ Disengaged Students

Disengaged students seem uninterested and uninvolved, but teachers often don't know the reason. The student may be upset, angry, hungry, bored, tired, or discouraged.

Quite often, disengaged students have little confidence in their ability to be successful. They may feel that art has no relevance to their lives, so why bother? When students have barely engaged in making art, teachers have little to assess. No Studio Habit can be learned by disengaged students, and even excellent instruction is likely to fail, because engagement is a prerequisite for learning. The immediate goal for teachers of these students is to motivate them to engage.

- Take the time to discover why the student is tuned out. Sometimes it is an issue with art class, and sometimes it is from factors beyond an art teacher's control. What is the issue for a particular student, and how can a teacher make the art class a safe space to be oneself?
- Capitalize on strengths—ideally in art, but other strengths can work—and build on these abilities or interests.
- Personalize content, giving students freedom to work with their preferred media and topics.
- Start small with work that can be completed in one class. Long-term assignments may feel overwhelming.
- Remain flexible about whether artworks are completed by students alone or in groups—for extreme introverts or extroverts, that can make a huge difference in their ability to engage.
- Assign the student a leadership position (small-group leader, cleanup czar, pencil-return police). Sometimes students "play" disengaged in order to gain attention—how can you turn the tables so that the student gets attention for a positive reason?
- Find contemporary artists who make art that may interest the student because of the media or subject matter choice.
- Go with the flow. Our starting point here is engagement—without it, learning can't happen. Student-level exceptions to project guidelines or class norms may be appropriate to spark engagement.

To illustrate how to reach a child who seems disengaged much of the time, let's look at Jack.

Jack is an active child who loves sports—he dreams of being a football player when he grows up, and this is Jack's and his family's top priority. Jack is diagnosed with ADHD and has a paraprofessional for support in the classroom (but not in art class). He avoids work whenever he can, using excuses to go to the nurse or get a drink of water. He is falling behind his classmates, including in art class. Jack sees no point in engaging in art class because he thinks it is "boring," it is not something his family values, and he doesn't see himself as good at it. His teacher reminds him to stay on task, but it's more fun to make his friends laugh than to make art. If he does finish an artwork, he throws it in the trash instead of taking it home.

As Jack's teacher, you want Jack to become engaged in his artmaking process, so instead of focusing on what Jack *isn't* doing, you can start with what he cares about and does well. Because he is a good football player, he understands teamwork and strategic plays. He is pretty funny, so humor is also a potential lever. What else does he do well? What does he do outside of football season? How can Jack's skills and interests in these areas help him become engaged in art class? Looking at the list of suggestions above, consider these suggestions for what a teacher could do for Jack.

Recognize that Jack has skills in areas that might be useful in art class (teamwork, strategy, humor). Then, reflect on your class activities—is there enough freedom within them for Jack to find his niche through subject matter? Jack might engage if he could create art about subjects that interest him (like football). Remember to be honest with Jack, and let him know that you want to work with him to make art class more interesting. What materials does he like best? Could he work with those materials, even if everyone else is doing something different? You can also partner Jack with a friend or team of three or four. Parallel to strategies in football, his role could be "quarterback," who calls the "plays" (makes the decision when the group is undecided). Or it could be "coach," who suggests possibilities (What if we . . . ? Do you think we could . . . ?). Or maybe he could be "tight end," who catches the ball and runs with it (I'll try this idea and show it to you in 5 minutes)? And, finally, don't forget that many artists express themselves using humor—show Jack some of these artists, like Lynda Barry or Red Grooms. If he doesn't find them amusing, keep searching for artists he can relate to. When you find an artist, let Jack take time to look at that artist's work and tell you what he likes about it. Ask Jack to list ideas he wants to incorporate into his own work.

❖ Extrinsically Motivated Students

Extrinsically motivated students are carrying out assignments dutifully and are more motivated to respond to rules than to learn. Students at this level ask questions such as, "Is this good?" or "Is it done?" or "Is it right?" and "Is this an A?" They seem to be operating on the principle of "You tell me what to do, I do it, and you tell me that it's good." They're not being curious or making their own judgments about the quality of their work. These students seem trapped by outside approval at the expense of their own natural interests. A teacher's first goal with these students is to help them switch from extrinsic to intrinsic motivation. Following are some teaching strategies:

- Be explicit with students about why you value intrinsic motivation. "The most important thing to me (the teacher) is that you (my student) are making art that means something to you. That's how learning happens. Tell me what you're excited about, and we'll look for ways you can make art with that."
- Be clear that learning can't happen if you're just going through the motions: artists have to use hand, mind, and heart together.
- Design lessons and units that emphasize personalization and offer choices in media and approach.
- Assess steps that lead up to final pieces, but do not assess the final piece itself. This boosts confidence in those perfectionist students who may be unsure about their final products. Adding a large, public celebration of the work with an important audience (parents, school board, in a public library) emphasizes that artists work on process thoroughly—not just to earn a good grade—but so real audiences can appreciate the final work.
- Create explicit lessons about how artists find ideas for their works, and model your own idea-finding process for making artworks in front of students.
- Show videos of contemporary artists talking about how their works are personally meaningful.
- Find ways for students to model for others what they are passionate about by posting their sources of inspiration on a bulletin board.
- Exhibit the final work along with the prior drafts and false starts to promote a growth mindset.

The example below shows how the teacher of extrinsically motivated Greta helped her develop intrinsic motivation.

In the early grades (K–2), Greta didn't stand out much in her choice-based art class. She blended in with the group, neither acting out nor being particularly invested in anything she made or in any particular medium or idea. Art did not seem to interest her, but being with her friends did—and her friends did art, so she did, too.

One day early in 3rd grade, Greta's art teacher, Diane Jaquith, invited the class to engage in the Attachment Test challenge (Douglas & Jaquith, 2009, 2018), making a sculpture by attaching materials together successfully without glue or tape. Diane set out a box of unusual materials for attaching: pipe cleaners, foam, spring, wire, brass fasteners, wood, beads, feathers, and foam. Greta was enchanted by the materials [Develop Craft: Technique]. She dived in and selected a foam square, pipe cleaners, beads, and feathers. She played with these materials [Stretch & Explore] and poked feathers and pipe cleaners into the foam, using the pipe cleaners to attach beads as eyes [Develop Craft: Technique]. Delighted with her "creature" [Reflect: Evaluate], she went on to make a family with two more [Engage & Persist] (see Figure 5.3A). Suddenly, Greta was invested in art itself, and not simply as a reason to be with her friends.

From that playful exploration [Stretch & Explore], Greta found a direction for what she wanted to pursue [Express]. This marks a shift in Greta's motivation from extrinsic to intrinsic. Diane's attachment test was developmentally appropriate and novel for 3rd-graders—just the right hook to engage Greta in making personally meaningful art [Engage & Persist].

Using pipe cleaners, Greta started exploring how to make a variety of creatures, including people and their environments [Stretch & Explore; Express]. She began exploring novel characters with fibers, such as a pillow-face and a pencil-person [Stretch & Explore; Express] (see Figure 5.3B). In 5th grade, she learned needle felting, and her commitment to fibers became complete [Engage & Persist; Develop Craft: Technique]. She made creatures and families of figures that she posted all around the room with the names she gave to them [Engage & Persist] (see Figure 5.3C).

This progression shows that, supported by Diane's introductions of new techniques and materials, Greta jumped from being extrinsically motivated to be with her friends, to being intrinsically motivated to develop her own artistic pursuit. Now Diane can return to the Studio Habits as lenses to identify and support strengths and gaps in Greta's artistic growth.

Make Habits Visible: Creating Studio Habit Profiles. Diane creates a Studio Habit profile to identify areas Greta should focus on. Table 5.1 documents how Greta is using Studio Habits after she discovered a passion for inventing creatures. We document her use of all Studio Habits here. But teachers may choose just to work with a few habits—the ones that are particular strengths or weaknesses for a student.

FIGURE 5.3. Greta's artworks. **A:** Her solution to the Attachment Test is a family of creatures. **B:** She explores wrapping with yarn to attach materials to a stick character. **C:** She expands her fiber arts skills to include sewing to make a pillow character.

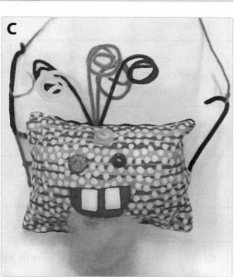

In classrooms where the Studio Habits are continually used for reflection, children become very aware of their own relative strengths and weaknesses. At least by Grade 3, students can begin to create their own habit profiles, alone as a self-reflection or in a mini-conference with a peer or teacher.

These profiles can provide fodder for conversations with students and parents. They can help students and teachers know which Studio Habits need to be developed and how to better understand each habit. Habit profiles can also be used to reflect on which Studio Habits were used in the creation of a particular artwork. Have students create these profiles after they complete an artwork,

whenever that's possible, even if it is only twice a year. The goal is for each student to develop the full set of Studio Habits to think with, and that begins with an awareness of which habits are already strengths and which areas need to grow. Making or having students make these profiles from time to time may be all teachers need to do to track extrinsically motivated students.

Focusing on One Habit. Sometimes students may need more attention for one reason or another. They may be stuck in a rut or frustrated; or they may have all Studio Habits in play and teachers want to know ways to support their deeper development within and across the habits.

TABLE 5.1. Greta's Habit Profile

Studio Habits	Rating (Strength or Area for Growth)	Evidence
Develop Craft: Technique	Strength	Greta developed strong skills with media, primarily fibers.
Develop Craft: Studio Practice	Strength	Greta always accesses and returns materials to the right places.
Engage & Persist	Strength	Greta is intrinsically motivated to create characters using a wide variety of materials and makes many of them.
Envision	Strength	Greta enjoys imagining new characters, their personalities, and their families.
Express	Area for growth	Greta's characters are expressive. She could begin to express her own perspectives and ideas deliberately through the characters.
Observe	Area for growth	What, if anything, is Greta looking at outside of school to influence her ideas? She could build awareness to become alert to these influences.
Reflect: Evaluate	Area for growth	Greta seems satisfied with her work and rarely examines it with a critical eye for improvement.
Reflect: Question & Explain	Area for growth	Greta is eager to discuss her characters with everyone, but not analytically.
Stretch & Explore	Strength	Greta is very playful and resourceful with materials.
Understand Art Worlds: Communities	Area for growth	Greta has become self-sufficient in her artmaking. She would benefit by connecting more often with her classmates, perhaps in a small critique group.
Understand Art Worlds: Domain	Area for growth	Greta would benefit by looking at the work of artists who develop characters, such as Takashi Murakami.

When teachers have the time, they can follow the suggestions listed below for how to think more deeply about students' areas of strength or weakness.

Following the creation of a habit profile, teachers can use the three elements of a thinking disposition (skill, inclination, alertness) to help students understand how to work on habits in need of growth or better use their strengths to help them grow. Table 5.2 defines these elements. If a habit is particularly strong or weak, teachers can select it as a Focus Habit and analyze its dispositional elements to understand its components. Strength or weakness could be a matter of *skill* development, but it also could be an attitudinal factor: whether or not students *want* to develop the ability (*inclination*) or whether they have understanding of the appropriate *contexts* in which to identify or make use of it (*alertness*).

TABLE 5.2. Dispositional Elements for Analysis of a Focus Habit

SKILL: *Can* they do it?	This question asks teachers to look at how skilled a student is with a particular habit. Any habit can appear in less or more skilled forms. For example, a student can observe quickly and superficially or look long and carefully. A student can reflect formulaically or in depth. A student can envision details but not consider how an entire composition would look.
INCLINATION: *Will* they do it?	This question returns to motivation, but this time it asks about motivation to use a particular Studio Habit. Think about how motivated a student is to use a particular habit and whether the student is driven to use that habit by extrinsic or intrinsic motivation. For example, is a student willing to stretch and explore to find new possible solutions to a setback, or does she just want to do what she's asked or settle for what she already knows?
ALERTNESS: Do they know *when* and *why* to do it?	This question asks whether a student recognizes opportunities to put a habit to use. This is the crucial question for students who are motivated and have a good deal of skill in many habits. The student may be skilled at Envision, for example, and motivated to use this habit, but he just may not notice times when he could benefit from envisioning by stepping back and imagining where he could go next. This element requires that a student use his ability in and attend to the context of a Studio Habit when not told to directly.

Choosing a Focus Habit. Since teachers don't have time to analyze the dispositional elements of every habit in a student's habit profile, we see two options in choosing one or two focus habits to analyze for a student who puzzles you:

1. *Choose a weaker habit.* Choose a habit where the student needs to grow. For example, in Table 5.3, we take an area for growth habit for Greta—Reflect: Question & Explain—and analyze it using the three dispositional elements so her teacher can develop personalized teaching strategies to help Greta use this habit better.

2. *Choose a stronger habit as an entry point to a weaker one.* Select a habit in which the student is strong and which could be used as an entry point to help a weaker habit grow. For example, strength in Develop Craft: Technique could be used to improve Express.

❖ Intrinsically Motivated Students

Teaching Strategies. Intrinsically motivated students are curious and joyfully engaged in making art for their own reasons. They are passionate about art and able to work independently and productively. Sometimes it's easy to help these students, because they are so genuinely curi-

ous, and sometimes their abundance of interest and enthusiasm means that they require special care and attention. Following are teaching strategies for intrinsically motivated students:

- Be clear that one's artistic thinking can always be improved and expanded—it's not good enough to rest on one's laurels!
- Use the habit profile to point out relative weaknesses among a student's many strengths, and support the student in making a plan to improve one habit or dispositional element.
- Analyze a habit in need of growth in terms of skill, inclination, and/or alertness and explain that to the student to help him see which elements can be strengthened.
- Allow individualized instruction for those whose high motivation and achievement require it—self-study in a particular medium or exploration of a particular topic, or extension menus (Byrd, 2017) in which students choose from a menu of possible assignments to find the right level of challenge.
- Carefully balance intrinsically motivated students' abilities to act as "teacher's assistant" or leader of a small group with their need and right to keep learning at the level that's right for them.

TABLE 5.3. Dispositional Analysis of Greta's Focus Habit—Reflect: Question & Explain

Dispositional Elements of Reflect: Question & Explain	Evidence
SKILL: *Can* Greta do it?	Greta's teacher Diane writes that she is already showing the skills of Reflect: Question & Explain when she talks about making her creatures. But when it comes to what her creatures mean to her, Greta is not articulate. She is unable to show skill in Reflect: Question & Explain when it comes to talking about her expressive intent. This is something Diane can point out to her. It might help to show her a video example of an artist reflecting about meaning (for examples, refer to the artist videos referenced in Chapter 1 under the habit Express).
INCLINATION: *Will* Greta do it?	Greta only reflects when she is assigned to do so and scaffolded by Diane. She reflects when a reflection sheet prompts her to "describe how you used and played with materials," or when Diane questions her directly by asking, "What makes you say that?" or in Talking About Art sessions when peers ask questions like "Which creature do you feel best about?" Diane doesn't see evidence that Greta cares enough about reflecting to integrate it into her work independently. Diane probably needs to continue assigning reflections until Greta practices enough to feel its benefits for herself.
ALERTNESS: Does Greta know *when* and *why* to do it?	Greta doesn't show visible evidence of independently knowing when and why to reflect. She doesn't use Reflect to make connections, think more flexibly about possibilities, or look at her work systematically. Diane might model this for Greta and, again, videos of artists reflecting might help her (for examples, refer to the artist videos referenced in Chapter 1 under the habit Reflect, both Question & Explain and Evaluate).

Studio Habit Profiles. Intrinsically motivated students also benefit from having a Studio Habit profile. Do this analysis just as you did for the extrinsically motivated students. As an example, we introduce Kai, who was intrinsically motivated in art. His habit profile (see Table 5.4) contrasts with Greta's because from kindergarten he revealed a strong, internal commitment to drawing [Engage & Persist]. He drew evocative geography, weather, and natural history narratives [Express] and patterns using strong color as he worked in oil pastel and watercolor [Develop Craft: Technique]. In a landscape from 1st grade (see Figure 5.4A), we see a complex narrative involving prehistory, dinosaurs, and extreme weather events [Express]. Kai selected a plastic dinosaur available in his classroom to draw [Observe], and when drawn, he decided to add the weather around it [Envision; Express].

By 2nd grade, Kai was layering landscape elements and color [Develop Craft: Technique] to continue his geographic narratives [Express] (see Figure 5.4B). In this watercolor and crayon resist, we see Develop Craft: Technique that is sophisticated for a 2nd-grader; Engage & Persist, because Kai worked continuously on the piece over multiple classes; Envision, because he imagines these scenes from his head; Express, because he imbues his work with a sense of space and power as an avalanche descends to destroy a town; and Stretch & Explore, because he is playing with textures using resist. He is also using Reflect in his artist statement to explain how he envisioned his painting and what it expresses: *"It's a terrible morning, because there is an avalanche and a big storm cloud. There are huge waves on the beach where there is pink coral and seaweed."* We wonder if he has seen Japanese woodblock prints, since the landscape and blue

TABLE 5.4. Kai's Habit Profile

Studio Habits	Rating (Strength or Area for Growth)	Evidence
Develop Craft: Technique	Strength	Kai is eager to learn technical skills in his preferred media of drawing.
Develop Craft: Studio Practice	Strength	Kai is reliable and conscientious in care for the studio.
Engage & Persist	Strength	Kai is highly focused and remains committed to an artwork, despite challenges.
Envision	Strength	Kai envisions by picturing ideas in his mind and revises his work once the main elements are in place.
Express	Strength	Kai uses a variety of techniques to express his interpretations of nature.
Observe	Strength	Kai's landscapes demonstrate that he keenly observes nature and reads about natural phenomena.
Reflect: Evaluate	Strength	Kai articulates his ideas in artist statements.
Reflect: Question & Explain	Strength	Kai is able to share the rationale behind the changes that he makes in his artworks.
Stretch & Explore	Area for growth	Kai has expanded his use of techniques in his drawings, but there is room for greater exploration of ideas and materials—such as 3-dimensional or time-based media (animation, video).
Understand Art Worlds: Communities	Area for growth	Kai would benefit by seeing examples of other artists' landscapes and artworks that focus on earth science. Ai Wei Wei's pieces about the Sichuan earthquake might interest him.
Understand Art Worlds: Domain	Area for growth	Kai likes to work alone. He could benefit from working with a small group at least sometimes to talk through his ideas.

waves are reminiscent of Hokusai [Understand Art Worlds: Domain]. We do not know much about Observe, but we know that he must be referencing what he reads and sees outside the classroom.

Kai's habit profile reveals that he is strong in many habits. His teacher has identified two that are areas for improvement: Stretch & Explore and Understand Art Worlds. Since Kai does not require specific interventions, this may be enough information for now. The teacher may choose to put these relatively weaker Studio Habits on a list that she keeps for the class so that she can remember to reference them in conversations with Kai. As he

FIGURE 5.4. Kai's artworks. **A:** In 1st grade he drew a dinosaur from observation and then added weather elements. **B:** In 2nd grade he spent several classes working on this multimedia drawing of an avalanche.

grows older, Kai can be responsible for focusing on one or more of these articulated goals when approached during Students at Work or Talking About Art. If the teacher chooses to go deeper in formative assessment with Kai, she could choose a Focus Habit and think about Kai's behavior in that habit using a dispositional elements approach. In Table 5.5, we show a way to approach Stretch & Explore with Kai.

GETTING CONCRETE

Teachers engage in assessment "on their feet." Formative assessment may seem overwhelming to many teachers. We hope that some of the strategies we describe below will be helpful. They can be implemented quickly and easily as you document, review, and analyze student work with the aim of helping students become better artistic thinkers.

TABLE 5.5. Dispositional Analysis of Kai's Focus Habit—Stretch & Explore

Dispositional Elements of Stretch & Explore	Evidence
SKILL: *Can* Kai do it?	Kai has incorporated new techniques into his work that his teacher introduced to the class (crayon-watercolor resist for drawing). What about going beyond 2-dimensional work?
INCLINATION: *Will* Kai do it?	Kai does not make sketches or practice pieces. He fully commits to each artwork, and once he starts, he sticks with it. He does not search for new materials or play with techniques to discover new ways of working. He stays with the same theme for all of his drawings. Maybe talk with him about his choice and suggest he might use another of his interests as a theme.
ALERTNESS: Does Kai know *when* and *why* to do it?	Kai seems content with his processes in drawing at the moment. Perhaps looking at artwork by other artists will inspire him to search for new ways to express himself with the same or different media.

◆ Documentation During Class Time

- Establish routines so students internalize protocols for documentation activities, such as planning, artist statements, and exit tickets.
- Maintain a pocket-sized notebook for each class and write down interesting things kids say and do in the moment or during gallery walks. Consider keeping a separate notebook for each class.
- Keep your phone handy to audio- or video-tape conversations with students to review later.
- Gradually build up the habit of written and spoken reflection with your students. Introduce these practices frequently and early in the year, making sure that students understand the criteria and purpose of reflection. This can be as simple as a daily "turn and talk" activity or writing/drawing sticky note comments, or it can be less frequent in-process gallery walks and written self-assessments at the end of a unit or every six to eight classes.
- Teachers cannot listen to every "turn and talk" or table talk discussion. Be strategic in your selection of a few students to observe during these times and note/record if possible.
- If you use online portfolios, teach children how to document their work with photographs, caption them, and upload them to online collections.
- Glance at students' writing for clarity while they are still in class so you can check in if something is not clear.
- Ask another adult to scribe for students who can't yet write; parent volunteers can help with artist statements for young children.

◆ Reviewing and Interpreting Work

- Write down brief notes during a break period or at the end of the day for each class before you forget.
- Sort and file assessment information into students' processfolios daily—don't let things pile up.
- Try to review the work of five or six students each day (one per class) using a simple checklist or notation system. Write down observations and questions you may have for that student and follow up in the next class. This is not a comprehensive portfolio review but rather a quick conversation. Keep track of these reviews on a class list so you get to everyone over time on a rotation.

◆ Using These Reviews to Inform Teaching

- Plan interventions. Scaffold instruction for students who demonstrate that they need more support—break down processes and concepts into simple steps and write or draw them out for the student. Or make YouTube videos of demonstrations that students can reference independently.
- Identify several students in each class to check in with during class time. Keep track and rotate students so you reach everyone every six to eight classes.
- Build assessments into your lesson plans (check for progress in specific goal areas during Students at Work).
- Review audio and video recordings and note what's interesting. (Student teachers would also benefit from doing this and summarizing for you.)

Quarterly. Periodically review and interpret what you've learned from the various assessment approaches. If the approach you've taken is not useful for teaching and learning, revise it. Decide what you really want to know and try again.

Annually. Strive for a portfolio review with each child at least once during the year. This does take significant time and may not be possible in large schools. Online portfolios make this review process easier because the work, over several years, is often accompanied by artist statements and other documentation. In preparation, students can look over their portfolio and reflect with a partner or in writing. It's even better if the student reviews with you, if you can make the time.

IF STUDENTS are to understand their learning, and if teachers are to be able to document student learning, it's vital to revisit student work over time. The elementary art teachers we've spoken with often say, "I get it—this is important—but it feels like so much work. How am I going to find time to get all of this done?" We realize that what is realistic for one elementary art teacher may be impossible for another, given the numbers of students they see and the schedules that limit their time. The recommendations we make are for an ideal teaching situation for a full-time art teacher with, on average, 400 students per week and planning time built into the school day. You would, of course, adjust your own expectations for what is realistic and possible based on your own school. You won't do much of what we recommend in your first year. Gradually, you'll be able to do more and more. Remember to set clear limits—four kids a day, for example. If you try too many, you might feel defeated and stop entirely.

CONCLUSION

What is the "product" of art education? We think it is the quality of the student's mind, with students' artworks as clues to understanding that. By teaching to enhance students' Studio Habits of Mind, teachers help students learn to create habit profiles to self-assess their work and work habits. The goal of this kind of assessment is to help students develop a set of artistic lenses through which to view the world.

Often, an elementary art teacher is the only experienced artist who sees a student's work develop—it can be a lonely sojourn. But these teachers can be supported by artists, student teachers, or art teachers from other schools, whether in person or via virtual media. Outsider perspectives are often valuable in examining student work, talking through issues about a student who is difficult to reach, or troubleshooting a lesson that didn't go as expected. Today, social media and distance learning platforms make it easier than ever for art teachers to connect and ask for guidance from others or to form professional learning communities.

Beyond assessing their students' work, elementary art teachers can leverage another potential benefit related to assessment—advocacy for their programs, as we explore more in Chapter 6. Because many elementary teachers may be the only art professional in their schools, art teachers have to educate many groups beyond their students, including colleagues, administrators, students' families, and the local community, all of whom need to understand what students are learning in art classes. Exhibitions of learning [Showing Art] can communicate with all of these audiences, assuming the audiences know how to see the learning. Sometimes, quality work that results from a thinking- and process-oriented curriculum may not look as polished as a Pinterest posting. To strengthen support for art programs, audiences need to understand what to look for in student work. Teachers can help them understand through signage, student artist statements, conversations, or notes sent home. Teachers can help administrators understand by sending notes to them, too. Assessment has tremendous potential for advocacy. When hallway displays and processfolios of work highlight specific Studio Habits that students develop as they make and reflect on their artwork, administrators, colleagues, and families take notice—and are more likely to offer support.

THINGS TO THINK ABOUT

1. What does compliance look like in a student? What does engagement look like? How can you tell the difference?
2. What are some extrinsic motivators for your students? What can you do, as a teacher, to minimize their impact on intrinsic motivation?
3. Think of a student who is disengaged. How could you approach this student, using one Studio Habit, to begin to build his or her confidence or interest?
4. Think about how your school district considers assessment. If necessary, how could you start a conversation to shift the district's criteria from skill, effort, and behavior to Studio Thinking?

CHAPTER 6

Beyond the Art Room
Studio Thinking for Advocacy and Integration

THUS FAR we have focused on how art teachers and students use the Studio Thinking framework. You've seen what the Studio Structures and Studio Habits of Mind look like in classrooms and in behind-the-scenes planning, and you've gained ideas for ways to assess student learning formatively. Now we show you how you can use the Studio Thinking approach as an advocacy tool so that parents, classroom teachers, and administrators come to recognize the important kinds of thinking going on in the art room. In this chapter, we also talk about how art teachers can work with classroom and other specialist teachers to integrate Studio Habits throughout the school.

MAKING HABITS VISIBLE

It always helps to advocate for arts education. Keeping your administrators, parents, and teaching colleagues aware of what is going on in the art room, in language that everyone can relate to, can help make an art teacher's job much easier in the long run. The Studio Habits provide language that is broad and, although it emerged from visual arts classrooms, is not arts-specific. No matter your background, you can think of an experience that required engagement and persistence. Everyone recognizes the importance of being engaged in a project and sticking it out over time. And perhaps once students learn to engage and persist in art, they might learn to use these dispositions outside the classroom. This kind of transfer of learning has not yet been empirically demonstrated, but it remains a reasonable possibility if teachers specifically teach for transfer. Speaking the language of Studio Habits, and making it ever-visible, helps advocate for arts education and provides a bridge for this kind of thinking across subject areas. There are many ways to make the Studio Habits more apparent to those in your greater school community, such as the following:

- Create public displays focused only on artistic thinking (without completed artworks). Put up quotations from students describing their working process [Reflect: Question & Explain] and their self-evaluative judgments [Reflect: Evaluate]. Displays of student artwork always get attention. But by sometimes showing just what students say about their work, you emphasize that thinking is as important as what artworks look like.
- Show final student products alongside their earlier drafts. Doing so highlights the thoughtful and effortful work process that led to the polished products.
- Always display student work with an artist statement or reference to the Studio Habits used during the process of making the artwork. When you and your students make decisions about what to show, remember that what you display reveals what you value. The point of arts education is to create artistic thinkers—how can you demonstrate that through what you exhibit?
- Give Studio Habits a center role at public exhibitions. Include them in artist statements and in any spoken or written announcements. Consider curating a show focusing on one or more particular habits, grouping artworks by the Studio Habit that they emphasize. Or center a show on just one Studio Habit—"all of these works started with a focus on Stretch & Explore" or "all of these works are inspired by other artists and helped us understand art worlds."
- Include Studio Habits in formalized documentation such as district and school curricula, student learning goals, district-determined measures, and summative assessments (progress reports and report cards). This emphasizes to parents and administrators that the visual arts have value beyond technical skills.

KEEPING PARENTS IN THE LOOP

Parents can be an art teacher's greatest allies. Keep families informed about the important thinking going on in your classes. It might seem that sometimes proactive communication (through newsletters, email blasts, or handouts sent home in backpack mail) falls on deaf ears, but you never know when a parent will take an interest in this information. New families and students enter your school community regularly, and making sure everyone gets the message (and gets it more than once!) that artmaking is about thinking can make a difference in how your art program is viewed by families and colleagues. These messages are vitally important to helping your school community understand why arts education matters—so please keep it up!

Most children in elementary school like art class and are eager to talk about why it is important (Hogan, Brownell, & Winner, in preparation). The most common reason children give is that it is fun—a perfectly good reason. But in some situations, a more academic rationale might be more effective. The second most common reason children give for valuing art class is that they learn technical art skills, such as painting or drawing. Assume that your students are already telling their parents how much fun art class is and about the art-specific technical skills they're learning. Spend your time focused on reporting about Studio Habits and artistic thinking.

❖ Open Up the Doors

An art class based on Studio Thinking may look quite different from art classes that parents in your school had growing up. The best way to demonstrate what you do in the art room is to invite parents and guardians in to see what goes on. Following are examples of how art teachers showed parents that artmaking is about thinking:

Create Volunteer Opportunities Outside of Class.
Parents at Emily Stewart's former school met once a month, right after student drop-off in the mornings, to help with art room responsibilities—cutting cardboard, sorting through donated materials, matting artwork, and doing other tasks needed in the art room. By becoming part of the art community, parents can develop greater investment in the art studio.

Create Volunteer Opportunities Inside of Class. In
Celia Knight's classroom (see Chapter 3), there seem to be adults everywhere—in one day, two parents and one retired science teacher from the community volunteered to help 5th-graders with their solar panel sculptures, and a paraprofessional gave up her free time to help with a class of 1st-graders.

A school's parent body has lots of resources—artists, craftspeople, and those who identify as neither but are eager to lend a helping hand. Mary Olson asks parents to come in and scribe children's artist statements. She gives parents a sheet of guidelines to help them do this well (see Figure 6.1).

Put on Informances. Jill Hogan, Emily Stewart, and the other specialist teachers at their former school invited parents in for a morning of "informances," inspired by the alternative approach to concerts in music education (Reese, 2009). Parents cycled through art, music, and dance classes with their children and had opportunities to make visual art, choreograph dances, and compose songs. There's no better way to help parents understand what is being learned in arts classes than by inviting them in to experience it for themselves.

Make Art-Centered School Events. The Cardboard Challenge has become a tradition at Julie Toole's school (Imagination Foundation, 2017; see Chapter 3). Each family comes to school on a Saturday and creates large structures from cardboard, some of which have been discussed and planned well ahead of time. This allows parents to see how engaged students become about artmaking and to experience some of that themselves.

Lead Parent Education. Julie Toole also helps parents understand how they can best help their children engage with art at home. She leads sessions about how to set up a studio at home, how best to talk with children about their art, and how to start conversations during trips to an art museum (Toole, 2013).

❖ Send Messages Home

Sometimes parents hear from art teachers only when it comes to the reporting of summative assessments—they see a grade or remarks from the art teacher alongside those from a half-dozen or more teachers. That may not be enough for parents to recognize the importance of making art, and we encourage teachers to communicate often on an individual, class, and schoolwide level as much as possible.

Positive Referrals. Steve Schaffner sends home a "positive referral" form to call attention to good things that are

FIGURE 6.1. Guidelines for helping students complete an artist statement created by Mary Olson.

HOW TO HELP STUDENTS COMPLETE AN ARTIST STATEMENT

What is an artist statement?

An artist statement is a written piece that tells the viewer about the artist's work. These are displayed at Art Night next to student work for all to see.

When helping students with their thinking and writing, please remember:

- The goal is for viewers to understand what the child wrote. Kid spelling is okay if you can understand what has been written, especially for K–2.
- If kids want help with spelling, you can write the word on a scrap of paper for them to reference.
- Scribe for the younger students if needed.
- Title is optional. Students can leave it blank or name it "Untitled."
- Encourage kids to use colored pencil to create their drawings. This is not required though.

Help students give specific details about their work.

If a child simply says, "I chose it because I like it," or "It's pretty," "It's awesome," etc., help them tell more about that. Ask them, "Tell me more. What makes it pretty?" etc.

happening in art class (see Figure 6.2). He places a check next to demonstrated behaviors (positive attitude, self-control, integrity, respect) and Studio Habits used. In a comments section, he describes how these habits surfaced, and there is a place for parents to respond if they wish. Steve explains how he uses positive referrals:

The positive referral form would be given to a student when they demonstrate a [Studio Habit] at a high level during a class period. I try to give out at least two of these for every class I see. I keep track of who gets them in order to make sure that I'm not giving them to the same students all the time—throughout the semester, EVERY student in my classroom will have earned at least one positive referral. To be specific, I gave one out last week to a student [in] 7th grade. She submitted a "final" work of art for grading that I thought needed to be more developed. It was truly a rough sketch, something done very quickly with a pencil. We had a conversation about it; she didn't even blink or fuss for a second, and then she went back to her desk to continue her artwork. She demonstrated 21st-century skills that day by thinking critically and problem solving to make her work better, and for the positive referral I emphasized her willingness to stay engaged and to persist.

Using Studio Habits to Talk About Student Performance. Julie Toole started using a one-point rubric (see Figure 6.3) to open up conversations with parents about their child during parent–teacher–child conferences. Similar forms could also be used to report progress or in other parent communications. Instead of just talking about the child's artworks, Julie and the child talk about the thinking skills that the child has learned, citing Studio Habits that are strengths and growth areas—those habits that are just starting to develop.

Newsletters. Many teachers send out newsletters in traditional hard copy form or in electronic forms like blogs. Such newsletters are another opportunity to educate parents about how children are not just engaging in technical art skills but are being taught important habits of mind.

In your newsletters and blogs, include which Studio Habits you're focusing on in the art room. It is useful to also include examples of student work or quotations or artist statements from students along with a description of the Studio Habits demonstrated in these. Make the entries short and simple—and keep track of which students you highlight so you can rotate through them all eventually. After a while, send home a note to ask parents what they've appreciated about the communication and what else they'd like to know about the art program. Their responses will surely inspire you to continue!

FIGURE 6.2. Steve Schaffner sends home a positive referral to highlight Studio Thinking accomplishments of students.

ART CLASSROOM, POSITIVE REFERRAL

Student: _____

Date: _2/16/17_ Grade: _6th_ Class: _Art_

STUDENT BEHAVIORS DEMONSTRATED:

_X_ Positive Attitude _X_ Self-Control _X_ Integrity _X_ Respect

ART STUDIO WORK HABITS DEMONSTRATED:

_____ Develop Skills _____ Express _____ Understand the World _____ Reflect

_____ Stretch & Explore _X_ Envision _X_ Observe _X_ Engage & Persist

Teacher Comments: _Great job sticking with the project when your pattern didn't turn out well ... AND a really nice observation to see something different in your painting to help you envision a new path for your Art! (☺)_

Teacher Signature: _Mr. Schaffner (8_

Parent Comments (optional): _I'm so pleased ____ is doing so well in Art. Thank you for taking the time to acknowledge it._

Parent Signature: _____

FIGURE 6.3. Julie Toole's one-point rubric identifies a student's strengths and areas for growth.

Studio Expectations and Studio Habits of Mind	Area of strength or Area of growth	Comments
Come up with an idea (Envision & Express)	Strength!	Always is inspired to create
Select & gather tools & materials (Develop Craft)	Strength	independent and knows the studio
Set up a Workspace (Develop Craft)	Strength	
Create (Develop Craft & stretch & explore)	Strength	Constantly learning and practicing new techniques
Clean up & store artwork (Develop craft, Understand Art World)	Strength	organized
Engage & Persist (work on art over time)	Strength	Does get frustrated at times but works until con
Revise, Edit and Reflect (Observe & Understand Art World)	Growth	I would like to see her take feedback and revise to go deeper with her work
Meet Deadlines and Share (Reflect & Understand Art World)	Strength	Loves to talk about her art and inspire others

COLLABORATING WITH THE SCHOOL COMMUNITY

In addition to educating parents and administrators about the thinking that goes on in the art class, classroom and other specialist teachers also benefit from knowing what habits of mind are being taught in visual arts classes. The best way for students to internalize habits of mind is to experience and hear about them in different contexts and from various teachers, especially when teachers make connections across their classes. When teachers plan together to use Studio Habits as points of integration, they make it more likely that students will understand them.

◆ Borrowing Studio Structures

The Studio Structures are formats that teachers of other disciplines can borrow. The tradition of some disciplines, with Teacher Presents for long periods of time, can be enhanced by using formats similar to those of the Studio Structures, which have shorter presentation sessions. In the visual arts, Teacher Presents happens for only brief periods. Students at Work takes up the bulk of classroom time, when students work on projects and the teacher circulates, observing and suggesting possibilities for improvement. This format can be used in any class; once students know what to work on, they can proceed independently or in groups as the teacher walks around, listens in on conversations, and makes just-in-time verbal interventions. Talking About Art—a reflection time for thinking critically about one's own and others' work—is a format that can be useful in all disciplines. Teachers of other subjects can borrow these ideas to bolster student involvement and success.

◆ Studio Habits as Points of Integration

Studio Habits are broad and useful in many contexts, and each of the Studio Habits can be used in every other discipline. In Table 6.1, we list some of our favorite points of overlap, but these are only suggestions. The possibilities for integration are endless.

Students are much more likely to make connections between art and other disciplines when teachers use the same language; the art teacher talks about "Observe" while looking at artwork, and the science teacher uses the word "Observe" when discussing careful examination of objects seen through a microscope. These points of integration are likely to stick only if teachers take time to discuss how to connect ideas across subject areas—including shared language and specific references to work being undertaken in other classes. For example, mathematics teachers can talk about how to use Observe or Envision in solving problems, or social studies teachers can consider how a particular textbook expresses the authors' attitudes and beliefs. Remember to start small—consider talking with just one other teacher, and see what you two come up with. Let the conversations grow from there. Or consider starting by using *Studio Thinking* (Hetland et al., 2013) in a book club with other teachers at your school, as was done at Kitty Conde's school in Chicago (see Chapter 3), or in department discussion groups, like the Acton-Boxborough teachers (see Chapter 4).

Make Classroom Teachers Aware of Your Art Themes. Look at the topics addressed in your art program—either those you select for projects or those that students develop through choice. Make a list of these and ask colleagues at your school if they connect to anything that they teach. You may be surprised by how many do! Find out more about what the teachers do in relation to those topics, and explain what you do. Then see if you can find ways to be more deliberate in making the connections visible to your students.

Formally Training Classroom Teachers. Alameda County, consisting of 18 school districts on the East San Francisco Bay in California, has created an Integrated Arts Learning Specialist Program (ILSP) of professional development. Co-designed by Louise Music's team at the Alameda County Office of Education, the ILSP helps classroom teachers integrate frameworks like Studio Thinking, Teaching for Understanding, and Making Learning Visible (all of which originated at Project Zero [n.d. b] at the Harvard Graduate School of Education). In the following section, we describe what happens at the Maya Lin School, which serves K–5 students and whose teachers have all participated in the ILSP.

COMMITTING TO STUDIO THINKING: A DAY AT THE MAYA LIN SCHOOL

Entering the Maya Lin School in Alameda, California, there's no question that the Studio Habits of Mind are integrated seamlessly into the school culture. They are visible not just in the art room but around the school hallways and inside classrooms. They are even prominently displayed in Spanish near the school's front door for those parents who prefer or need the translation (see Figure 6.4).

In this section, we walk you through a number of classrooms at Maya Lin School so you can see how the Studio Habits are thoughtfully integrated throughout this

TABLE 6.1. Studio Habits Integration

Develop Craft	Science	In science class, students need to learn how to use tools like microscopes, magnets, gears, and test tubes. And they need to learn to care for these tools and store them in organized ways.
	Library	In the school library, children need to learn some fundamental skills: how to find a book, how to check it out to take home, and where to put books they don't want. They also need to learn to take good care of library books—for example, not writing in them and not folding back the cover.
Engage & Persist	Library and Language Arts	Students learn tricks for finding "just right" books—books that are neither too hard nor too easy and that keep them engaged. They may also learn which sections of the library they are most likely to enjoy (e.g., fiction, nonfiction, science, or biography) so their attention can be captured by the books they choose.
	Social-Emotional Learning	When students see how much they improve through persistence, they realize that they can get "smarter" with effort. In psychology, this is called a growth mindset (Dweck, 2006). Having such a mindset, instead of the belief that you are either good or bad at something, inspires self-confidence and a willingness to keep going.
Envision	Social Studies	Learning about another culture requires students to develop historical imagination—to envision what it would be like to live in that culture. What does it look like, sound like, smell like, feel like?
	Science/ Engineering	When children are asked to build a structure out of Lego blocks that will not fall over when bumped, they have to envision various possible forms. Envisioning as they work means that what they do is not just trial and error. Rather, they are mentally testing how well their envisioned structures may stand.
Express	Language Arts	Students' stories are more compelling if they are written to convey a mood, an atmosphere, and a personal voice.
	Music	Just like artists use the elements of art to create expressive messages, musicians use the elements of their discipline such as dynamics, tempo, phrasing, and form to convey images and emotions.
Observe	Science	When students are learning about science, they need to observe—they're looking closely at plants to identify them, through microscopes to analyze the structures of cells, and at the comparative behaviors of animals to understand their behaviors' functions.
	Physical Education	To become better athletes, students need to be aware of how their bodies move. By watching others closely and paying attention to what's going on in their bodies, they can improve their abilities.

TABLE 6.1. Studio Habits Integration (*continued*)

Reflect	Mathematics	In mathematics classes in Japan, students are often asked to explain to their class how they solved a problem. This leads to discussions about approaches to solving and finding problems.
	Creative Writing	When students write their own stories, they can be asked to start with a first draft and then edit that draft and create a new one. They can be asked to write a "writer's statement" about what they were trying to achieve, how well they achieved that, and what they learned that might help them to improve future work.
Stretch & Explore	Mathematics	Students can be given brain-teaser problems in mathematics and asked to come up with solutions. They do not need to worry about coming up with the right answer—they learn just by trying out different solutions. Teachers can use these experiences to show them the value of error—how it offers new ideas and helps them figure out what's not working and how to change that.
	Music	Students can be asked to create an invented form of notation so that they can remember their own or others' compositions. There are many good ways to do this—they just have to come up with something to help them remember or to describe the sounds to someone who hasn't heard the piece before.
Understand Art Worlds	Science	Questions are products of the domain of science, so students in science class can be shown that the questions asked of them in a science lesson (e.g., Can this insect see colors? Why does this animal have fur that blends into the environment? Why do leaves change colors?) are similar to those designed by professional scientists in their efforts to create scientific understanding (Domain). Students can also take on different roles as they carry out experiments in small groups (Communities).
	Mathematics	Students in mathematics classes can come to understand how the world of professional mathematicians connects to them by seeing examples of what they're learning being used in real-world contexts. Show them how mathematics is used in bridge building, in musical notation, or to describe the cycles of the moon.

school environment. The result is that students are aware of how these habits of mind appear across their subjects and in their daily lives.

❖ Morning Art Classes

We start the morning in the art room with Constance Moore and her 1st-graders (see Figure 6.5). This year, stu-

dents are focused on the throughline "How do artists change the world?" All students in the school are creating masks that convey messages that are personally meaningful to the children who made them. These works have gone through a process that included idea generation through brainstorming, notes and sketches in visual journals, and reflection to help students choose ideas on which to expand. Students are beginning to papier-mâché

FIGURE 6.4. The Studio Habits are displayed in Spanish for parents who need or prefer a translation.

light up, and she focuses on her pipe cleaner flowers: "These are tulips, because I made them out of straws here. This is a beautiful purple rose! And this, this here is just a great big, huge flower" (see Figure 6.6).

Classes switch, and the younger students are replaced by 4th-graders. As this happens, the issues being tackled show more maturity. Malakai is using a pencil to poke holes in a shoebox. The others at his table stop their work and look up to watch. One student asks what he's doing. He doesn't respond, but another student surveys the work, and says, "He's making bullet holes." Another student pipes up, "That's a pretty powerful statement against racism." Eventually, Malakai responds that "this is about the police killing Black people for no reason." When asked how a viewer would know that from looking at the artwork, he says, "because there's blood here. It's red."

The schoolwide mask assignment allows students to express personal meaning, with the aim of affecting change when their artwork is viewed. When the masks are completed, Constance's room becomes more choice-based—she opens different studios, and students make individual works in various media, still centering on the year's question of how artists can change the world. Mask-making serves as practice for the bigger projects to come later in the year.

FIGURE 6.5. Art teacher Constance Moore and 1st-grader Greyson discuss his sketch.

the bases of their masks so that they will be ready for the addition of paint and other surface elements.

Some of these artworks tackle big issues—homelessness and global warming—and others are focused on smaller scale, 1st-grade problems. Constance talks about one student who is worried about how frozen food can become unfrozen. She encourages the student to go with this concern, because it matters to and engages him.

During Students at Work time, 1st-grade student Serafina is eager to talk about the issue that motivates her artwork. "Some people, and I'm not trying to be mean about this, but some people just pick too many flowers, and then we don't have any flowers, and then the bees die. And that's not okay." Serafina is clearly transported as she points out the different elements of her work. Her eyes

❖ An Afternoon in Second Grade

After lunch, the 2nd-graders process through three classes, all of which reference the Studio Habits. They begin in the library and discuss how the resources of a library can help with a creative inquiry process about how artists can make change in the world [Envision]. Then they watch a video of contemporary artist Aida Sulova, who created an anti–plastic bag campaign, and they discuss both how she is using her art to effect change and which Studio Habits likely went into the creation of her artwork [Understand Art Worlds: Domain]. Because the students are used to hearing about the Studio Habits, they list off ideas readily.

The class then heads to the art room, where they get to work on their masks, as the other classes have done. Their works convey social messages, just like Aida Sulova's did in the video they just watched [Express]. The issues important to these students and displayed in their in-progress artworks include pollution, endangered animals, and war, among many other topics.

Art class ends, and the students head back to their classroom with teacher Brian Dodson. Brian's room shows ample evidence of the Studio Habits. Cabinet doors in the classroom contain sentence stems that students can pull from to reflect on classwork they complete (not just artwork!) (see Figure 6.7). Today, the students are responding to the final result of an ongoing project. Working in

FIGURE 6.6. Serafina enthusiastically describes her artwork, centered on the preservation of bees.

FIGURE 6.7. Brian Dodson uses sentence stems and prompts about each Studio Habit to reflect on class activities.

small groups, students were each assigned to make the case for a particular imaginary student to take the one remaining spot in their classroom at the Maya Lin School. The imaginary students each have unique and dire cases to plead—they want to move to Maya Lin because their current schools don't have money for supplies or lunch, because they are violent, or because the students are desperately bored. Students at Maya Lin wrote letters on behalf of the imaginary students, created visual images of them, and became immersed in the situation of who would be allowed to "immigrate" into the school. Today, one of these imaginary students was chosen, and the class received letters letting them know who was selected. That news created one small group of happy students and a bunch of unhappy ones. Brian gave students the choice of responding to this decision by making an artwork, poem, or piece of creative writing, all of which focused on the Studio Habit of Express.

❖ Meanwhile, in First Grade

Down the hall, Emily Roberts is teaching a 1st-grade mathematics lesson about shapes and patterns, and about the similarities and differences among patterns. Like Brian's classroom, Emily's has the Studio Habits visible in many places. The class begins by looking at examples on the projector of four boxes, each filled in with multiple shapes (see Figure 6.8). Students observe and share what they notice.

> "So first, we're looking closely," says Emily. "We're observing. No hands; just looking. Giving people time to look." When the time comes, Emily asks for observations.
> "I think block D is different because it has a black shape."
> "I notice that A has two of the same shape."
> "I think A because it doesn't have a sideways shape."

After several examples and lots of observations, the activity transitions to desks, where students use paint to

FIGURE 6.8. First-graders observe differences and similarities.

create their own shapes, colors, and patterns. Emily gives directions:

> On this paper, if you want to do a quick sketch or plan for your painting, you may. If you feel like you just need to envision in your mind what it's going to look like, and then just paint, that's also fine [Envision]. . . . Take a second and make a picture in your mind. Make a plan. You have available to you cyan, magenta, and yellow. (Emily knows that mixing primary colors with tempera results in dull, lifeless secondary colors, so she substitutes colors that mix well into orange, green, and violet [Develop Craft: Technique].) You know how to mix those. I can also bring around black and white [Develop Craft: Technique]. You need to know, as you envision in your mind, what you will have available to you.

Students then approach Emily for paper, one by one. As they arrive, Emily asks them their plans in terms of subject matter. Students reply with themes of fruit, dots, trucks, feelings, vegetables, nature. "I hear a lot of fruit ideas. I think you guys are inspiring each other," says Emily [Understand Art Worlds: Communities].

The students sit down and begin work. "Swirl, swirl, swirl, swipe, swipe, swipe, tap, tap tap," Emily says, reminding students about the proper way to get enough paint on the brush. "I see purple! You guys are getting good at developing your craft. Look at your color mixing. I like to hear friends helping each other to mix colors [Develop Craft: Technique; Understand Art Worlds: Communities].

The students continue to work, and Emily approaches Ronen, who has completed his work quickly, making a different face in each of his boxes—happy, sad, nervous, and angry. He sits quietly and observes his work for a bit. Then he considers further additions. "I'm going to add tears to the sad one," he tells Emily. "And I'm going to add a sun to the happy person." A bit later, Emily approaches again (see Figure 6.9). Ronen has added what look like blobs of purple next to the nervous face, and she asks what he's adding. "Grapes. Because they're purple. Nervous is purple." Emily doesn't miss a beat, "Nervous feels like purple to you? That's a great way to express feelings—colors" [Express].

As students finish up, they wash their brushes and palettes and return to the rug [Develop Craft: Studio Practice]. As the group reconvenes, they reflect about which Studio Habits they used, and students volunteer various answers.

"I used Observe because I needed to know if I needed to change anything."

"I stretched and explored because I tried drawing a new thing . . . a Pokemon."

"I used Envision to imagine what my work would look like."

The conversation closes, and students head to retrieve their backpacks and jackets for dismissal.

WE HOPE we have convinced you that Studio Thinking is useful both in and outside the art classroom. The habits can be integrated into any subject area. When teachers make links between thinking in the visual arts and thinking in other areas, students have more opportunities to connect their learning. The power and breadth of the habits also can be used as advocacy for the importance and seriousness of arts education. We hope that you will come to view your art classroom through the lenses of Studio Thinking, and that you will help others to see your classroom through the same lenses.

FIGURE 6.9. First-grade teacher Emily Roberts and Ronan talk about his shapes.

THINGS TO THINK ABOUT

1. This chapter describes a number of ways that teachers can advocate for their art programs by making the thinking that goes on in the art studio visible to audiences outside the classroom. Which will you implement? What else can you design that will help educate your school community?

2. Think about your public displays. What do you normally include in an exhibition? Does what's on the bulletin boards represent to others the most valuable aspects of an art education? If not, how can you include other artifacts to better advocate for thinking and learning in art class?

3. Think about your parent community. What assets could they bring to your art program? What would make them and you feel most comfortable? If parents are not already involved in the art program, make a plan to invite a small group of parents in over a short period of time and assess how it goes. Offer options for how and when they can help in the art studio. Use parent feedback from these experiences to continue offering opportunities that are beneficial to both you and the parent community.

4. Which colleagues in your school might be willing to identify Studio Thinking concepts in their own classrooms? Who are you already friendly with? Who teaches a curricular area that is particularly interesting to you? Think of how you might approach these colleagues. What could you say if they ask why integration would be a good idea for student learning?

Resources for Teachers

Teachers from around the country have generously shared resources they've created for their particular classroom situations. Of course, not all of these ideas will fit perfectly in your classroom—they may require adaptation or reconceptualization to suit your needs. Use them as springboards for your own ideas. Since these are not our creations, we may not always agree with the chosen wording or concepts articulated in these resources. In addition, in Appendix F we provide a reference chart connecting the National Core Arts Standards and the Studio Habits. We hope these materials, along with the additional resources on our website at www.studiothinking.org, will help you integrate the Studio Thinking framework into your teaching practice.

APPENDIX A. Making Studio Habits Visible

GAMES, SONGS, AND ROUTINES FOR YOUNGER CHILDREN

Call and Response. When art teacher Jessica Kitzman first introduces Studio Thinking, she highlights one new habit in each class, repeating a call and response interaction: "When I say artists, you say OBSERVE!" Her goal is to introduce the Studio Habits language and encourage students to think of themselves as artists. The Studio Habits call and response is so popular that she continues to use it throughout the year.

Studio Habits Scavenger Hunt. Jessica Kitzman has also developed a scavenger hunt in which she has printed the names of each Studio Habit on paper and hidden them in plain sight around the classroom. These clues are treasures for scavenger hunt activities. Jessica places Understand Art Worlds: Communities by the bulletin board that features contemporary artists, because it shows how they work together. Understand Art Worlds: Domain can be found in the art library with art history books. Develop Craft: Technique is attached to the technique poster hanging on the wall. Students search to find the hidden habit and then discuss with others why their teacher may have placed it in that location.

Studio Habits Desk Cards. During Students at Work, Roni Rohr (introduced in Chapter 1) circulates and, as she sees a student using a Studio Habit, or sees an opportunity to use a Studio Habit, she alerts the student with a printed prompt (see Figure A.1).

INTRODUCING THE HABITS TO OLDER CHILDREN

Cynthia Gaub designed a Habits Around the Room game to introduce her middle school students to six of the Studio Habits (see Chapter 1). Each table is set up with an activity that highlights one way to use the habit. Students rotate through each activity, one at a time, spending 10–20 minutes at each table. Table A.1 shows an adaptation of a lesson plan developed by Cynthia for this game.

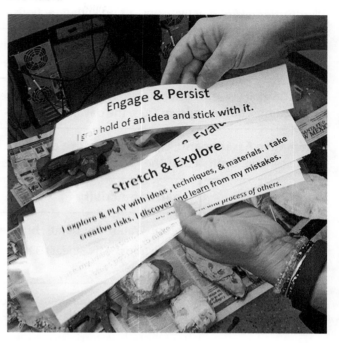

FIGURE A.1. Studio Habits desk cards, with definitions, remind Roni Rohr's students to use the habit.

TABLE A.1. Lesson Plan for Studio Thinking Around the Room, by Cynthia Gaub, Grades 4–8

Objective: To quickly introduce students to the Studio Habits of Mind while doing hands-on activities based on the habits.

National Core Art Standards VA:Cr1

Students can generate and conceptualize artistic ideas and work.

Essential Question: What conditions, attitudes, and behaviors support creativity and innovative thinking?

Materials

- Student sketchbooks and pencils
- *Observe Center:* Books from the *I Spy* series (Marzollo & Wick, various dates) and/or microscopes with interesting slides
- *Express Center:* Oil pastels, 4 × 5" black construction paper, adjective word cards
- *Develop Craft Center:* Tempera cakes or watercolors in only primary colors, 4 × 4" squares of watercolor paper, brushes, water cups
- *Envision Center:* Basic drawing supplies, 4 × 5" drawing paper, noun word cards
- *Explore Center:* Quick sculpture supplies, such as foil, pipe cleaners, cardboard, yarn, masking tape, scissors, and a spinner with prompts

Motivation: Explain the Studio Habits with a definition and a guiding question. Have the kids Think, Pair, Share with each question to list ways they think artists would use each habit. Tell the class that they are going to test out these habits while exploring some art activities.

(continued on the next page}

TABLE A.1. Lesson Plan for Studio Thinking Around the Room, by Cynthia Gaub, Grades 4–8 *(continued)*

Review the Centers: Share your procedures and expectations for each center. Cynthia uses a PowerPoint with a picture of the center activity and a sign with directions at each center for reminders.

Rotate Through the Centers: Rotate through the activities, spending between 10 and 20 minutes at each center. After the students do the activity, have them write some observations or discoveries in their sketch books or notes.

Reflecting: If you are continuing to new centers on different days, begin the next class with a quick sharing of observations and discoveries from the day before.

Summative Assessment: End the unit with a quiz where students identify which artistic habit is being used in a short scenario. Cynthia uses the ideas her students share in their class discussions.

Habit	Learning Activity
Develop Craft	*Setup:* Watercolor paints, brushes, and paper. *Instructions:* Mix at least 3 new colors with watercolor paints and add to the community color wheel.
Envision	*Setup:* Students generate a list of words that are printed, cut into strips, and placed in a bag. *Instructions:* Pick 2 word cards from the bag. Combine them into ONE drawing using your sketchbook. Return cards to the bag.
Express	*Setup:* Put words into a bag that might include the following: <ul><li>Political</li><li>Adventurous</li><li>Melancholy</li></ul> <ul><li>Assertive</li><li>Flowing</li><li>Sporty</li><li>Calming</li></ul> <ul><li>Mesmerizing</li><li>Vibrant</li><li>Swirling</li></ul> *Instructions:* Pick a word prompt from the bag. Draw it with oil pastels. Return the word to the bag.
Engage & Persist	*Setup:* Collect blocks. *Instructions:* As a group, build the tallest block structure you can that won't fall down. Keep trying to use all the blocks.
Observe	*Setup:* Gather *I Spy* books (Marzollo & Wick, various dates). *Instructions:* List all the things you can find on one page. Draw at least one item in your sketchbook.
Stretch & Explore	*Setup:* Make a spinner with prompts: <ul><li>Something to wear</li><li>Something to play with</li><li>Something real</li></ul> <ul><li>Something weird or creepy</li><li>Something musical</li><li>Something that moves</li></ul> *Instructions:* Spin the spinner and make sculptures based on the prompt. Use only materials at this table.

APPENDIX B. Student Planning and Reflection

PLANNING WORKBOOK

Agusta Agustsson (see Chapter 1) designed a planning workbook to guide students as they envision and later reflect on their artworks. She created a small book out of folded paper. Figure B.1 shows what students read and respond to (by either drawing or writing). She puts each of the rows in the table as a separate page in the workbook.

FIGURE B.1. Planning Workbook, by Agusta Agustsson

Imagine	How will you express your idea? Will it be 2-dimensional or 3-dimensional? What materials will you need?	
Sketch	Draw a sketch for your idea here.	
Inspire	Where will you get your ideas? Brainstorm some ideas for the subject of your work.	
Create	What skills do you need to create your idea? Will you collaborate with others?	
Checklist (*to remind students about criteria to include in a finished artwork*)	☐ Personal ☐ Original ☐ Carefully crafted ☐ Received feedback	☐ Took time (at least 3 classes) ☐ Photographed well ☐ Written reflection ☐ Uploaded to Google Classroom
Reflect	How can you make your idea better? Write down some feedback you have gotten from a peer while your work was in process.	
Share	How and with whom will you share your idea? Will you display it? Make it look its best.	

EXIT TICKETS

Exit tickets prompt students to reflect on something from the class session that went well, a challenge they faced, or a surprising discovery. At the end of class, students respond to questions on a form such as the one shown in Figure B.2, or on sticky notes collected by the teacher.

These reflections accomplish multiple things: students practice reflection, their teachers read these tickets immediately to plan for the next class, and when students review them several times a year, they can remember where they were and recognize the progress they have made.

FIGURE B.2. An exit ticket created by Julie Toole.

EXIT SLIP

Name: _____   Date: _____

What I accomplished **today**

Problems that arose today

What I **plan** to accomplish next art class

Help I need from Ms. Toole

APPENDIX C. Reflecting on Completed Works

STUDENT RUBRICS

Sometimes teachers use rubrics to help students reflect on their process and product. In Figure C.1 and Table C.1, we show two teachers' examples.

Diane Jaquith developed a form where students could either describe a "mess-up" in their work and how they resolved it using a Studio Habit or describe a part of their work that turned out well, name the Studio Habit that helped them succeed, and explain how it helped them (see Figure C.1). Dale Zalmstra uses a rubric for examining the Studio Habits (see Table C.1).

FIGURE C.1. Successes and Challenges, by Diane Jaquith

Directions: Respond to either Part A or Part B. Choose one of the Studio Habits that helped you succeed or resolve the mess-up, circle it, and explain how the habit helped you.	
Develop Craft **Envision** **Engage & Persist** **Express**	**A.** Describe a problem or mess-up in your artwork today and how you resolved it using a Studio Habit. Circle the Studio Habit from the list on the left and explain how the habit helped you.
Observe **Reflect** **Stretch & Explore** **Understand Art Worlds**	**B.** Describe a part of your work today that turned out really well. Circle the Studio Habit from the list on the left and explain how the habit helped you.

TABLE C.1. Studio Habits of Mind 3-Point Rubric, by Dale Zalmstra

	Master	**Apprentice**	**Novice**
Stretch & Explore	I experiment, ask questions, take risks, challenge myself.	I experiment and ask questions with my artwork.	I find it hard to experiment.
Engage & Persist	I choose work, focus, problem solve, and persist with my work.	I choose work, focus, and persist with my artwork. I usually work on skill-builders.	I find it hard to focus.
Observe	I take the time to look carefully and use what I see in my work in unique ways.	I take the time to look carefully and use what I see in my work.	I need support to look and use what I see in my work.
Develop Craft	I persist in improving my art skills. I have good craftsmanship.	I have basic art skills and craftsmanship.	I need support to use basic skills.
Express Ideas & Feelings	I use materials to clearly communicate complex art ideas that interest me.	I use materials to communicate art ideas that interest me.	I need support to communicate my ideas.
Envision	I begin with a plan (draw/write). I can explain how my plan develops over time.	I begin with a plan (draw/write).	I have a plan in my head.
Reflect (Writing)	I can write an artist statement using art words.	I can answer written questions about my work with specific answers using art words.	I can't really answer the questions. I don't understand.
Artist to Artist (Critique)	I can discuss the ideas in my artwork and in the artwork of others using art words.	I can discuss my artwork and the artwork of others using art words.	I need support to discuss my art and the art of others. I need support to use art words.
Artist to Art World: Connect	I can find artists in history and contemporary artists and show how they connect to my work.	I can find artists in the art world and show how they connect to my artwork.	I need support to find artists in the art world and show how they connect to my artwork.
Artist to Studio: Community	I am respectful and responsible for myself, my classmates, materials, and tools. I help the class as a whole to work well together.	I am respectful and responsible for myself, my classmates, the materials, and tools that I use.	I need support to stay on task. I don't respect or take responsibility for myself or the materials.

ARTIST STATEMENTS

Many teachers ask their students to write artist statements for each work that is exhibited during Showing Art, and they create forms for students to use to complete their statements. We show a variety of approaches using teacher-created forms in Figures C.2, C.3, and C.4.

FIGURE C.2. Mary Olson created guidelines to help her Grade 3–6 students write artist statements.

ARTIST STATEMENT GUIDELINES

An artist statement is a written piece that tells the viewer about your art.
These are displayed at Art Night next to your work for all to see.

You may use the questions below to clarify your thinking:
- What have you learned while creating this piece?
- What do you want viewers to know or notice about your work?
- Where did you get your idea?
- Share any problems or challenges you experienced.

Tips:
- View exemplars from your grade level.
- Include art vocabulary in your statement.
- Speak from your heart.
- Sketch your piece in the box. Use colored pencils for biggest impact.

FIGURE C.3. Third-grader Sylvie describes a success (canine teeth) and a concern (spots that make her animal look like a leopard instead of a cheetah) on her artist statement.

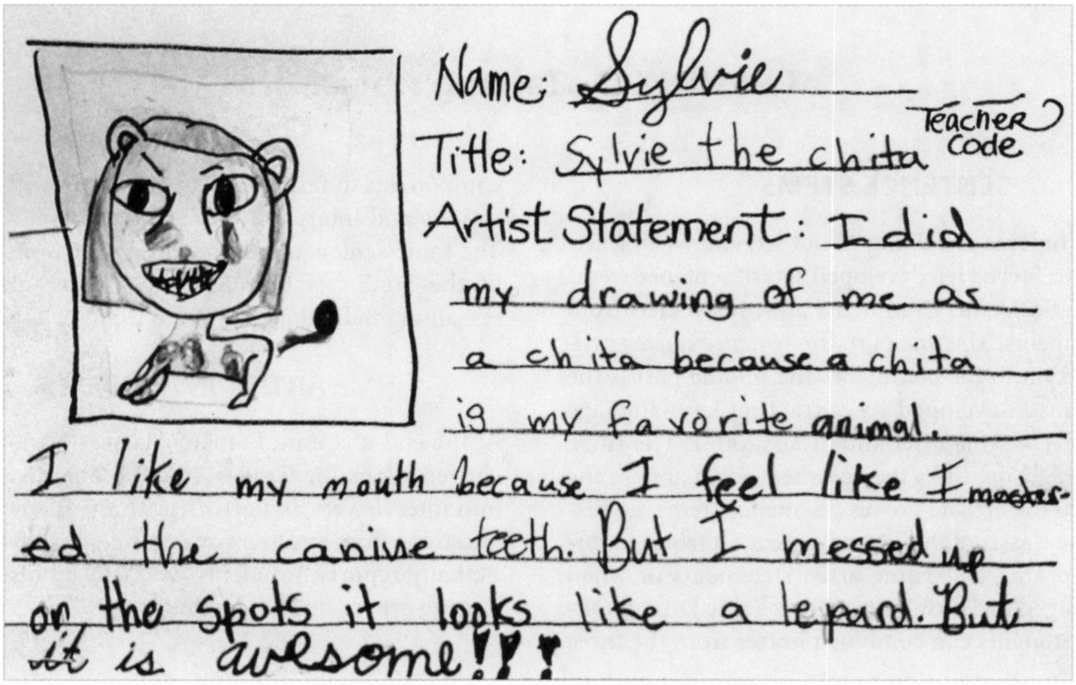

Name: Sylvie
Title: Sylvie the chita   *Teacher Code*
Artist Statement: I did my drawing of me as a chita because a chita is my favorite animal. I like my mouth because I feel like I mastered the canine teeth. But I messed up on the spots it looks like a lepard. But it is awesome!!!

FIGURE C.4. An artist statement form for Grades 1 and 2 created by Ianthe Jackson.

ARTIST STATEMENT FORM

Name: _____   Class: _____

I made a . . .

Drawing   Collage   Painting

Sculpture   Fiber Art Piece   Print

My artwork is a . . .

Portrait   Self-Portrait   Group Portrait   Abstract

Imagination   Landscape   Something I Observed

To make it I used . . .

Paper   Paint   Markers   Crayons   Pencil   Cardboard

Tape   Glue   Scissors   Pastels   Wood   Other

My idea was important to me because . . .

APPENDIX D. Talking About Art

SENTENCE STEMS

To support students in Talking About Art and writing artist statements, Steve Heil developed sets of sentence stems for each Studio Habit. Comments are constructed from three components. The first part, the *sentence starter,* provides an entry into the comment. The middle part is the *stem*—a phrase developed by extracting key language from *Studio Thinking* (Hetland et al., 2007). The third part, the *connection,* links the comment to an area in the artwork or to the artistic process. Sentence stems are displayed on the classroom walls and appear on tables as students are working or writing artist statements or when they are engaged in Talking About Art. Table D.1 demonstrates how students can combine phrases from the three components to respond to a peer's work with their observations and interpretations for the habit Develop Craft. The same sentence starters and connections serve for all of the Studio Habits. Sentence stems specific to the remaining individual habits are listed in Table D.2.

ARTIST INTERVIEWS

At the end of a unit, Bethany Haizlett Narajka structures conversations for Grades 4 and 5. She divides the class into interviewers and artists, with the interviewer asking questions first, and then switching roles after 3 minutes. Bethany reports, "Students who can be resistant to discussing art are thrilled by this activity."

TABLE D.1. Using Sentence Stems in Talking About Art: Develop Craft, by Steve Heil

Sentence Starters	*Develop Craft* Sentence Stems	Connections to Art or Work
I like that you are . . . I see that you are . . . I notice that you are . . . I can tell that you are . . . It seems to me that you are . . . Could it be that you are . . . ? I wonder if you are . . . ? Would you be . . . ? What if you were . . . ?	using a variety of tools in a range of different ways . . . using tools in a skilled and mindful way . . . choosing tools best suited to creating what you wish to make . . . applying what you learn about artistic conventions . . . shading, cross-hatching, using perspective, etc. using ideas such as cubism, abstraction, color scheme, asymmetrical balance, etc. caring for tools and materials . . .	when you . . . where you . . .

TABLE D.2. Additional Sentence Stems for Talking About Art, by Steve Heil

Engage & Persist Sentence Stems	*Observe* Sentence Stems
• connecting to your work personally . . . • persisting in your work through difficulty . . . • committing to an art task over time . . . • breaking out of ruts and blocks . . . • showing openness to new ideas and unexpected solutions . . .	• observing closely, representing the surface aspects of what you see . . . • observing closely, representing the underlying structures of what you see . . . • observing closely, representing what you imagine, but cannot see . . . • seeing not just what's literally there in [the] artwork, but also seeing underlying processes . . . • seeing not just what's literally there in [the] artwork, but also seeing implied lines or forms or underlying meanings . . .
Envision Sentence Stems	
• planning how your artwork will look . . . • envisioning possibilities and changes to better express what you want . . .	
Express Sentence Stems	*Reflect* Sentence Stems
• expressing ideas and feelings . . . • expressing a sense of mood . . . • expressing a sense of sound . . . • expressing a sense of time . . . • expressing a sense of emotion . . .	• explaining your intention for the art . . . • explaining the problem you are trying to solve . . . • describing the process and decisions made in your artwork . . . • evaluating the effectiveness of artwork . . . • comparing artwork fairly with other artworks . . .

(continued on the next page)

TABLE D.2. Additional Sentence Stems for Talking About Art, by Steve Heil *(continued)*

Stretch & Explore Sentence Stems	*Understand Art Worlds* Sentence Stems
• welcoming unexpected ways of solving problems in art . . . • discovering new techniques through play . . . • asking "What would happen if . . . ?" • courageously facing fear of failure . . . • courageously facing fear of making mistakes . . . • going beyond familiar ideas, tools, or techniques . . .	• learning about art history and current practice . . . • interacting as an artist with other artists . . . • interacting as an artist with local arts organizations, such as markets, galleries, and museums . . . • interacting as an artist with an audience . . . • becoming aware of how your artwork may be received . . .

APPENDIX E. Documentation—
Collecting and Keeping Everything Together

PROCESSFOLIOS

How do you document student work so that it makes learning visible, and so that the work is readily accessible? The Arts PROPEL Project at Project Zero (Winner & Simmons, 1993) advocates using processfolios—portfolios that collect work in process such as drafts, revisions, and final works, as well as reflections written by the student during and outside of classes. Traditional portfolios store a student's "best work," but processfolios store all of the drafts that precede a final work, dated in time order, so that there is a record of process. San Francisco art teachers Caren Andrews and Jennifer Stuart (see Chapter 4) maintain processfolios for every student. These contain sketches, sticky notes, evidence of conversations, photos, written reflections, arts-based research notebooks, and any other documentation of artistic process.

At the beginning of the year, establish a processfolio system that works for you to maintain collections of students' process work—sketches, entrance/exit tickets, and self-assessments. Some of these items may be small and easily lost—consider a manila envelope or folder with edges stapled together, or an online storage system, or a simple box. Find the system that works for you.

TOOL BOOKS

Starting in 3rd grade, students in Dale Zalmstra's art classes collect evidence of their learning in small Tool Books—stacks of pages made from one-third of a piece of cardstock, bound with one ring (see Figure E.1). For Dale, with 750 students who meet daily for a week and then not again for 6 weeks, it is essential that her students do much of their own documentation. Students can set goals, plan, store ideas and information, and reflect, using the card appropriate for their own work. Several cards are added per art week, maintaining the collection over 3 years. Students can review what they've learned in prior years to remind themselves about processes, concepts, and techniques. The Tool Books are being continuously refined by Dale and her colleague, Kat Potter, who introduces them mid-year in Grade 1. They share ideas for individual cards:

- Reference cards: Studio Habits in a Novice/Apprentice/Master rubric
- Isolated Studio Habit with rubric as a week's focus (5 classes)
- Studio Habit vocabulary used in process
- Ideas/Envision/Goals/Plan
- Idea card: Blank idea card or card with prompts (i.e., favorite toy, game, etc.)
- Point of View card: Taking an idea to composition—up close, far away, mapped, etc.
- Thinking maps for brainstorming
- Media cards: Draw (shading, portraits, overlapping, etc.), Paint (Color Theory, i.e., mini-color wheel, tints, shades), Collage, Clay, Sewing, Weaving, Origami, Sculpture (Attaching), Papier Mâché, Printmaking

- Compare/Contrast: For example, Elements and Principles of Art, as seen across various artists, styles, cultures, points in history
- Understand Art Worlds: Information card about an artist, style, or culture with an image
- Studio Habits rubrics

- Redraw card: Draw what you did in box, name it, write a sentence
- Reflection card: Blank reflection card or card with reflection prompt question on board
- Artist Statement card

FIGURE E.1. Dale Zalmstra and Kat Potter designed Tool Books bound by a ring and maintained by students over multiple years.

APPENDIX F. Connections Between the Studio Thinking Framework and the National Core Arts Standards

The Studio Thinking framework is parallel in striking ways to the National Core Arts Standards (National Coalition of Core Arts Standards, 2014). Indeed, *Studio Thinking: The Real Benefits of Visual Art Education* (Hetland et al., 2007) was one of the resources used by the committee that created the standards. We have created a table that provides a "crosswalk" from the National Core Arts Standards for Visual Arts to the Studio Habits of Mind. In using this table, teachers can start from whichever approach is most comfortable and familiar to them—the standards or the Studio Habits. We do not address the Studio Structures in the table, since every structure can be used to address any of the standards. The table is available for free download and printing from tcpress.com/studiothinking and/or www.studiothinking.org

References

Arnheim, R. (2006). *The genesis of a painting: Picasso's Guernica*. Oakland, CA: University of California Press.

Art 21. (2005, September 23). *Memory* [Video file]. Available at https://art21.org/watch/art-in-the-twenty-first-century/s3/memory/

Art 21. (2008, September 25). *On museums* [Video file]. Available at https://art21.org/watch/extended-play/kerry-james-marshall-on-museums-short/

Art 21. (2010, May 14). *Mural* [Video file]. Available at https://art21.org/watch/extended-play/julie-mehretu-mural-short/

Art 21. (2011). *Chaman. Shahzia Sikander*. Available at https://art21.org/read/shahzia-sikander-chaman/

Art 21. (2014, May 23). *A subtlety, or the marvelous sugar baby* [Video file]. Available at https://art21.org/watch/extended-play/kara-walker-a-subtlety-or-the-marvelous-sugar-baby-short/

Art21. (2015, May 1). *Diana Al-Hadid plays the classics*. Available at https://art21.org/watch/new-york-close-up/diana-al-hadid-plays-the-classics/

Barrett, J. (1978). *Cloudy with a chance of meatballs*. New York, NY: Aladdin Paperbacks.

The Be Like Brit Foundation. (2017). [Home page]. Available at https://belikebrit.org/

Berry, B. (2007, October 13). What is WOW work? Message posted to https://groups.yahoo.com/neo/groups/TAB-ChoiceArtEd/conversations/messages/28288

Boone, L. E. (1992). *Quotable business: Over 2,500 funny, irreverent, and insightful quotations about corporate life*. New York, NY: Random House.

Blythe, T., & the Teachers and Researchers of the Teaching for Understanding Project. (1998). *The teaching for understanding guide*. San Francisco, CA: Jossey-Bass.

Byrd, I. (2017). Offer choice with extension menus [Blog post]. Available at http://www.byrdseed.com/offer-choice-with-extension-menus/

Calkins, L., & Mermelstein, L. (2003). *Launching the writing workshop*. Portsmouth, NH: First Hand.

Center for Responsive Schools. (2016). *Responsive classroom for music, art, PE, and other special areas*. Turners Falls, MA: Center for Responsive Schools.

Council of Arts Accrediting Associations. (2007). *Achievement and quality: Higher education in the arts*. Council of Arts Accrediting Associations. Available at https://www.arts-accredit.org/wp-content/uploads/2016/04/AchievementandQuality-2007SepDoc.pdf

Cyran, P., & Gaylord, C. (2012, October 5). *The 20 most fascinating accidental inventions*. Available at https://www.csmonitor.com/Technology/2012/1005/The-20-most-fascinating-accidental-inventions/Post-its

Douglas, K. M., & Jaquith, D. B. (2009). *Engaging learners through artmaking: Choice-based art education in the classroom*. New York, NY: Teachers College Press.

Douglas, K. M., & Jaquith, D. B. (2018). *Engaging learners through artmaking: Choice-based art education in the classroom* (2nd ed.). New York, NY: Teachers College Press.

Dweck, C. (2006). *Mindset: The new psychology of success*. New York, NY: Random House.

EL Education. (2017). Praise, question, suggest critique protocol. *EL25*. Available at https://eleducation.org/resources/praise-question-suggest-critique-protocol

Exploratorium. (2018). Strandbeest: The dream machines of Theo Jansen. Available at https://www.exploratorium.edu/strandbeest

Farago, J. (2015, April 9). Hokusai and the wave that swept the world. *BBC Culture*. Available at http://www.bbc.com/culture/story/20150409-the-wave-that-swept-the-world

Gaub, C. (2016). Printmaking around the room [Blog post]. Available at http://www.artechtivity.com/printmaking-around-the-room/

Gaub, C. (2017). Artistic habits video [Blog post]. Available at http://www.artechtivity.com/artistic-habits-video/

Godrèche, D. (2013, November 26). Speaking with clay, mud and clowns: Pueblo potter Roxanne Swentzell. *Indian Country Today*. Available at https://indiancountrymedianetwork.com/culture/arts-entertainment/speaking-with-clay-mud-and-clowns-pueblo-potter-roxanne-swentzell/

Gunther, R. (2012). Faith Ringgold on Tar Beach quilt [Television series episode]. In C. Sauvion & P. Bischetti (Producers), *Craft in America*. Los Angeles, CA: PBS.

Harmon, W. (2016). Artists stretch and explore [Blog post]. Available at http://huffmanart.squarespace.com/blog/2016/9/25/artists-stretch-explore

Hench, J., & Van Pelt, P. (2009). *Designing Disney (A Walt Disney Imagineering Book)*. New York, NY: Disney Editions.

Hetland, L., Winner, E., Veenema, S., & Sheridan, K. (2007). *Studio thinking: The real benefits of visual art education*. New York, NY: Teachers College Press.

Hetland, L., Winner, E., Veenema, S., & Sheridan, K. (2013). *Studio thinking 2: The real benefits of visual art education*. New York, NY: Teachers College Press.

Hogan, J., Brownell, H., & Winner, E. (in preparation). Fourth graders' rationales for keeping art, music, and physical education in the school day.

Howitt, S. (2013). Cornelia Parker [Television series episode]. In R. Bright (Producer), *What do artists do all day?* BBC.

Imagination Foundation. (2017). Cardboard challenge. Available at http://cardboardchallenge.com/

Kerzner, H. (2013). Industry specific: Disney theme parks. In *Project management: A systems approach to planning, scheduling, and controlling*. Hoboken, NJ: John Wiley & Sons.

Krechevsky, M., Mardell, B., Rivard, M., & Wilson, D. (2013). *Visible learners: Promoting Reggio-inspired approaches in all schools*. Hoboken, NJ: John Wiley & Sons.

Lavache, C. (2017, July 28). *10 things every true J. K. Rowling fan should know by now*. Available at http://www.cosmopolitan.com/entertainment/books/a10372546/jk-rowling-facts/

Marshall, J., & D'Adamo, K. (2011). Art practice as research in the classroom: A new paradigm in art education. *Art Education, 64*(5), 12–18.

Marzollo, J., & Wick, W. (various dates). *I Spy* [Series of books]. New York, NY: Scholastic. Available at http://www.scholastic.com/ispy/books/

McDonnell, B. (2017, July 2). Interview, photos and video: Kehinde Wiley's 'A New Republic' makes its final stop at the Oklahoma City Museum of Art. *NewsOK*. Available at http://newsok.com/article/5554966

MoMA. (2017). Instant Photography: 2003–Today. Notes from exhibition of Stephen Shore.

Moore, G. (1891). *Impressions and opinions*. London, UK: David Nutt.

Naghshineh, S., Hafler, J. P., Miller, A. R., Blanco, M. A., Lipsitz, S. R., Dubroff, R. P., et al. (2008). Formal art observation training improves medical students' visual diagnostic skills. *Journal of General Internal Medicine, 23*(7), 991–997.

National Coalition of Core Arts Standards. (2014). National Core Arts Standards. Available at http://www.nationalartsstandards.org/

Patterson, F. (2008). *The Guild: Publishers & Distributors of Fine Art Limited*. Available at http://theguildpublishing.com/fp_statement.htm

Perkins, D. N., Jay, E., & Tishman, S. (1993). Beyond abilities: A dispositional theory of thinking. *Merrill-Palmer Quarterly (1982–)*, 1–21.

Pogrebin, R. (2015). Sarah Sze aims for precise randomness in installing her gallery show. *New York Times*. Available at https://www.nytimes.com/2015/08/24/arts/design/sarah-sze-aims-for-precise-randomness-in-installing-her-gallery-show.html?_r=0

Pollack, B. (2012, November 14). Diana Al-Hadid makes a sculpture. *ArtNews*. Available at http://www.artnews.com/2012/11/14/diana-al-hadid-makes-a-sculpture/

Project Zero. (n.d. a). *Artful thinking*. Available at www.pzartfulthinking.org

Project Zero. (n.d. b). *Thinking routines*. Available at http://www.visiblethinkingpz.org/VisibleThinking_html_files/03_ThinkingRoutines/03a_ThinkingRoutines.html

Reese, J. (2009). Lift the hood and get dirty! A closer look at informances. *Music Educators Journal, 96*(2), 27–29.

Reynolds, P. (2003). *The dot*. Nottingham, UK: Candlewick Press.

Ritchhart, R., & Perkins, D. N. (2005). Learning to think: The challenges of teaching thinking. *The Cambridge Handbook of Thinking and Reasoning*, 775–802.

Rog, L., & Kropp, P. (2004). *The write genre: Classroom activities and mini-lessons that promote writing with clarity, style and flashes of brilliance*. Ontario, Canada: Pembroke Publishers.

Rutherford, P. (2012). *Instruction for all students*. Alexandria, VA: Just ASK Publications.

Saltzberg, B. (2010). *Beautiful oops!* New York, NY: Workman Publishing Company.

State Education Agency Directors of Arts Education. (2015). *National Core Arts Standards*. Available at http://www.nationalartsstandards.org/

Studio tour with Betye Saar. (2017). *Los Angeles Times*. Available at http://www.betyesaar.net/media.html or http://www.latimes.com/visuals/video/86980912-132.html

Texas Education Agency. (2013). *Texas Essential Knowledge and Skills for Fine Arts*. Available at http://ritter.tea.state.tx.us/rules/tac/chapter117/index.html

Toole, J. (2013). The home–school connection. *Arts & Activities, 154*(4), 7.

van Gogh, V. (1882). *To Theo van Gogh. The Hague, Saturday 9 September 1882*. Available at http://vangoghletters.org/vg/letters/let261/letter.html

van Gogh, V. (1884). *Letter to Theo van Gogh. Written early June 1884 in Nuenen*. Translated by Mrs. Johanna van Gogh-Bonger, edited by Robert Harrison, number 370. Available at http://webexhibits.org/vangogh/letter/14/370.htm

Wiggins, G. (2010, June 10). What is a big idea? [Blog post]. Available at http://www.authenticeducation.org/ae_bigideas/article.lasso?artid=99

Wiggins, G. P., & McTighe, J. (2005). *Understanding by design*. Alexandria, VA: ASCD.

Winner, E., Goldstein, T. R., & Vincent-Lancrin, S. (2013). *Art for art's sake? The impact of arts education*. Educational Research and Innovation. Paris: OECD Publishing.

Winner, E., & Simmons, S. (Eds.). (1993). *Arts PROPEL: A handbook for visual arts*. Cambridge, MA: Project Zero at the Harvard Graduate School of Education and Educational Testing Service.

Wiske, S. W. (Ed). (1998). *Teaching for understanding: Linking research with practice*. San Francisco, CA: Jossey Bass.

Index

About the Authors

JILLIAN HOGAN is a Ph.D. student in Developmental Psychology in the Arts & Mind Lab at Boston College. She holds an M.M. and B.M. in Music Education and Clarinet Performance from Boston Conservatory and has additional training in Montessori and Orff-Schulwerk approaches. In her research, she uses mixed methods to investigate what we learn through arts education and how those findings align with public perceptions. Her primary interest is the teaching and learning of habits of mind in visual arts and music education, which is informed by teaching for 6 years in schools that specialize in gifted, inclusion, and autism spectrum disorder populations. A happy introvert, she wrote this book under the watchful eyes of her two cats. www.jillhoganinboston.com

LOIS HETLAND, Ed.D. (Harvard, 2000), is Professor of Art Education at the Massachusetts College of Art and Design and an Affiliate of Harvard Project Zero (Researcher 1992–2000; PI 2001–2010, Senior Research Affiliate, 2010–present). With undergraduate degrees in music and visual arts, she taught elementary and middle school students for 17 years. Her research as a cognitive and developmental psychologist focuses on learning, teaching, and assessment in arts and other subjects; she currently consults with Abt Associates on an evaluation of nine partnerships among community arts organizations, universities, and schools in Wisconsin and Alaska. Prior research includes teaching for understanding in the disciplines (1989–1998); meta-analytic reviews of art's effects on non-arts learning (1997–2000); three US DOE-funded grants in Alameda County, California (2003–2010); *Qualities of Quality: Understanding Excellence in Arts Education* (2005–2008); and an evaluation of Art21 Educators (2010–2013). She has published five books (*Studio Thinking, Studio Thinking 2, Educating for Understanding,* and *The Project Zero Classroom,* volumes 1 and 2) and more than 100 articles, and she has coauthored (with J. C. Hamlin) a chapter in *Arts Evaluation and Assessment: Case Studies of Program Evaluation in Schools and Communities* (R. S. Rajan and I. C. O'Neal, eds., 2018). She co-led the Studio Thinking Network, a monthly online conversation among educators who use the Studio Thinking framework (2012–2014); was founding Education Chair of Project Zero's annual summer institutes (1996–2005); and consults widely.

DIANE JAQUITH is an Instructor in Art Education at Massachusetts College of Art and Design, where she also directs the Teaching for Artistic Behavior Summer Teacher Institute. She has been a visual arts educator for 30 years, with over 20 years at the elementary level, blending choice-based pedagogy with Studio Thinking. She is co-author of *Engaging Learners through Artmaking: Choice-Based Art Education in the Classroom,* co-editor of *The Learner-Directed Classroom: Developing Creative Thinking Skills Through Art,* has written numerous articles, and authors a blog, *Self-Directed Art: Choice Based Art Education.* A co-founder of the Teaching for Artistic Behavior organization, she frequently presents on the topics of choice-based art education, Studio Thinking, and creativity at regional and national conferences.

ELLEN WINNER is Professor of Psychology at Boston College, Director of the Arts and Mind Lab at Boston College, and Senior Research Associate at Harvard Project Zero. She received her Ph.D. in Psychology from Harvard University in 1978. Her research focuses on learning and cognition in the arts in typical and gifted children. She has published more than 100 articles and chapters and four books: *Invented Worlds: The Psychology of the Arts* (1982); *The Point of Words: Children's Understanding of Metaphor and Irony* (1988); *Gifted Children: Myths and Realities* (1997; translated into six languages and winner of the Alpha Sigma Nu National Jesuit Book Award in Science); and *How Art Works* (2018). She has co-authored two other books: *Studio Thinking: The Real Benefits of Visual Arts Education* (Teachers College Press, 2007); and *Studio Thinking 2* (Teachers College Press, 2013). She received the Rudolf Arnheim Award for Outstanding Research by a Senior Scholar in Psychology and the Arts from the American Psychological Association. She is a Fellow of the American Psychological Association (Division 10, Psychology and the Arts) and of the International Association of Empirical Aesthetics.

Develop
Craft

Engage
&
Persist

Envision

Observe

Reflect

Stretch & Explore

Understand Art Worlds